# Don't Stop Believin'

# Don't Stop Believin'

## Pop Culture and Religion from *Ben-Hur* to Zombies

*Edited by Robert K. Johnston, Craig Detweiler,
and Barry Taylor*

WESTMINSTER
JOHN KNOX PRESS
LOUISVILLE · KENTUCKY

*1st edition*
Published by Westminster John Knox Press
Louisville, Kentucky

12 13 14 15 16 17 18 19 20 21—10 9 8 7 6 5 4 3 2 1

*Book design by Sharon Adams*
*Cover design by designpointinc.com*
*Interior art:* "Elvis Presley" © *Culver Pictures, Inc./SuperStock;* "Martin Luther King Jr. and Malcolm X" © *Science Faction/SuperStock;* "Thoughtful Mary in Still from Mary Tyler Moore"* © *CBS Photo Archive/CBS/Getty Images;* "Rehearsals for 43rd Annual Golden Globe Awards"* © *Ron Galella/Ron Galella Collection/Getty Images;* "Dalai Lama" © *Marka/SuperStock;* "Comedy Centrals 'Indecision 2008: America's Choice'" © *Brad Barket/Getty Images Entertainment/Getty Images*
*Cover art:* "On the Set of Ben-Hur" © *42-28096202: Photo M.G.M./Collection Sunset Boulevard/ Corbis;* "American Football" © *Anthia Cumming/istockphoto.com;* "Statue of Mother Theresa in India" © *Fotosearch/SuperStock;* "1981 President Ronald Reagan Speaking" © *ClassicStock .com/SuperStock;* "Star Trek" *(US Series CL-17772)* © *9000044066-001: Photo Paramount Pictures/Collection Sunset Boulevard/Corbis;* "Facebook App on iphone" © *Marc Müller/dpa/ Corbis;* "Tie Dye" © *nolimitpictures/istockphoto.com;* "South Africa, Politics, Portrait of Former President Nelson Mandela" © *Eye Ubiquitous/SuperStock;* "Red Scream" © *Diane Diederich/ istockphoto.com*

**Library of Congress Cataloging-in-Publication Data**
Don't stop believin' : pop culture and religion from Ben Hur to zombies / edited by Robert K. Johnston, Craig Detweiler, and Barry Taylor.
    p. cm.
  ISBN 978-0-664-23505-5 (alk. paper)
    1. Popular culture—Religious aspects—Christianity. 2. Popular culture—United States—History—20th century. I. Johnston, Robert K., 1945– II. Detweiler, Craig, 1964– III. Taylor, Barry, 1956–
  BR115.C8D665 2012
  261.0973—dc23

2012013167

Most Westminster John Knox Press books are available at special quantity discounts when purchased in bulk by corporations, organizations, and special-interest groups. For more information, please e-mail SpecialSales@wjkbooks.com.

To inspirational sources, however unlikely,
and to their Source

# Contents

# Introduction: Don't Stop Believin'

Why does the song "Don't Stop Believin' " keep playing on our iPods, on our TV screens, and in our stadiums? Is it the keyboards ushering us into a tale of "a small town girl living in a lonely world?" Perhaps we empathize with the plight of a city boy from South Detroit. In their beloved top-ten hit from 1981, Journey invites us to identify with these strangers taking a "midnight train goin' anywhere." The rousing chorus arrives late, summoning us to join these streetlights/people, to not stop believing.

But what are these beliefs that we're supposed to hold onto? There is no creed, no rationality even. Beliefs are primarily a feeling mirrored by the lilting sound of Steve Perry wailing above Neil Schon's guitar. A desperate hope bonds the winners and losers inhabiting Journey's boulevard. The goal seems to be finding emotion, holding onto the sense of being vitally alive. The song never references the hereafter. These beliefs are things worked out among people on the margins, in the streets, acutely aware of how few promises life offers. Can we persist in the midst of ample reasons to abandon hope? Journey taps into the inchoate longings of teenagers (and their parents!) who face daunting circumstances every single day. Religious people may have a specific language by which to address their disappointments. Prayers offered to God may be tied to promises from the Divine. But increasingly, such lofty language strikes us as too easy. We want something earthier than platitudes.

Journey's fans may be surprised to discover that the biblical Psalms share the sense of desperation haunting small-town girls and city boys. Their loneliness is reflected in these pleading lyrics from Psalm 22: "My God, my God, why have you forsaken me? / Why are you so far from helping me, from the words of my groaning?" (v. 1). Their searching after dark is mirrored by the psalmist's quest, "O my God, I cry by day, but you do not answer; / and by night, but find no rest" (v. 2). Hanging from a cross, gasping for air, Jesus turned to the Psalms for solace. The enduring power of Psalm 22 reaches across the centuries, but today's teens may have heard those words a few hundred times less than Journey's "Don't Stop Believin'." Aren't both songs a desperate cry for solace and meaning? This book seeks to find the commonalities between ancient prayers and contemporary pop songs, to point out how the religious resides amid our most resonant movies and shows. We turn to pop cultural figures as a form of ritual, for the emotions they engender so faithfully. But we also want to find the reasons behind these feelings, to join theological words and concepts to these pop cultural beliefs. We are trying to discern a mystery—why certain artists and performers inspire such religious feelings.

When *The Sopranos* needed a compelling conclusion, executive producer David Chase reached back to Journey's anthem. When *Glee* needed a compelling beginning for its series pilot, the writers updated "Don't Stop Believin'" as the cry of creative high school outcasts. The Chicago White Sox rode the triumphant chorus all the way to their 2005 World Series championship. It caps off Broadway's celebration of 1980's metal in *Rock of Ages*. The malleability of such a seemingly disposable pop song suggests that we may not know what will still sound relevant and refreshing thirty years from now. A suicidal folk singer who toiled in obscurity like Nick Drake may have his songs resurrected to sell Volkswagens. Vincent Van Gogh's modest art sales to his brother may be shattered by one $50-million offer from the Getty Museum. What lasts? What matters? Which songs, shows, and stories will resonate across time? Perhaps most importantly, what artists continue to nourish our soul? We have chosen to focus on 101 pop cultural icons that stir up something in our spirit. It could be joy or sorrow, comfort or pain. But they spark frenzied opinions and demonstrate enduring influence. At their best, they usher us into a transcendent space. They prompt us to respond to Steve Perry's plea: "Don't Stop Believin'."

This book will likely make little sense to those born a thousand years from now. Yet, beneath the specific pop cultural examples, we hope the core theological truths shine through. We explore books, movies, music, shows, plays, people, products, and games as an entry into ultimate questions—and answers.

Times have changed since *The Gospel according to Peanuts* was published in 1965 by a small Presbyterian publishing house. Ten million copies later, pastors and churches (and publishers!) discovered our longing to connect our pop cultural passions with our spiritual practices. Now, we have Gospels according to all kinds of sources, from Harry Potter to *Twilight*. And we've carved out plenty of permission to look for God in unlikely places. Our goal has never been merely searching, but finding. We have never longed for mere examples or intimations, but strong, mediated experiences of the divine. And our hunger for God compels us not to limit the times or places the Wholly Other may appear. We follow a free-range God, delighted to surprise us.

Our project began in the sunlight of southern California. Perhaps that explains why we've developed a sunny attitude toward pop culture. We tend to look toward the spiritual upside of movies, music, and TV, rather than their nefarious power. Fuller Seminary's proximity to Hollywood has given us remarkable access to movie directors, television producers, and pop song-writers. Some may think that a close encounter with the entertainment industry would engender even greater cynicism toward pop cultural projects. Yet we have found our conversations with the creators of films, TV shows, and video games to be remarkably enlightening.

The passion and care poured into the most enduring songs and shows humbles us. Yes, a classic pop song can arrive in a single hook, or a memorable line may be improvised on the set. But the most important writers, directors, and performers have also polished their craft through countless hours, working hard to disguise the blood, sweat, and tears they've invested. Creative brilliance is supposed to appear spontaneous and effortless. Memorable lines are uttered as if they've sprung from the top of an actor's head rather than from hours a writer spent at a keyboard. But we've found that inspiration usually arrives after considerable perspiration.

This book may appear to have a dashed-off quality. The entries are short. The subjects are broad and well known. Yet we poured over the table of contents, editing and pruning until we felt confident that 101 theologically significant figures and trends emerged. We limited our reach to the television era, a moment when history began to be captured on tape as well as film. So our entries run from the 1950s of Elvis Presley and Marilyn Monroe up to present day. We have chosen artists whose work feels (nearly) complete. While Lady Gaga offers countless provocations for theological consideration, we do not feel conclusions can already be drawn regarding her message or impact. We also chose artists or subjects of considerable renown. While we love Neutral Milk Hotels' *In the Aeroplane over the Sea*, we recognize that its pleasure retains a smaller, cult-like status (at least in this century!). So we majored on the majors.

We recruited experts who have published much more detailed tomes about their respective subjects, such as the authors of *The Gospel according to the Beatles; What Would Buffy Do?* and *Killing the Imposter God: Philip Pullman's Spiritual Imagination in His Dark Materials*. We invited contributors to hone in on the most salient, spiritual traits of a series or songwriter. In some cases, a theological truth may emerge from an unlikely subject (the cool jazz of Miles Davis). In other cases, a person or thing was chosen to exemplify a larger phenomenon (Rick Warren for the rise of the megachurch, or Tom Cruise for Scientology).

We recently hosted contributor David Dark in southern California. Having been asked countless questions about our critical method, we invited David to explain his methodology. How come his books will cram Radiohead, St. Augustine, The Simpsons, and Flannery O'Connor into the same volume? How are those hoping to adopt similar approaches in their teaching and preaching to determine what matters? Dark offered a simple apologetic: "I write about the things I love." We focus on the songs or shows that move us, analyzing the artists who prompted us to pay attention. We also consider cultural touchstones that have captured the popular imagination. While we may not have been the target market for the Twilight series, we believe such massive phenomena are worthy of theological study. Jesus repeatedly directed his parables to those who have eyes to see and ears to hear. So this project is an exercise in watching closely and listening carefully, contemplating what is popular and endeavoring to determine why.

When we began our theological projects over a decade ago, we felt the need to write elaborate introductions. We sought an alternative to the blanket condemnation of Hollywood coming from some religious circles. And yet, reducing films or shows to sermon illustrations also seemed a disservice to what can be remarkably complex art forms. In his book *Reel Spirituality*, Robert K. Johnston put theology and film into mutually beneficial dialogue. In *A Matrix of Meanings*, Craig Detweiler and Barry Taylor expanded the conversation to include television, music, celebrities, advertising, fashion, and art. We challenged our readers to receive the pop cultural artifacts as creative gifts, laden with theological potential. Rather than reading pop culture through the lens of the Bible, we suggested that thoughtful Christians and spiritual seekers consider how the most enduring songs and shows might sharpen our understanding and appreciation of Scripture. And so we present this survey of theological possibilities, cutting across formats, genres, and eras. We are not baptizing these subjects as holy, but using them as occasions to pause for theological reflection.

Has our attention to entertainment come at the expense of timeless truths? Undoubtedly. Our personal bandwidth is far less than the networks that bring us Internet access. While we're glad to have provided space where less justification is necessary to love the things we love, we recognize that the need for caution remains. Not just regarding the content of shows, but the sheer volume of content. Our books could be turned into theological license for blanket indulgence. We tend toward cultural gluttony rather than restraint. The freedom that we encourage can be abused. And with the rise of Google, You-Tube, and Facebook, we are veering toward information—or at least entertainment—overload. Smart phones and iPads have meant that the "show" that comprises our collective posts, links, and texts almost never stops.

An era of too much information requires a step back or at least a break in the action. With less time to reflect, we must actively schedule time to discern what matters. A constant flow of electronic inputs can leave us bloated and bleary-eyed. So consider this compendium an exercise in restraint. Perhaps we need to think even more carefully about the things that surround us. Artists we take for granted as touchstones could be ripe for reassessment. Others, like Sister Corita Kent, are ripe for rediscovery. A constant diet of the new may leave us exhausted by the pressure to catch up, to chase relevance. A weekly Sabbath or media fast provides a way to process all the links headed our way.

Yet, rather than turn from the electronic empire, we expand our interests into even more arenas. Video games offer an even larger canvas for creators to play with. Transformative design reflects the glory of the Designer. And we're just coming to understand how the Internet serves as one giant book we never finish reading or one giant screen, with endless programming, always available on demand.

As knowledge fragments into ever-smaller bites, we present a theological sampler. It can be read front to back or by skipping around, following your pop cultural bliss. By organizing things chronologically, then alphabetically, we were delighted to discover our entries ranged from *Ben-Hur* to Zombies. Some may see a natural devolution, from a blockbuster celebration of Jesus' sacrificial life to a haunting metaphor for a living hell. Others may find such bookends remarkably resonant. Both subjects deal with our struggles to overcome the gnawing grip of death. The book can be perused in any order, but we invite readers to consider the shifts across time.

Note how our understandings of gender, sexuality, and the divine have been conveyed across mediums and throughout the decades. Religious institutions are continually challenged to respond to our electronic inputs. We've presented an array of formats (movies, music, TV, advertisements, sports, video games) at a moment when boundaries are collapsing. Our students could be introduced to *The Lord of the Rings* through the movies, the video games, or the books. They may watch/read/experience all three simultaneously, working from an iPad—and they may not worry about which format it started in. New delivery devices make previous format categories useless. As Pandora recommends an unexpected artist or Netflix suggests a classic film, this dictionary may prove a helpful companion. It may include artists who deserve closer attention. We hope it may prompt a search for answers that leads toward a Bible handbook or concordance as well.

Our area of interest remains general revelation/common grace/natural theology. We try not to confuse a transcendent moment in a movie with the Transcendent source behind it. We want to worship the Creator, not the creation, and we don't want to raise the creators contained in this book to god-like status. Even a guitar god like Eric Clapton knows that his fingers are not omniscient or omnipresent. At the same time, we have heard so many stories over the years where God used unlikely means to communicate remarkable callings.

We've met a pastor who was called out of his hippie commune thanks to *Easy Rider*. He saw through the purple haze of Dennis Hopper and Peter Fonda into a different calling. We taught a graduate student in psychology who applied to Fuller Seminary because of *Lars and the Real Girl*. The compassionate care extended to Lars prompted a commitment to the helping professions. We're just starting to meet the generation prompted to service by seemingly dismissible video games. By shining a spotlight on these 101 pop cultural icons, we open up a window of possibilities. We would never prescribe a response or predict a reaction. But hopefully we offer the Spirit room to move into our hearts and minds, even when we least expect it. This dictionary invites us to expect more than we may have previously believed.

Craig Detweiler, with Robert Johnston and Barry Taylor

# Contributors

**Tim Basselin** holds a PhD in Theology and Culture from Fuller Theological Seminary. He currently adjuncts at various schools in the Chicago area. His first book is *Flannery O'Connor: Writing a Theology of Disabled Humanity* (2013).

**R. W. Bonn** worked as a development executive in Hollywood before serving as senior editor of HollywoodJesus.com and development director for Reel Spirituality. His articles have appeared in *Prism, Christianity & Theatre*, and on various Web sites. His graphic novel, *Meow Meow Jones*, will be published in 2013.

**Alexis L. Boylan,** PhD, is an Assistant Professor in Residence at the University of Connecticut. She is the editor of *Thomas Kinkade: The Artist in the Mall* (2011). Her forthcoming book, *Man on the Street: Masculinity, Urbanism, and Ashcan Art*, examines the Ashcan circle of artists and their visual commentaries on urban masculinity.

**Eric Bumpus** is the coauthor of *Cease Fire, the War Is Over!* (2005). In 2008, he cofounded CeaseFireStrategies, which encourages "positive Christian interaction with media and culture" through the audio program, Cultural Diplomacy. Eric's BA is in Communications, and he is pursuing an MBA in Applied Management. He works as a videographer and editor.

**Kutter Callaway,** PhD, is the Director of Church Relations and an Adjunct Assistant Professor of theology and culture at Fuller Theological Seminary. He was a contributing author to *Halos and Avatars* (2010) and is the author of *Hearing Images*, a study on the theological significance of music in film (2012).

**Caroline Cicero,** PhD, is an expert on the social and policy implications of the aging population, especially Baby Boomers. She directs the Southern California Health and Aging Public Policy Institute (www.socalhappi.org) and the Center for Visual Gerontology. Her blog can be found on the Huffington Post Web site.

**David Dark,** PhD, lives and teaches in Nashville, Tennessee. He is the author of *The Sacredness of Questioning Everything* (2009), *The Gospel according to America: A Meditation on a God-blessed, Christ-Haunted Idea* (2005), and *Everyday Apocalypse: The Sacred Revealed in Radiohead, the Simpsons, and Other Pop Culture Icons* (2002).

**Craig Detweiler,** PhD, directs the Center for Entertainment, Media, and Culture at Pepperdine University in Malibu, California, where he is Associate Professor of Communication. He edited the original book on theology and video games, *Halos and Avatars* (2010), is the author of *Into the Dark* (2008), and coauthor of *A Matrix of Meanings* with Barry Taylor (2003).

**Gabriel Ferrer** is an Episcopal priest and visual artist who lives in Los Angeles, California, with his wife, Debby. They have four grown children.

**Eddie Gibbs,** PhD, an ordained minister in the Anglican Church, has served as Home Director of the South American Missionary Society, worked with the Bible Society in the UK, and taught at Fuller Theological Seminary for twenty-six years. He has led seminars in preparation for Billy Graham events both in the UK and U.S.

**Mark Hayse,** PhD, directs the undergraduate Honors Program at Mid-America Nazarene University in Olathe, Kansas, where he is Professor of Christian Education. He has written on religion, ethics, transcendence, and video games for several volumes, including *Halos and Avatars* (2010), *The Legend of Zelda and Theology* (2011), and the two-volume *Encyclopedia of Video Games* (2012).

**Gareth Higgins,** PhD, is a northern Irish writer, film critic, festival director, and peace activist. He lives in North Carolina and works at the intersection of justice, spirituality, and art; which, he believes, is where we all work as well.

**Daniel White Hodge,** PhD, is assistant professor of Youth Ministry and Popular Culture and Director of the Center for Youth Ministry Studies at North

Park University where he teaches on religion, race, hip hop, and youth culture. He is the author of *Heaven Has a Ghetto* (2009), *The Soul of Hip Hop* (2010), and coauthor of *The Hostile Gospel* (2012).

**Robert K. Johnston,** PhD, is Professor of Theology and Culture at Fuller Theological Seminary, where he teaches students how to engage theologically with movies, popular culture, and contemporary fiction. A past president of the American Theological Society, his books include *Reframing Theology and Film* (editor, 2007), *Useless Beauty* (2004), and *Reel Spirituality* (2000, 2006).

**Jason King,** PhD, is chair of the Theology Department at St. Vincent College in Latrobe, Pennsylvania. He coauthored *Killing the Imposter God: Philip Pullman's Spiritual Imagination in His Dark Materials* (2007).

**Matthew Kitchen** is a freelance writer in New York who contributes articles on sports, style, relationships, and more to publications including *Sports Illustrated* and Esquire.com. He's also a writer and editor for the NBC Olympics site and is working on his second play, because why not?

**Caitlin Lawrence** serves as Visiting Instructor in Communication at Pepperdine University in Malibu, California, where she received both her undergraduate and graduate degrees. Her master's thesis is titled "Fairy Tale Faith: 'Cinderella's' Power to Draw Young Women toward an Internalization of Biblical Truths." Today she continues researching the relationship between media and religion.

**Elizabeth Lin**, PhD, recently completed the clinical psychology doctoral program at Fuller Theological Seminary, where she also earned master's degrees in psychology and theology. An alumna of the University of Michigan, she loves popular culture, college football, and *Parks and Recreation*. You can find her on Twitter at @curiousliz.

**Terry Lindvall,** PhD, is the C. S. Lewis Endowed Chair of Communication and Christian Thought at Virginia Wesleyan College. Among his published books are *Sanctuary Cinema* (2007) and *Celluloid Sermons* (2011), as well as other works on humor, film, and religion. He is presently working on *In the Seat of Scoffers: Religion, Laughter, and Satire from the Hebrew Prophets to Stephen Colbert.*

**Anthony R. Mills** recently completed his PhD in Theology and Culture from Fuller Theological Seminary, writing on Marvel comics and films in light of American hero mythology and theological anthropology. He considers himself an all-around geek and lover of almost anything in the sci-fi, fantasy, superhero, and zombie/horror genres.

**Christopher D. Min** is a conceptual artist and photographer based in Los Angeles, California. He has worked as an entertainment professional, producing content for numerous media channels such as MTV. He holds a MA in Theology from Fuller Theological Seminary and a BFA in Theater from the University of Southern California.

**Rose Pacatte**, FSP, MEd, is the Director for the Pauline Center for Media Studies in Los Angeles, California. An award-winning coauthor of the Lights, Camera, Faith series and columnist on faith and film for the *St. Anthony Messenger* and the *National Catholic Reporter*, she has appeared each season on the NBC/GSN TV show *1 vs. 100*.

**Mark I. Pinsky,** longtime religion writer for the *Orlando Sentinel* and the *Los Angeles Times,* specializes in evangelical Christianity. He is the author of *The Gospel according to* The Simpsons, *The Gospel according to Disney*, and *A Jew among the Evangelicals*. His commentaries appear in *USA Today*, the *Wall Street Journal*, and the *Harvard Divinity Bulletin*.

**Jana Riess** is currently the director of publishing for Patheos Press, and prior to that was an acquisitions editor at Westminster John Knox Press. She is the author of several books, including *Flunking Sainthood* and *What Would Buffy Do?* She is currently tweeting every chapter of the Bible as a daily humor project. She has a PhD in American religious history from Columbia University.

**Leah Buturain Schneider** seeks to "dwell in possibility, a fairer house than prose," pursuing wisdom's beauty as Senior Researcher for the Luce Sacred Imagery Project at Fuller Theological Seminary, where she is a Brehm scholar of theology and visual culture at the Brehm Center for Worship, Theology, and the Arts. She is also a gerontologist.

**Mindy Coates Smith** is the Codirector of Youth Discipleship at Bel Air Presbyterian Church in Los Angeles, California. She recently finished her doctoral work at Fuller Theological Seminary with an emphasis on youth, family, and culture.

**Jeanette Reedy Solano,** PhD, was born in Hollywood, California, the capital of popular culture. Today, as an Associate Professor of Comparative Religion at California State University, Fullerton, she now punches the same numbers into her remote every 108 minutes, hoping to find a series with half the brilliance, intrigue, and depth as *Lost*.

**Steve Sudeth** fills his days teaching and writing about the intersections of philosophy, culture, and spirituality. After earning degrees from Pepperdine University and Fuller Theological Seminary he has turned his attention to teaching his nephew about David Bowie. He currently lives with his wife and record collection in Redondo Beach, California.

**Eugene Suen** is a filmmaker, producer, and the Codirector of Reel Spirituality at Fuller Seminary. Raised in Taipei and Chicago, Eugene has codirected the City of the Angels Film Festival and is a member of Almond Tree Films, the team behind the award-winning film *Munyurangabo*. He recently produced the feature *Abigail Harm* and contributed a chapter in the newly released book *FilmCraft: Editing*. He is active in filmmaking and ministry.

**Lisa Swain** is an Associate Professor of Cinema and Media Arts at Biola University. She came to academia after a successful career in the film industry as a production supervisor on such films as *Big Fish* and *Anger Management*. She is currently working toward a PhD in Media Psychology at Fielding University.

**Barry Taylor,** PhD, is Artist-in-Residence at the Brehm Center for Theology, Worship, and the Arts at Fuller Theological Seminary; Senior Associate Rector at All Saints' Episcopal Church in Beverly Hills, California; Codirector of the Center for Creative and Emerging Ministry for the Episcopal Diocese of Los Angeles, California; and a lecturer in Advertising at Art Center College of Design in Pasadena, California—different hats, but all of them exploring the intersections of life, faith, and culture.

**Steve Taylor** is Senior Lecturer at Flinders University and Director of Missiology at Uniting College of Leadership and Theology. He is author of *Out of Bounds Church?* (2005), a film reviewer for *Touchstone* (since 2005), and chapter contributor in *Bible in/and Popular Culture* (2010) and *Exploring U2* (2011).

**Steve Turner** has written on music and popular culture for many publications, including *Rolling Stone, Mojo, Q,* and the (London) *Times*. He is the author of *The Gospel according to the Beatles* (2006), *Imagine: A Vision for Christians in the Arts* (2001), and *A Hard Day's Write: The Stories Behind Every Beatles' Song* (1999).

**Robert Velarde** is author of *The Wisdom of Pixar* (2010), *Conversations with C. S. Lewis* (2008), *The Heart of Narnia* (2008), *Examining Alternative Medicine* (2001), and more. He received his MA from Southern Evangelical Seminary and is an adjunct faculty member of Denver Seminary.

**Lauren F. Winner** is the author of several books, including *Still: Notes on a Mid-Faith Crisis* (2012) and *Girl Meets God* (2002) . She has a PhD from Columbia University and is Assistant Professor of Christian Spirituality at Duke Divinity School.

# The Fifties

$T$he fifties are remembered as an idyllic time when families (father, mother, and their two children) together watched *Father Knows Best, The Adventures of Ozzie and Harriet, The Honeymooners,* and *The Burns and Allen Show. I Love Lucy* lived up to its title, with audiences celebrating the birth of "Little Ricky" to Lucille Ball and Desi Arnaz. The Eisenhower era was a period of rising prosperity for suburbanites with affordable homes, higher educational levels, and profound medical advances (e.g., polio vaccine and organ transplants). Equality for Jews and Catholics became more common, and with *Brown vs. Board of Education of Topeka*, the concept of "separate but equal" was outlawed. In refusing to give up her seat, Rosa Parks sparked the Montgomery bus boycotts. Viewers sat transfixed in front of their TVs as Orval Faubus, the Governor of Arkansas, tried to resist the desegregation of Little Rock High School. Martin Luther King Jr. and the Southern Christian Leadership Conference started their long march to justice.

Those who came of age in the fifties were not simply the "silent generation." James Dean in *Rebel without a Cause* and Holden Caulfield, the angst-filled student in J. D. Salinger's 1951 novel *Catcher in the Rye,* emerged as counter-cultural heroes. Allen Ginsberg let out a collective "Howl" on behalf of "angelheaded hipsters burning for the ancient heavenly connection." By locating the holy amid junkies, homosexuals, beatniks, and the mentally ill, Ginsberg was tried for obscenity and became a symbol for free speech. The fifties also gave rise to other forms of rebellion like rock & roll. Preachers railed against a musical euphemism for sex, yet Bill Haley and the Comets' "Rock Around the Clock" still rings in the ears of those raised during this decade. Network censors couldn't silence the screams generated by Elvis's gyrating hips on *The Ed Sullivan Show.*

Conservatives embraced Ayn Rand's Rational Egoism and Objectivist philosophy articulated in her 1957 novel, *Atlas Shrugged.* Pioneering television priest Bishop Fulton J. Sheen insisted that *Life Is Worth Living* even as sci-fi films like *Invasion of the Body Snatchers* tapped into collective paranoia. The phrase "under God" was added to the pledge of allegiance. And producer Cecil B. DeMille installed the Ten Commandments in civic spaces as a way to promote his blockbuster film.

Yet, all was not as peaceful as it might have seemed in Pleasantville. The Cold War was heating up. With the Soviet launch of the Sputnik satellite in 1957, the fifties also saw the widespread construction of personal bomb shelters and anticommunist sentiment ranging from McCarthyism to the fear of brainwashing.

# *Ben-Hur*

The film *Ben-Hur* (1959) held the record for most Oscars for close to half a century until it was equaled by *Titanic* (1999) and *Lord of the Rings: Return of the King* (2003). Its story, however, doesn't trace to the 1950s when the movie came out, but to the late nineteenth century, when former Union General Lewis "Lew" Wallace chanced upon the notorious agnostic, Robert G. Ingersoll. The free-thinking humanist challenged Wallace's professed faith, causing the latter to examine what he really believed. Wallace wrestled with his understanding of the New Testament. After a period of intense personal investigation, Wallace wrote the bestselling novel *Ben-Hur, a Story of the Christ*, situating a bold fictional character within an authentic biblical setting.

This biblical epic captured the hearts and imaginations of readers around the world, including in the Vatican; it was the first work of fiction blessed by a Pope. The book has never been out of print since its publication in 1880. *Ben-Hur* lingers in the popular imagination, though this is more for its cinematic glory than for its nineteenth-century pious historical narrative. Its spectacle has attracted all the attention; yet quietly, *Ben-Hur* endures much more as an intimate spiritual journey or road novel, leading its protagonist from Jerusalem to Rome and back again. Wallace's iconic protagonist, Judah Ben-Hur, grapples with personal and political problems not unlike the author's own, trying to grasp how this historical figure of Jesus might fit into a world of violence, failure, adventure, and salvation. In the process, the story becomes a map for all of its myriad fans on their own pilgrimages of faith.

*Ben-Hur* has been adapted for both stage and film multiple times. In 1899, American theatrical entrepreneurs Marc Klaw and Abraham Erlanger persuaded the reluctant Wallace to allow a stage presentation with treadmills and moving backcloths at Manhattan's Broadway Theatre, though Wallace did reject a proposal to develop a Ben-Hur amusement park on Staten Island. Significantly, in an era in which some Christian resistance to theatre and film lingered, the play received a favorable welcome. In 1905, the famous director Sidney Olcott illegally commandeered Wallace's story to produce the first film version, a series of theatrical tableaux that merely watched events taking place, with people pointing at off-screen chariots zipping by. Two significant film versions followed, including a silent version for MGM in 1923 and the more prominent and impressive William Wyler production of 1959. Starring Charlton Heston, the film won a record eleven Academy Awards, including Best Picture.

*Ben-Hur* offers a double pleasure: it tells two tales, although the film versions play down the biblical Christ story, relegating it to a cosmic backdrop.

The other story concerns the eponymous Jewish hero, Judah Ben-Hur, whose stark individualism and resistance to Rome mark him as a political threat. On one level the narrative regales spectators with the testosterone-filled adventures of the noble Jewish merchant in contrast to his Roman best friend and nemesis, Messala. But amid the staggering scale of action sequences, chariot races, and sea battles, a small and intimate story emerges. Readers and spectators see what each of the central characters must suffer—family separations, unjust accusations, tests of loyalty to one's own people, motives of revenge, fears of disease and loss, and the pain of romance.

If the story were only Ben-Hur's story, readers and viewers would be stuck in his pain and ire. Like Alexander Dumas's *The Count of Monte Cristo*, which had inspired Wallace, the narrative trajectory is motivated by a desire for revenge. Anger keeps Ben-Hur alive and moving, struggling against the political, cultural, and spiritual powers aligned to thwart him. Falsely accused and enslaved, he is marched to the galley ships. Exhausted, he is refused water by all except one, one whose face we never see but whose hand extends a cup of cold water for the parched Jew. With the special lighting effects and crescendo of Miklós Rózsa's exquisite musical score, the moment transcends. We know we have seen Jesus, even if obliquely and in the corner of the screen. This is the power of *Ben-Hur* as a film and as a novel: the quietly bracketed story of Jesus of Nazareth, the Messiah prophesied in the Hebrew Bible.

TERRY LINDVALL

# Johnny Cash

"Hello, I'm Johnny Cash." With these words one of America's most famous musical sons would introduce himself to his audience, in spite of the fact that virtually the entire world could have recognized him by his trademark black clothing and the sound of his deep bass-baritone voice. His career, which began in country music, encompassed many other musical forms from rock and roll to blues, gospel, and folk.

Johnny Cash was born February 26, 1932, in Kingsland, Arkansas, the fourth of seven children. He was actually given the initials J.R. at birth because his parents could not agree on a name. It was only upon entering the United States Air Force, which refused to accept initials as his name, that Cash chose John R. Cash as his given name.

A 1954 move to Memphis, Tennessee, to pursue a career in radio announcing led to Cash's initial foray into music, playing guitar with two musicians known as the Tennessee Two. An early attempt at a recording career was thwarted by Sun Records's studio owner Sam Phillips, who deemed him unmarketable. "Go home and sin, then come back with a song I can sell," Phillips is reputed to have told Cash. Although this story is probably apocryphal, it hints at some of the lifelong conflicts captured in Cash's life and music. Cash did eventually win the famed producer over with some new songs he had written.

In 1956, Cash recorded *Folsom Prison Blues* and *I Walk the Line*, the former reaching number five in the country charts while *I Walk the Line* rose to number one in both the country and pop charts. After this, Cash became the first artist on Phillips's label to record long-playing albums, but his growing frustration with the constraints of Phillips's autocratic approach to recoding led Cash to a lucrative deal with Columbia Records.

As his career continued to grow, he had a number of chart hits and even a television program, *The Johnny Cash Show*, which aired from 1969 to 1971. The successful music variety show underscored his crossover popularity. As his career developed, so did a struggle with addiction to both drugs and alcohol, though it didn't seem to stifle his creativity.

A spiritual epiphany in 1968 forever changed Cash and introduced the world to a different kind of artist. He had attempted to commit suicide whilst under the influence of drugs and found his way to the Nickajack, a partially flooded cave in Marion, Tennessee. He passed out in the cave and upon waking described a sense of God's presence in the darkest moments of his life. Although he battled addictions more than once after this conversion experience, it changed the course of his life. After this encounter he lived at the home of the Carter Family (one of the first families of country music) and eventually married June Carter. They wrote, toured, and sang together until June's death in 2003.

By the early 1970s, Johnny Cash became the Man in Black. He generally performed wearing black, which stood in marked contrast to the gaudy rhinestone suits and flashy cowboy boots of most of his country music contemporaries. He wrote a song, "The Man in Black," to explain his dress, saying "just so we're reminded of the ones who are held back/ up front there ought to be a man in black." He went on to sing that he wore black on behalf of the poor and hungry, the imprisoned, the elderly, and those betrayed by addictions and the "lives that could have been." He expressed his theology and lived out the complexities and dichotomies of his own life and faith through the songs he sang and the clothes he wore. Fellow country singer Kris Kristofferson told the *New York Times* after Cash's death in 2003 that the singer was "as comfortable with the poor and prisoners as he is with presidents. He's crossed over all age boundaries. I like to think of him as Abraham Lincoln with a wild side."

Cash was a devout but troubled man whose life was characterized, like the songs he sang, by sorrow, tribulation, and redemption. He wore his faith quite literally on his sleeve and sang of it without any hesitation. Of himself he said, "I am a Christian, don't put me in another box." A complex Christian, but one nonetheless.

BARRY TAYLOR

## Walt Disney

Since 1938, few institutions outside organized religion have played a greater role in instilling values in young children around the world as the Walt Disney Company—from its early animated shorts through the opening of Disneyland in 1955 and especially through its full-length, animated feature films.

Walt Disney (1901–1966) always called himself a Christian, but his biographers agree that, as a result of being raised in a fundamentalist home, he was skeptical about organized religion and as an adult he rarely set foot inside a church. He insisted that any narrow portrayal of Protestant Christianity (or any religion, for that matter) in his animated features was box-office poison, particularly in lucrative overseas markets. More broadly, Walt's fear was that explicit religiosity might needlessly exclude young viewers, while a watered-down version might at the same time offend the devout.

Yet the studio's founding genius also understood that, from the ancient Greeks to the Brothers Grimm, successful storytellers have needed supernatural intervening agents to resolve plots. So, Walt decided, Disney's cartoon protagonists would appeal not to Judeo-Christian religion but to magic, which was more palatable in the ticket-buying world. It is no coincidence that Disney's marquee theme park is called the Magic Kingdom, or that there are no churches on Main Street, USA.

On one hand, there were good fairies, godmothers, wishes upon a star, and, later, a fast-talking blue genie. On the other were witches, wizards, sorcerers, and malign spirits and spells. Critically, however, while evil and the dark side existed, they never, ever triumphed over good. Over the decades a more comprehensive, hopeful theology evolved around that single, unshakable tenet.

In addition, Disney characters had to have faith in faith. That is, they had to believe in themselves, as well as in something greater than themselves. That greater something was nonspecific, vaguely defined in terms of human values and moral lessons rather than particular religious creeds.

This secular 'toonism became the Disney Gospel, and most Christian leaders and parents accepted its trade-offs. At first, there was some resistance from Christian leaders, beginning with the release of Disney's first full-length animated movie, *Snow White and the Seven Dwarfs*, in 1938. Reviewers at the time voiced similar worries about the dark magic in that groundbreaking feature. And in the 1960s, there was some notable resistance from the left in such books as *How to Read Donald Duck: Imperialist Ideology in the Disney Comic*, by Ariel Dorfman and Armand Mattelart.

The long rapprochement between Christian leaders and Disney has occasionally frayed. In 1996, the Southern Baptist Convention launched a nationwide (and ultimately unsuccessful) Disney boycott. It protested that the conglomerate, under Michael Eisner and Jeffrey Katzenberg's leadership, had betrayed Walt Disney's family-friendly legacy. Among other complaints, they charged that the full-length animated features *Lion King* and *The Little Mermaid* contained subliminal sexual messages and that the company extended health benefits to same-sex partners.

Before the boycott began, Eisner and Katzenberg—both Jews—had already taken a 180-degree turn from Walt's religion-averse policy in the company's signature releases. They believed it was possible to animate faith without caricaturing it. In 1996's *The Hunchback of Notre Dame*, Disney writers and artists turned Victor Hugo's anticlerical classic on its head, making the studio's most explicitly pro-Christian feature ever. While the Baptists applauded—and took credit for—this aspect of *Hunchback*, they were considerably less enamored with the films that showcased different belief systems, all in positive, respectful lights: *Mulan* (Confucianism), *Pocahontas* (animism), *Hercules* (paganism), and *Brother Bear* (shamanism).

After *Brother Bear* in 2003, Disney seemed to give up on hand-drawn, 2D animated features. When it purchased Pixar in 2006, a studio that specialized in computer-generated imagery (CGI), some wondered if the glory days of Disney-identified animation were over.

Those concerns were answered in 2009 with the release of *The Princess and the Frog*, a classic animated feature that featured a young African American heroine. While the Walt Disney Company no doubt expected kudos for breaking racial barriers in what turned out to be a modest holiday hit, the entertainment giant found itself receiving stinging criticism from some Christians. HollywoodJesus.com said the animated feature's preoccupation with voodoo, black magic, bloody amulets, and Ouija boards was "too dark and extreme for this kind of kids' film." ChristianAnswers.net rated the movie "Offensive"; citing a Tarot card reading, soul transfer, and implied reincarnation, the site called the film "demonic." But in fact, the film embodied all of the elements of the studio's cartoon cosmology. When the hard-working heroine demonstrated that she believed in herself, a voodoo fairy godmother intervened, making things right.

MARK I. PINSKY

# Charles and Ray Eames

Long before terms like "organic" and "sustainable" began to describe "green" architecture, Charles and Ray Eames were busy creating designs with humanity and nature in mind. They figured out how to bend but not break wood to conform to human sizes. This husband and wife team of American designers graduated from the Cranbrook Academy of Art in Bloomfield Hills, Michigan, and worked in both architecture and furniture design. They are renowned as innovators, developing new design technologies and working in modern materials like fiberglass, plastic resin, wire mesh, and particularly molded plywood. Together they defined midcentury modern design and transformed the way Americans furnished their homes. For almost four decades they contributed to and shaped virtually every facet of American daily life.

A move to California in 1941 saw Charles initially working in the movie industry and his wife creating cover designs for *California Arts and Architecture* magazine. Charles experimented with molded plywood; he was searching for a way to create a flexible product that could be manipulated in multiple shapes and forms. He built an apparatus named the Kazam! Machine to mold plywood, but it didn't function well and was abandoned. In the midst of his experimentation, Charles was commissioned by the U.S. Navy to develop mass-produced and lightweight plywood splints for injured servicemen. Access to military technology helped Eames to resolve the design challenges he had not been able to conquer to that point.

Having overcome the design issues that had hindered them, the Eameses turned their attention to furniture design. Their first product was a simple chair produced by the Herman Miller Company. The low-slung chair was called the Lounge Chair Wood (LCW). It appeared modest in its ambitions, close to the floor, with no tall back to announce its importance. But sitting in the chair was a nearly miraculous experience. How could something so simple and basic be so comfortable? It remains in production today. They quickly added other furniture products to their catalog—Dining Chair Wood (DCW), Dining Chair Metal (DCM), and Aluminum Group furniture. The Eames Lounge Chair became a status symbol for executives eager to impress their clients. Its black leather can be seen on the sets of *Mad Men*, *Frasier*, and *House*, communicating taste, style, and success. Charles and Ray's furniture designs met the need of consumers eager to embrace a more modern existence after the struggles and deprivations of the early decades of the twentieth century. Their work was crafted with real people in mind.

Once they had established their furniture business, Charles and Ray expanded into architecture. The housing demand in America had been around since the Great Depression, but the return of soldiers after the war exacerbated the crisis. The *Arts and Architecture* magazine developed a project aimed at solving the crisis by inviting young architects to design and build case study homes. In 1951, the Eameses built Case House Study #8 in the Pacific Palisades, which became their family home. They used off-the-shelf parts found in steel manufacturers' catalogs because of the shortage of traditional building materials. Their house's industrial feel, combined with a flexible interior with maneuverable spaces rather than fixed room arrangements, became a model of postwar modern architecture. It captured how we aspired to live in harmony with nature and each other. Esteemed architect Eero Saarinen recognized the "spiritual function" in what they created.

Alongside furniture and architectural design the Eameses also were involved in fabric design and filmmaking, particularly with corporate communication films. They had been making films together for most of their marriage, documenting their interest in things like collecting toys and their travels to various places. Their film *Glimpses of the USA* was shown in the Soviet Union in 1959. The beguiling short, *Powers of Ten*, took viewers from a park in Chicago to the edges of the cosmos in exponential, ten-second intervals. Films like *Contact* and *Wall-E* borrowed heavily from Charles and Ray's vision. While they are renowned as American designers, their influence was truly global.

In 1958 Charles and Ray were asked to put together a curriculum for the National Institute for Design in Ahmedabad, India. The "Eames Report," as it was known, was influential in modern Indian architecture. In it, the two noted that the major impact on design in India was not influence from the West or East but the "phenomenon of communication . . . that affects a world, not a country." A central message was an intensely modern one that still holds true today—that "security lies in change." This was the philosophy that the Eameses lived and worked by.

A third curricula idea was that rather than being based on composition, design should be focused on expression. This idea liberated design from the rules that kept it limited to certain appearances and forms. In 1970–71, Charles gave the Norton Poetry Lectures at Harvard where he told a story about the banana leaf, which is the most basic dish that people eat off of in southern India. He explored the progression of its design from simple functionality into something beautiful and ornate. This was classic Eames rooted in the organic and underscored his views on design as expression.

Communication, change, and expression—simple ideas that transformed the world of design and ushered in the ideology of modern culture. Charles and Ray Eames essentially took wine and made new wineskins, understanding that the key to accessing the future was moving into it.

BARRY TAYLOR

## *Gojira (Godzilla)*

Etymologically, the word "monster" involves two overlapping meanings: to show and to warn. The monster engages us both with a spectacle and with a foreboding sense of terror accompanied by admonition. As with all monsters, Godzilla fascinates, frightens, and forewarns.

The 1945 bombing of Hiroshima and Nagasaki produced Godzilla, the iconic giant lizard-like monster of Japan's premiere sci-fi film director, Ishiro Honda. Almost ten years after the holocaustic devastation, Honda released *Gojira* in 1954, its monster intent on wreaking havoc on the citizens of Tokyo, the rebuilt capital.

This movie invokes memories of American nuclear testing near the Marshall Islands. In 1954, an American nuclear blast off the Bikini Atoll contaminated an unsuspecting Japanese tuna fishing boat, the *Daigo Fukuryu Mary*. More than a thinly veiled symbol, the "monster" erupts out of legends and history to confront us with our sin, since Honda's Gojira is created from just this type of nuclear accident.

In the American version, Godzilla emerges dramatically out of a radioactive and foamy sea, stepping onto Japanese soil and stomping into Tokyo itself. Full of rage, terror, and destruction, the monster is more than a symbol of the dark, iridescent seas; it conjures up the consequences of everything evil done by humanity (even if done for noble reasons), with the boomerang-ing effect of sin returning to haunt us. Somewhere between *Pogo*'s "we have met the enemy and he is us" and *The Shadow*'s "The evil that men do lives after them" hovers the warning of this classic Japanese film, trying to show us the curious relationship of ourselves to our monsters. If we are not the monsters, the film suggests, then we at least have created them.

The Japanese horror film that began the franchise originally appeared as *Gojira*, whose name combined the Japanese words for "whale" and "gorilla." *Gojira* comes across as both serious and solemn, unlike its campy and badly re-edited, dubbed, and butchered 1956 American version, *Godzilla, King of the Monsters!* Starring a pompous, pipe-smoking Raymond Burr as a stuffy journalist, the American adaptation erased any trace of the original's scath-ing anti-American sentiment. Monster movie aficionados revere the original source, *Gojira*.

In *Gojira*'s now-familiar plot, American nuclear testing has given rise to a 150-foot tall engine of destruction, breathing atomic fire and hell-bent on destroying Tokyo before taking on the world. Assembling the army and all of the modern science Japan can muster, the Japanese battle the rampaging monster to the film's inevitable conclusion: Gojira is destroyed, but at great human cost. The original version offers much more than the classic monster going berserk and wreaking havoc on civilization; it speaks to the corruption of human nature and the groaning of nature itself.

Starring the veteran Kurosawa actor, Takashi Shimura (*Seven Samurai*), as a prescient scientist who reflects on the meaning of the monster's sud-den appearance, *Gojira* does not resemble the man-versus-monster movies of the American Cold War period. Instead, *Gojira* is a meditation on nuclear devastation and the pursuit of weapons of mass destruction. Furthermore, it is about answering why this monster emerged and what can be done about it. When the heroine's tormented fiancé must descend to the monster's watery lair with his oxygen destroyer to wipe out the king of the monsters, we rec-ognize that a life must be sacrificed for this evil we produced.

Godzilla, played in the U.S. film by an actor in a rubber suit and with a hand puppet, still elicits terror, but is tempered with sadness. Pathos for the monster grows, even as catastrophic incidents destroy not only trains and famous Tokyo buildings but also innocent women and children. The movie evokes a melancholic atmosphere as Godzilla hovers against the electric grids and fire-cast shadows looming in the background. Although the cheesy special effects of the lumbering monster will make contemporary viewers smile, this smirk will be quickly erased by scenes of sheer wonder, such as when Gojira stares at a huge clock in the original Japanese film, seemingly reflecting on the nature of time, before trying to devour it. Or again, Rudolf Otto's idea of the holy will be evoked as Gojira peeks over the mountains before it begins its rampage of death and devastation.

As recounted in William Tsutsui's book *Godzilla on My Mind,* Tojo Studio producer Tomoyuki Tanaka explained that his theme for *Gojira* was "the terror of the bomb; mankind had created the bomb, and now nature was going to take revenge on mankind." Showing the hubris of modern science, the military, and the government, *Godzilla/Gojira* warns viewers that our own monstrous nature can unleash untold cataclysms of suffering, which will require the personal sacrifice of a life.

TERRY LINDVALL

## Billy Graham

Which evangelist has a star on the Hollywood Walk of Fame? Not Pat Robertson or Oral Roberts, but Billy Graham. Graham also shares the distinction, along with the president of the United States, of the U.S. postal service delivering his mail with just his name and country as the address. Such is his iconic status!

Born in 1918, Graham grew up on a farm near Charlotte, North Carolina. Within that small-town, Southern culture, racial segregation was accepted as a cultural norm, supported by religious conviction. The people of the town represented a churchgoing culture, with regular revival meetings to restore spiritual backsliders. Graham dates his conversion to the revival meetings of Mordecai Ham in 1934.

From obscure beginnings, raised in legalistic, separatist fundamentalism, Graham rose to occupy a unique place on the American religious stage, and indeed around the world. He has preached to more people than any other Protestant, become a trusted friend of U.S. presidents, and been welcomed by many world leaders. He first came to national attention through a Hearst newspaper piece "puffing" his 1949 Los Angeles crusade. His influence grew until he was addressing crowds of tens of thousands to a quarter of a million in New York's Central Park in 1991, and over a million in Seoul, Korea. His radio and TV programs and syndicated My Answer newspaper column reached millions and kept his name before the public.

Graham never claimed to be a theologian. His primary calling remained that of an evangelist, to which he remained committed over the decades of his ministry. The greatest intellectual challenge to his theological position came from his close friend Charles Templeton, with whom he worked at Youth for Christ. Templeton had increasing doubts concerning the Bible's authority once he was introduced to higher criticism and neoorthodoxy at Princeton Theological Seminary in 1948. Eventually he declared himself an agnostic. Graham knew that he was no match for Templeton's sharp intellect, but he was determined to accept the authority of the Bible by faith even while seeking increased understanding.

Remarkably, Billy Graham played a key role in forging an evangelical identity and consensus, beginning in the 1950s. He achieved this through his gracious spirit and his ability to establish a climate of trust. He also broadened the evangelical agenda to include issues of racial reconciliation and social justice. In 1953 in Chattanooga, Tennessee, he removed the ropes separating the white and black sections at his crusade, a move that shocked many Southerners. He held meetings around Alabama following the Selma march in 1965, and he visited Watts neighborhood in 1965 after the Los Angeles riots. In 1960 he refused to include South Africa on his African visit as a protest against apartheid. Graham maintained a friendship with Martin Luther King Jr., who counseled Graham to preach his message in the stadium, while he would march in the streets.

Billy Graham's influence in establishing an evangelical alternative to liberalism on the one hand, and legalistic fundamentalism on the other, was promoted by establishing *Christianity Today* in 1956 (as a counterpoint to *Christian Century*) under the editorship of Carl Henry. Influencing Graham's thinking during this time was his contact with evangelical scholars who had not been exposed to the kind of fundamentalism of Graham's early years: Harold John Ockenga of Park Street Church in Boston; Leighton Ford, who became Billy's brother-in-law; Anglican pastor/scholar J. R. W. Stott of London; and Scottish theologian J. D. Douglas. *The Lausanne International Conference on World Evangelization* in 1974, sponsored by the Billy Graham Evangelistic Association that brought together evangelical scholars from around the world, produced *The Lausanne Covenant,* which for several decades was evangelicalism's most accepted theological position statement.

In the post-Graham era the question arises as to whether the mass-evangelistic meeting will continue to play a significant role in Christian life, as an increasing percentage of the population becomes distanced from institutional religion. Perhaps his youth appeal of increased crowd participation and contemporary music might point to the future, but this is unclear. Also uncertain is the question of unity: In the 1970s, one popular description of Evangelicalism was all those who agreed with Billy Graham. Today it remains an open question whether Evangelicalism can retain the cohesion of earlier decades or fragment under the pressure of divergent biblical, theological, and political viewpoints. Already in evidence is evangelicalism's increasing partisanship, as groups align with the political right or left, succumbing to increasing polarization and strident culture wars.

EDDIE GIBBS

# Alfred Hitchcock

Jesuit film critic Richard A. Blake proposes that the Catholic "afterimage," which emerges in the works of several American filmmakers, reveals that Catholic faith, training, and culture have marked these filmmakers' work. This is certainly true of British film director Alfred Hitchcock. Coming from a Catholic family and schooled by Jesuits, he later said that what he chiefly learned from his religious background was fear. His only intention as a film director therefore became "to simply scare the hell out of people." In the words of film critic David Thomson, Hitchcock "taught America to love murder."

When Hitchcock was six years old, his father, William, sent him to the local police precinct in London with a note for the officer about an infraction. He was to place the young boy in a cell for five minutes to teach him what happens to naughty boys. Hitchcock insisted for years that this was the source for his themes of false imprisonment, isolation, fear of enclosure, unjust punishment, and anxiety about any kind of pursuit.

His mother, Emma Jane, seems to be responsible for Hitchcock's fixation with confession, guilt, ritual, and the psychological intimacy of a not-quite-normal mother-son relationship in films such as *Notorious* (1946), *North by Northwest* (1959), *Strangers on a Train* (1951), *Psycho* (1960), *The Birds* (1963), and *Frenzy* (1972). Each evening, even after he left school and was working, Hitchcock had to stand at the foot of his mother's bed and answer "detailed questions with detailed replies." As for insecurity, terror, darkness, and loneliness, essential elements of the horror genre, these seem to come not only from his parents but from Hitchcock himself. He admitted often that he was always frightened.

Pauline Kael, the most unambiguous voice ever to emerge from American film criticism, described Hitchcock as "an ingenious master builder of mouse-traps, and more often than not, the audience is caught tight."

Hitchcock designed every script, even noting the editing to be done, and seldom wavered from that vision. Although Kael—who made these observations in the 1970s when the influence of less-stylized French New Wave filmmaking was on the rise—saw this as a negative, Hitchcock's influence on the actual practice of "blueprint" filmmaking is normal today.

Hitchcock, for all his brilliance, was a deeply conflicted man and this inevitably emerged in his art. Although he was married and the father of a child, biographers attest to his preference for young, blond women, pointing out that his sexual desires and frustrations frightened young actresses and assistants. His methods to achieve a desired effect could be cruel, such as causing actress Tippi Hedren to have a physical breakdown by repeatedly filming the final attack by real birds. This shut down production of *The Birds* for a week. His films are often voyeuristic and explore criminal and sexual transgressions, their possibilities and consequences, as well as guilt. All of a film's elements, from camera angle to music and sound, were calculated for effect. Though Hitchcock claims not to have trusted psychoanalysis (*Spellbound* in 1945 notwithstanding), Freudian themes and motifs, from the Oedipus complex to repression of traumatic memories, recur in his films. Carl Jung's ideas about dreams and the shadow-self are also present in Hitchcock's films and provide keys to their interpretation. *Marnie* (1964), especially the rape scene, seems almost a synthesis of Hitchcock's own pathological psychology.

Alfred Hitchcock made fifty-three films over six decades. It seems incredible that he was nominated for the Academy Award for Best Director five times, yet never won. He did receive the Irving G. Thalberg Memorial Award for Lifetime Achievement in 1967, but it had to be seen as a consolation prize.

Hitchcock's influence on filmmakers continues today: consider his use of the MacGuffin, a plot element that keeps the action moving, even though it has no intrinsic importance (*The 39 Steps*, 1935; *Notorious*, 1946; *North by Northwest*, 1959). But it is his film *Psycho* that perhaps most changed the face of filmmaking. More than any other film, it made horror, noir humor, murder, nudity (using an impressionistic montage), blood (using chocolate syrup), and swirling toilets (this was the first one ever allowed in American film under the Motion Picture Production Code) acceptable to mainstream American audiences. The censors were so confused by the ninety shots from seventy different camera angles in the 45-second shower scene that they let the film pass. And the rest is history!

Hitchcock's most easily identifiable religious film was *I Confess* (1953). But as Blake notes, Hitchcock was more interested in a good thriller than theology. At best, Hitchcock's Catholic "afterimage" sheds light on secular realities and the human condition.

ROSE PACATTE

# C. S. Lewis

The life of C. S. Lewis reveals many paradoxes. An atheistic professor of medieval literature at the beginning of his career, Lewis later gained world renown as an author of children's literature with distinctly Christian themes. In another unusual dichotomy, despite being a high-church Anglican, he is greatly adored by American evangelicals who somehow see past his belief in the actual presence of Christ in the Eucharist, his anti-inerrantist views, and his enjoyment of a good beer and smoke. Most surprising, though, this self-defined "high-brow academic" wrote literature that has found great currency in popular culture, particularly with Walden Media's release of films based on his Narnia series. *The Lion, the Witch, and the Wardrobe* (2005); *Prince Caspian* (2008); and *The Voyage of the Dawn Treader* (2010) grossed well over $1.5 billion in theatres worldwide.

Much of Lewis's appeal results from his peculiar talent for expressing complicated matters in simple and reasonable ways. He was able to turn thick theological concepts into fiction, as with *Till We Have Faces* (1956), his space trilogy, and of course *The Chronicles of Narnia* (1950–1956). Also, in nonfiction works like *Mere Christianity* (1952) and *A Grief Observed* (1961) he made complicated arguments for faith lucid enough that many recognize him as the leading Christian apologist of the twentieth century. Lewis moved effortlessly between the "high" academic and church cultures where he spent his time and the "lowly" worlds of children's literature and popular culture. This talent for simplification without falsification, however, does not fully explain his popularity.

American evangelicals have also embraced Lewis because his theological works have expressed their discontents with modernity. In "Meditation in a Toolshed," Lewis draws an analogy from a beam of light entering a dark shed. He notes the difference between looking *at* the beam of light and putting one's eye in the light and looking *along* the beam to see through the hole to the world outside. Critiquing modernity's preference for looking *at*, he notes, "It has even come to be taken for granted that the external account of a thing somehow refutes or 'debunks' the account given from inside." For

Lewis, it was important to recognize that the experience of being in love is quite different from the scientist's observation of the boy in love. The being in love, the looking *along* the beam, provides at least as clear an understanding of true reality as does the looking *at*.

A similar argument in *The Abolition of Man* furthers the point. Lewis believed with Aristotle that, as the Greek philosopher taught in his *Ethics*, the purpose of education was "to make the student like and dislike what he ought." Modern education, in contrast, dismisses any connection between a student's belief and a reality beyond the self, thus discrediting belief as mere opinion. The result, Lewis argues, is that students are left with only intellectual opinions and bodily appetites. By extracting any sense of a reality beyond the physical, modernity consequently breeds human beings incapable of courage, honor, and drive, for they have no hearts. In writings like these, Lewis gave evangelicals a reasoned and respectable voice in their defiance of modern theological movements that attempted to remove all mystery from Christianity and strain it into mere moral teachings. Lewis was, in short, a friend of faith and mystery.

Lewis's influence on popular culture can be traced along the same trajectory. Though his apologetic prose spoke eloquently into his modern context, culture has largely turned away from reasoned evidence for the gospel. Narrative enticement has since proved more constructive, and it is Lewis's fiction that has catapulted him into popular culture.

Lewis was at ease using both his reason and his imagination. In "Bluspels and Flalansferes," he wrote, "reason is the natural organ of truth; but imagination is the organ of meaning." Developing this organ of meaning was the purpose of the Inklings' weekly gatherings at a local pub, where J. R. R. Tolkien, Charles Williams, Lewis, his brother Warren, and others gathered to read their unfinished works to one another. They spoke of baptizing people's imaginations and enlivening in readers what Lewis came to name *Sehnsucht*, the longing and melancholic joy for true reality that we all possess. In doing this, they hoped to help people look along the beam of light, to know truth in more than just our minds. For this reason, Lewis's fiction, particularly *The Chronicles*, will outlast his other works. Lewis did not simply tell us about truth, he helped us feel it in our chests and imagine it could be true for us.

TIM BASSELIN

## *The Lord of the Rings* and J. R. R. Tolkien

"Stop possessing it," instructs Gandalf the Grey to Bilbo Baggins as they first discuss the ring that animates one of the most significant literary works of the twentieth century: J. R. R. Tolkien's *The Lord of the Rings* (LOTR). While it's true that Tolkien's world (or interpretations of it) have engaged the public's imagination since initial publication in 1954 and 1955 through animation, video games, and a hugely popular blockbuster film series, these creative responses are no more definitive or final in their representations of Tolkien's witness than is a single production of a Shakespeare play. Friends don't let friends see the LOTR films without reading the source material. The lyrical authority and the comprehensive scope of Tolkien's vision are gifts that keep on giving.

In the first book of the trilogy (*The Fellowship of the Ring*), Gandalf counsels Bilbo that the ring of great power, which Bilbo possesses, may in fact possess him. "It has . . . far too much hold on you. Let it go!" This is years before the Council of Elrond, the reappearance of Sméagol, and the siege of Gondor, but in microcosm, this exchange is at the heart of Tolkien's moral vision. After flipping out for a moment, indulging in harried equivocation, and even referring to the thing as his "precious," Bilbo surrenders the ring, following the gesture with a tired look of relief and a laugh. In typical Tolkien fashion, Gandalf describes the scene of Bilbo's struggle to Frodo years later ("He hated it and loved it, as he hated and loved himself") and does so in such an offhanded way that the cosmic significance of the moment only dawns upon the reader gradually. Of all the beings in the ring's history, it is only Bilbo, Gandalf observes, who gave it up willingly.

That which Hobbits like Bilbo, Frodo, and Frodo's friend Samwise Gamgee seem to perform almost unknowingly is the work Gandalf himself seeks to emulate—the creative capacity for open-handedness. This is not unrelated to the habit of self-emptying (*kenosis*) whereby Jesus, according to Philippians 2:7, made himself nothing and took the form of a servant, not considering the life of divinity something to be grasped at. The urge to seize and control through the assertion of will and force is ever with us, but life and liveliness demand a different path to be discerned anew in every situation, every relationship.

There's the issue of Gollum (formerly called Sméagol), for instance, which the various members of the Fellowship of the Ring (Frodo, Aragorn, et al) have to sort through. Would it not make a certain sense to put the poor creature out of his misery? Apart from the terror he will doubtless bring, he had also murdered his relative Deagol to first obtain the ring, so a quick death might even be better than he deserves. Gandalf will have none of it:

"Many that live deserve death . . . Some that die deserve life. Can you give it to them? . . . Do not be too eager to deal out death in judgment. For even the wise cannot see all ends." As a steward, not a ruler, of all that might yet flower and bloom, Gandalf is committed to a deeply redemptive attentiveness to the world as it is; *not* as it might be remade: "I have not much hope that Gollum can be cured before he dies, but there is a chance . . . the pity of Bilbo may rule the fate of many." Even when he has the opportunity to take out his wizard rival, Saruman, Gandalf refrains: "I do not wish for mastery."

In fiction, scholarship, and correspondence, Tolkien often appears to be our most eloquent and prophetic critic of the well-intentioned but tragically misguided will to domination, the tale that in a 1951 letter to his editor he termed, "the Fall, Mortality, and the Machine." The desire to move beyond "the satisfactions of plain ordinary biological life" leads to the "bulldozing" of humans and other living things. Such desire dedicates itself to presumed efficiency and paved-over meadows people on committees once referred to as "development." As Tolkien teaches us, the more knowingly incarnate work of redemptive cultivation is an artfulness that always eschews such mastery. Like the magic practiced by the most faithful denizens of Middle-earth, "Its object is Art not Power, sub-creation not domination and tyrannous reforming of creation."

DAVID DARK

# Mickey Mantle

Becoming a sports hero is never easy. However, it is far more difficult to become a sports legend—an athlete whose presence both on and off the field transcends the tidy confines of the game. Likewise, winning a batting title is not easy. However, it is far more difficult to win a Major League Triple Crown—the highest batting average, the most home runs, and the greatest number of RBIs in both the American and National leagues in a single season. In the whole of professional baseball history, only five players have accomplished this feat. In 1956, Mickey Mantle (1931–1995) became the last player to do so. Yet, even though history remembers Mantle as a baseball great, his rise to legendary status was far from meteoric. After he took the place of the beloved Joe DiMaggio in center field for the New York Yankees, the impassioned fans and unfriendly press in the Big Apple were initially resistant to the young Mantle. He was too green, too unpolished, too "country" to thrive in the spotlight that shone on ballplayers in this booming metropolis.

As his career progressed, however, baseball aficionados in both New York and across the country could no longer deny his greatness. In addition to Mantle's Triple Crown, he won seven World Series, took three American League MVP titles, and was selected to play in sixteen All-Star games. Moreover, Mantle captured the public's heart by not only establishing the all-time record for walk-off home runs but also by hitting some of the longest long balls in Major League history. Indeed, the tape measure home run originated from an attempt within the Yankees' organization to determine the length of Mantle's heart-stopping dingers. By the end of his career Mantle was more than a ballplayer; he was firmly ensconced within the mythic annals of America's pastime. Thus, when we consider Mickey Mantle, we are no longer speaking of a mere baseball player; we are standing in awe of a legend.

Within popular cultural, exceptional athletes like Mantle are not merely admired. They do not simply serve as role models. Rather, they are revered, adored, and worshiped as sports "gods." Could it be that we divinize these mythic heroes because, on a fundamental level, we are concerned with the infinite possibilities of our existence? As we celebrate the spectacular, the sensational, and the super-human, it is as if, deep within us, we sense that there is a larger meaning to human life and activity. Thus, much like the ancient Greeks with their pantheon of gods and demigods, we follow our sports heroes religiously, hoping for a touch of the divine—a foretaste of the infinite. In doing so, we invest these cultural figures with a transcendent significance, standing dumbstruck in the presence of their greatness.

It therefore comes as a surprise when these legends display the same weaknesses as the humans they routinely amaze. Mantle, who was the son of a domineering father, was notorious for his rampant alcoholism and even spurning children who were seeking his autograph. In part, his lifelong struggle with alcohol led directly to the significant statistical decline that marked the end of his otherwise illustrious career. His indiscretions were such that, not only did his wife and each of his sons become alcoholics, but he attended his induction ceremony to the Hall of Fame with his wife on one arm and his mistress on the other. To be sure, our sports legends are inspiring, but they are also all-too-human.

Despite the fact that his private life was anything but exemplary, the public continues to revere Mantle. Why? Perhaps this impulse to willingly overlook or even deny the failings of our sports heroes resonates with a basic longing to venerate those who are unbound by the fetters of humanity's brokenness. Perhaps our adoration of sports figures like Mantle offers a glimpse into a more substantive reality that we can intuit but only dimly see. That is, through our adoration of these sports "gods," it may be that we encounter a mythic symbol of the *means* by which we are able to enter into this untarnished reality—a divine human whose humanity remains unmarred and whose divinity is intimately bound up in the human condition. For that would be a hero we could worship, a person whose failings we would never have to overlook.

KUTTER CALLAWAY

# Marilyn Monroe

Permanently seared into the contemporary cultural consciousness is an image of Marilyn Monroe standing over a subway vent in *The Seven Year Itch* (1955). Sporting a flirtatious smile, an almost careless demeanor, and a halter-neck dress that is either unwilling or simply incapable of abiding by the laws of gravity, she exudes both a playful innocence and a brooding sexuality. Here, frozen in time, is both the paragon of pulchritude and the epitome of a prurient modern-day siren enticing all passersby with her tacit-yet-palpable sensuality. As many have convincingly argued, it is this still frame that solidified Monroe's status as an icon within American popular culture. Apparently, this image (and, by extension, this woman) embodies all that we consider to be true, good, and beautiful.

In a somewhat fateful twist, though, it is this same image that reduced Monroe to little more than her own visage. In truth, Norma Jeane Mortenson (1926–1962) always longed to be and, indeed, always was more than a sex symbol. Yet in spite of her desire to be taken seriously as a dramatic actress, she was routinely cast to play the part of eye candy, even to the point where contemporary critics believed she was the victim of exploitation. Although a few of her fellow actors would occasionally note her quiet ambition and pronounced intelligence, she could never fully escape the cultural (and economic) reality that, ultimately, *Gentlemen Prefer Blondes* (1953) and *Some Like It Hot* (1959). Even though she won a Golden Globe for the latter of these two films, as far as filmmakers and the broader public were concerned, Monroe remained the quintessential dumb blonde, whose primary function was to entice the audience's gaze in the same manner as her photo on the cover of the first issue of *Playboy*.

In other words, it was the iconic sex goddess that the public wanted, and, given Monroe's aspirations, an image that she willingly provided. Over time, her persona increasingly reflected an image of female sexuality that the public idolized. Men wanted her and women wanted to be her. In addition to her three marriages (to policeman Joe Dougherty, baseball star Joe DiMaggio, and playwright Arthur Miller), her celebrity was bolstered by rumors that she had affairs with, among others, John and Robert Kennedy. In the closing moments of her career, she filmed the infamous pool scene in *Something's Got to Give* (1962), posed for nude photographs in *Vogue* magazine, and delivered a breathless rendition of "Happy Birthday" to President Kennedy in a skin-tight sequined dress. In doing so, this object of love, desire, and devotion captivated our collective cultural gaze. In the person of Marilyn Monroe, the icon had become an idol.

Thus, the tragedy of Monroe's story is rooted not so much in the untimely nature of her death, but in the fact that her image—much like her very life— had been commodified, fetishized, and consumed to such a degree that she was ultimately reduced to an American idol. At the age of thirty-six, Marilyn Monroe's life ended due to a drug overdose, but it may very well be that we idolized her to death.

This invites theological consideration not only of our cultural icons and idols but of our culturally embedded conceptions regarding what it means to be fully, authentically, and essentially human. If an idol is that which captures our devoted gaze but is inherently limited by the inadequacies of human vision, then an icon is something (or someone) that clarifies our vision by allowing the visible to become saturated with the invisible. The idol limits our gaze; the icon enlarges it, granting us the ability to peer through the porous boundary between the material world and the world of deeper, richer meanings that resides just beneath the surface. The icon floods our experience with its excess and, in doing so, offers a critique of our thin and underdeveloped visions of life and its meaning.

In this way, through her tragic death, Monroe's life has emerged as something of an icon in the religious sense of the term. The basic dis-ease that her death evokes within us serves as the very means by which we are opened to a deeper dimension of our own humanity. Surely, we are urged to conclude, this human being possessed more value than her image could contain; surely, we cry out, women are infinitely more beautiful than this picture of raw sexuality suggests. Monroe's iconic figure thus confronts the image-bound world of modern celebrity with a truly scandalous notion regarding our basic humanity: our daughters, sisters, mothers, and, indeed, even our idols are not loved because they are lovely; they are lovely because they are loved.

KUTTER CALLAWAY

# Norman Vincent Peale

Born into the poor family of a Methodist circuit minister in Ohio, Norman Vincent Peale (1898–1993) rose to prominence in the years immediately following WWII, becoming arguably the leading figure of mainline American Protestantism. Peale's Horatio Alger story-arc made tangible what he preached. He was always the eager toastmaster at Horatio Alger Awards dinners, reassuring all present of their ability to succeed through positive thinking and extolling America as the God-given land of opportunity. Preaching his gospel of success for over seventy years, he gave practical advice about the power within us and from God to overcome whatever adversity we face in order to reap material reward. He often told the story of his fifth-grade teacher who counseled the class that they had the power to erase the *t* in *can't*. But for this to take place, they had to "believe."

Peale wrote forty-three books, including *The Power of Positive Thinking* (1952), which sold over a million copies in the Eisenhower era. He did not consider himself a writer, and certainly not a theologian. Instead, he saw himself as a practically oriented preacher, and his writings as do-it-yourself manuals. The wounds of WWII needed healing. Families had been separated, weddings postponed. Women had had to work long hours in industry jobs, and soldiers had returned traumatized. The Depression was an all-too-recent memory. Across the nation there was, in the decades following WWII, nostalgia for normalcy, even while a growing unease continued to settle in. Religion in general was thought a helpful antidote. Even President Eisenhower spoke famously of the value of having "faith in faith."

Speaking with his context in mind, Peale argued that if you believe in God and in yourself, you could "make life what you want it to be." And people listened by the millions. At the peak of his influence and long before the advent of the Internet or social media, Peale's weekly newspaper column was read by ten million people; three million heard his almost daily radio and TV programs; 500,000 subscribed to his magazine *Guideposts*; and 150,000 regularly received copies of his weekly sermons. Meanwhile, his church for fifty-two years, Marble Collegiate in New York City, became an early megachurch, packing in 4,000 worshipers each Sunday. Peale was Mr. Protestantism.

Peale proclaimed that Jesus was your friend and that you could tap into that divine energy. He provided a "practical Christianity" for the masses, one that focused on personal fulfillment through belief—both in Jesus and in yourself. Though his message of simple optimism was light on sin, Peale still believed himself to be telling the old Gospel story. But Peale's twin themes of Christian reassurance and cosmic unity also had strong cultural roots. His message sprouted in American soil—in William James, whom he often quoted, and in Ralph Waldo Emerson. Believing that America was a nation uniquely blessed by God, he spoke during the time when the nation voted to add the words "under God" to its pledge of allegiance. Peale's uniquely American gospel of success fit in well with what many wanted to believe.

Norman Vincent Peale sought to fill the spiritual hunger of a growing middle class who had come to expect more and anticipated a better standard of living. His critics have called his message "cultural narcissism," fixated as it was on the pursuit of happiness. But like Robert Schuller, who would follow in his footsteps several decades later with his "possibility thinking" televised on *The Hour of Power*, Peale saw himself as making Protestant Christianity relevant to a wider public.

Peale's therapeutic Christianity presaged the rise of other electronic evangelists who would later become household names, including Jim Bakker, Jimmy Swaggart, and Joel Osteen. Like Peale, these televangelists usually appealed to viewers wanting to improve their own lives. Also like Peale, they often argued for conservative politics, as Jerry Falwell and Pat Robertson did in creating the Moral Majority. It could be argued that Peale's self-help focus was even an influence in the success of contemporary self-help teachers like Deepak Chopra. Certainly Peale found a worthy successor in Rick Warren, whose practical manual, *The Purpose-Driven Life,* sold millions of copies with its combination of simple biblical principles, unsophisticated theology, and self-help advice. Peale's therapeutic Christianity was definitive in its day; it also proved, both for good and for ill, a bellwether of more to come.

ROBERT K. JOHNSTON

# Pablo Picasso

Pablo Picasso (1881–1973) died at age 91 in Mougins, France, while he and his wife, Jacqueline, entertained friends for dinner. His final words were, "Drink to me, drink to my health, you know I can't drink anymore." He spent most of his years creating art, and he left behind an astonishing 50,000 works in different media, more than any other artist in history.

His life can be divided in different ways: the first half by artistic periods, the second half by a list of wives and lovers. To his public, he marketed himself and became the portrait of the modern man. Self-assured, prodigious, and sexually and fiscally omnivorous, he was a true celebrity and an ever-changing icon of wealth and prosperity. To those who knew him privately, there was another side: jealous, unsure of his friends, more unsure of his lovers, fraught by betrayal, hounded by the specter of artistic impotency, and running from old age and death.

Picasso's early years in Spain were spent under the tutelage of his father, an art teacher. A child prodigy, he quickly outgrew the help of any local and then national mentors. Finding his way to Paris at the age of nineteen, Picasso was quickly overwhelmed, especially when a close friend committed suicide. He embarked on his Blue Period, marked by many austere melancholy paintings of prostitutes and beggars, borrowing heavily from the style of El Greco and Henri de Toulouse-Lautrec. This was followed by the Rose Period, marked by a more cheery palette. This transformation is usually attributed to a new girlfriend, Fernande, as well as an increased exposure to other artists, especially Henri Matisse, with whom he had a lifelong combative, challenging, and ultimately rewarding relationship. Matisse was the only other living artist that Picasso ever considered his equal (or, in his more reflective moments, his superior).

What drew Picasso to stretch himself beyond his own bourgeois self-constraint is uncertain, but it is clear that African Tribal Art opened him up to a world that exploded on the 1907 Paris art scene with Picasso's seminal large-scale painting, *Les D'moiselles d'Avignon*. Did the spiritual power contained in the African religious rituals release him from European or Catholic constraints? Regardless, it is universally acknowledged as the birth of Modern Abstraction. Picasso was twenty-six years old. What Paul Cézanne had hinted at years before, Picasso achieved with full force: fragmented forms and colorful distortions masking as the sensual forms of the shape and beauty of the prostitutes favoring a well-known Barcelonan street.

The next year, Picasso paired up with a painter named Georges Braque, and the two of them founded cubism. They broke their subjects into fragments, reflecting the speed and movement of the era. Why should artists be confined by a single point of reference? Couldn't painting (and thought and life and even religion) be better appreciated from multiple perspectives? Prototype cubism quickly gave way to analytical cubism, which was followed by synthetic cubism. All these developments employed alternate and multiple perspectives to represent three-dimensional objects on a two-dimensional surface, something that had never been tried by European artists.

After his years with cubism, Picasso returned to a neoclassical period, then moved through surrealism, quickly picking up and synthesizing styles as needed or desired. He was a painting machine. If he could think of it, he could paint it, and everything in his life—his women, children, animals, or friend Matisse—all became fodder and a foil for his art.

All along the way, Picasso was seducing the major art collectors in the city—Gertrude Stein, her brother Michael, the Cone sisters, and others, all patrons of Matisse. All became Picasso's new fans. There were also many lovers, mistresses, and wives—all intertwined into an artistic life that was all-consuming. As the years rolled by, Picasso's love affair with Eva Gouel gave way to a marriage in 1918 with ballet dancer Olga Khokhlova (who bore him a son, Paulo). This was followed by Picasso's seventeen-year-old lover Marie-Thérèse Walter (who delivered a daughter, Maia); followed by photographer Dora Maar; who was displaced by Françoise Gilot (with whom Picasso had two more children, Claude and Paloma) and then Geneviève Laporte, more than four decades his junior. Finally it was his second wife, Jacqueline Roque, who was with him in his final years. These tumultuous relationships are summarized in the title of the 1996 biopic, *Surviving Picasso*.

What could capture Picasso's attention beyond his interpersonal affairs? The 1937 bombing of the Basque town of Guernica, Spain, provided Picasso with the creative outrage that became his masterwork, *Guernica*. An immense mural measuring eleven feet in height and twenty-three feet in width, it is a commentary on death, brutality, helplessness, and the horrors of war, all in shades of black, white, and gray. A horse and a bull are intertwined with severed limbs and screaming mothers surrounding them. *Guernica* is a memento mori for innocent civilians—especially women and children—caught in geopolitical crossfire. It is a passionate protest against military technology and a poignant plea for peace. It was exhibited in July 1937 (just three months after the bombings) at the Paris International Exposition. *Guernica* called attention to the Spanish Civil War and traveled around the world throughout the 1950s as a rigorous antiwar statement. At Picasso's request, *Guernica* was entrusted to the Museum of Modern Art in New York City until it was eventually returned to Spain in 1981.

Asked to explain its symbolism, Picasso said, "It isn't up to the painter to define the symbols. Otherwise it would be better if he wrote them out in so many words! The public who look at the picture must interpret the symbols as they understand them."

GABRIEL FERRER

# Elvis Presley

Elvis came in as an eruption of gyrating sensuality, terrorizing the parents of the first generation of Americans who called themselves "teenagers," cleaning up his reputation via military draft (doing exactly what those postwar parents might most want), and colonizing the record and film industries. He defined beauty and eroticism, the personification of the intersection between black traditional gospel music and "white blues," a mama's boy and sexual threat rolled into one.

Two decades after it began, it was over. The very incarnation of what it meant to be young, rich, and famous was, at forty-two, waiting to die. The bloated figure of a pills-addicted, greasy-haired, musical legend lazed on his couch with a revolver in hand, embalmed in paranoia though still alive, or at least *living*, humming about a love either tender, hunking and burning, or that he can't help falling into. Elvis Aaron Presley died in his bathroom, several years into an ultimately failed comeback based mostly in Las Vegas, his body enlarged partly because of the drugs he had first turned to while in the army. Americans' projection of the broken parts of their psyche onto one individual perhaps never seemed so tragic, until Elvis's curse found its way to Michael Jackson's door.

Elvis wanted to entertain, and to this there can be no challenge: when he was on form, there was no one like him. The 1970 concert film *Elvis: That's the Way It Is* features an astonishing sequence in which the man sings "Love Me Tender" while walking through an audience that includes Cary Grant—a more publicly circumspect sex symbol, to be sure, but a sex symbol nonetheless. Elvis touches the hand of every woman who offers one. He keeps walking, he keeps singing, and no one looks at Cary Grant. Why would they? This audience knows it's in the presence of greatness. Women faint and cry at his touch, reminding us of the religious power of celebrity.

Elvis offered a sea of change to social attitudes—while rooted in a gospel tradition, his music's tactile contours compelled its proponents to raise their hands in the air, to sway, to jump up and down, and to shout "Glory, Glory Hallelujah!" He was paradox in a Mississippi boy's frame. He could sound holy while sensualizing the sex-negative popular culture of the 1950s; he could make racist white America like "black" music without realizing it; he could offer to inform on the Beatles' drug habits to President Nixon while hooked himself (one record says he was prescribed 10,000 doses of various pharmaceuticals in an eight-month period).

Elvis won his lifetime achievement Grammy at age thirty-six. His career had come of age when only a handful of figures could dominate the culture, and music lovers basically had to choose between him and Frank Sinatra. When, despite Sinatra's own ambivalent personal life, he denounced rock'n'roll as a "rancid-smelling aphrodisiac," people who came of age between 1955 and the early 1960s knew who they would root for. Elvis made them dance and gave them a focus for displaced desires.

Amazingly, decades after his death he still does so. You can get married at the private chapel in Graceland, stay the night at his Heartbreak Hotel, and visit the grave that has been turned into an ashram for celebrity. The only American home that gets more visitors in a year is the one where the President lives—another place where the powers-that-be seek to sanitize an image, no matter who happens to be in residence. Elvis remains a question mark: did he help break the color barrier by making black music accessible to an audience that might otherwise denounce it, or did he plunder African American culture? Does his inability to maintain stable personal relationships make his love songs into sad jokes? How should we respond to the fact that the expectations his militaristic manager, "Colonel" Tom Parker, created in the audience led to him consuming salt tablets before concerts in order to fake the requisite on-stage sweat? Elvis is still always on our mind, but when we hear him questioning divine providence—saying, "I mean there *has* to be a purpose . . . there's got to be a reason . . . why I was chosen to be Elvis Presley. . . . I swear to God, no one knows how lonely I get. And how empty I really feel"—maybe the only appropriate response is for the public to admit that maybe we didn't love him quite as well as we should have.

GARETH HIGGINS

# The Sixties

*B*ob Dylan knew something was "Blowin' in the Wind" and Sam Cooke predicted "A Change Is Gonna Come," but neither singer could have envisioned how tumultuous an era would follow. The sixties began with visions of Camelot as the Kennedys entered the White House—John, Jackie, Carolyn, and John-John. Feel-good musicals like *My Fair Lady* and *The Sound of Music* reinforced viewers' contentment. While Nikita Khrushchev was banging his shoe on behalf of the Soviets, JFK encouraged Americans to "shoot the moon." The space race reflected the tensions already building via the arms race. In October 1962, the Cuban Missile Crisis ended with Khrushchev withdrawing missiles in Cuba in exchange for the United States removing tactical warheads from Turkey. In the March on Washington in August of 1963, Martin Luther King Jr. set forth his dream of an equitable future where "justice rolls down like waters and righteousness like a mighty stream." Such optimism came crashing down in November of 1963 when Lee Harvey Oswald assassinated President Kennedy. With the subsequent shootings of MLK and RFK ("Bobby" Kennedy) and the growing quagmire of the Vietnam War, the days of wine and roses were over.

The sixties became a time of social ferment. In warning against pesticides in *Silent Spring* (1962), Rachel Carson sparked the rise of environmentalism. With the 1963 publication of *The Feminine Mystique*, Betty Friedan fueled the burgeoning call for women's liberation. The Second Vatican Council ushered in significant changes in the Latin liturgy of the Catholic Church. The Free Speech Movement at the University of California at Berkeley sparked student sit-ins across college campuses. Birth control pills hastened the sexual revolution. The counterculture connected "free speech" to "free love."

Beatlemania swept the globe, causing John Lennon to infamously quip that the group was "more popular than Jesus." John Coltrane summoned his creative energies into a masterful celebration of "A Love Supreme." The Grateful Dead provided a psychedelic soundtrack for Ken Kesey and the Merry Pranksters' Acid Tests. Music became equated with enlightenment.

While some celebrate the 1969 Woodstock festival's idyllic vision of "3 days of peace + music," others remember the sixties as too much "Sympathy for the Devil" unleashed at the Rolling Stones' tragic Altamont concert later that year. In Hollywood, the Hays Code gave way to a rating's system aligned with controversial films like *The Graduate*, *Bonnie and Clyde*, and *Easy Rider*. In 1969, *Midnight Cowboy*, an X-rated movie about a bisexual male prostitute and his heroin-addicted best friend, won the Oscar for Best Picture. The era ended a long way from *Mary Poppins*.

# Muhammad Ali

*"I'll be floating like a butterfly, and stinging like a bee."*

From a young age, Muhammad Ali, born in 1942, was both a gifted boxer and magnetic entertainer. As an amateur boxer, Cassius Clay Jr. (Ali's given name) won the gold medal in the 1960 Summer Olympic Games. As a professional, he became the youngest fighter to wrest a title from a reigning heavyweight champion. His highly publicized matches with Joe Frazier and George Foreman were among the most anticipated bouts of all time. With the aid of boxing promoter Don King, Ali's bouts became cultural spectacles. Rather than mere heavyweight championships, Ali participated in "The Fight of the Century," "The Thrilla in Manila," and "The Rumble in the Jungle."

In part, Ali was compelling because of his signature one-two punch: an unorthodox fighting style combined with a series of masterfully crafted verbal taunts. On the one hand, Ali's rope-a-dope method required a fighter to absorb and endure repeated blows until his opponent was physically exhausted. On the other, his braggadocio displayed a level of self-confidence that bordered on arrogance. Both, however, demanded a level of strength and commitment few opponents could muster. Thus, Ali constructed a boxing persona that epitomized a particular expression of masculinity. A *man* was proud, he was defiant, he was overpowering. A *man* never backed down from a fight.

*"Your hands can't hit what your eyes can't see."*

Yet, Ali was magnetic, not simply because he exuded a preternatural self-confidence but also because he was unabashedly expressive. Just like his movement in the ring—graceful and rhythmical, powerful and flowing—his trash talk was far from rubbish; it was inspired, beautiful language. A man who pummeled others for a living could in fact be more than a prosaic caricature; he could also be poetic. Indeed, so captivating are his one-liners that not only have they become imbedded in our cultural imagination, but they have provoked subsequent artistry. From documentary films, to dramatic representations, to the celebrity-obsessed art of Andy Warhol, Muhammad Ali is now a contemporary objet d'art.

*"I shook up the world."*

Perhaps, then, it should not be surprising that Ali's life outside of boxing followed a trajectory of unmistakable beauty. A highly visible African American figure living in the midst of the civil rights movement, Ali became a lightning rod for controversy when he joined the Nation of Islam in 1964 and declared himself a conscientious objector to the Vietnam War on the basis of religion. Here was a strong, eloquent, black man of faith who spoke for the minority, calling out from the fringes to those who had ears to hear: "Wars of nations are fought to change maps. But wars of poverty are fought to map change." The voice of the "Louisville Lip" had now shifted registers, from the poetic to the prophetic.

Upon being diagnosed with Parkinson's disease, Ali's prophetic role enlarged. With the entire world watching him light the Olympic torch in Atlanta in 1996, Ali emerged as not only a figure for minorities but a figure for the vulnerable and the impaired—one whose very steps embody the dignity inherent in every human being, even, as we read in Matthew 25:40, "the least of these."

*"I am the greatest. I said that even before I knew I was."*

According to some, Muhammad Ali is one of the greatest heavyweight champions to have ever entered the ring. Yet Ali was always more than a boxer. In and out of the ring, his life became emblematic of the strength, vitality, and dignity of the human spirit. Repeatedly, Ali rose from the bloodstained mat of life in order to fight once more—in order to challenge those modes of thinking and those structures of power that were once thought indestructible. In the person of Muhammad Ali, we are able to see not only why sports are so compelling but why they are transformative.

In other words, Muhammad Ali is a cultural icon. In a certain respect, his own transition from pugilist to poet to prophet to peacemaker charts a parallel course to our evolving notions of masculinity in contemporary society. Ali presents us with a robust image of masculinity—one that not only incorporates previous ideals but enlarges and expands them. Men may very well be braggadocios, but they are also beautiful. Moreover, as an icon, Ali allows us to look *through* what he represents into something much deeper. That is, whether we are male or female, black or white, Christian or Muslin, as we reflect on Muhammad Ali the icon, we catch a glimpse of our own soul. And in so doing, we learn how to be human once again.

KUTTER CALLAWAY

# The Beatles

It's impossible to give an account of Western life in the 1960s without some-where referencing the Beatles. Not only were they the most popular group of the decade with their music permeating every area of life, but they seemed to encapsulate the era from its joyous early optimism through consciousness-altering experimentation to eventual disillusionment, bickering, and fragmentation.

When they began recording in 1962, American rock and roll had lost its early bite. Elvis had gone to Hollywood, Little Richard had gone to church, Chuck Berry had gone to jail, and Buddy Holly had gone to his grave. Into the vacated space came various Billys, Tommys and Bobbys who had the right haircuts but the wrong attitude. The Beatles took the original American rock-and-roll style, brought back the bite, Anglicized it a little, and sold it to the world.

Perhaps because of their more complete education (John Lennon had been to art school and Paul McCartney had studied advanced-level Eng-lish literature) they were able not only to write their own songs but to pro-gress artistically in terms of range, depth, and innovation. They made the previously unheard-of transition from touring pop idols to recording studio artists.

*Rubber Soul* (1965) saw them incorporate subjects other than love; *Revolver* (1966) displayed a complex musical imagination that drew on styles ranging from chamber music and Motown to folk and the avant-garde; and *Sgt. Pepper's Lonely Hearts Club Band* (1967), the first album to be made after their retirement from live performance, was consciously pro-duced as a work of recorded art rather than as a template for future concerts.

Along with Bob Dylan and the Rolling Stones, the Beatles dominated the popular music of the 1960s and their choices of fashion, girlfriends, drugs, music, and belief were highly influential on Baby Boomers. Each album they released was anticipated as a new indication of the way forward for a genera-tion desperate for leadership in a time of uncertainty.

In spiritual terms, the Beatles were a paradox. On the one hand they were irreverent, openly atheistic, and symptomatic of the break with so-called traditional values. When John Lennon claimed in 1966 that the Beatles were "more popular than Jesus," he vocalized the fears of many believ-ers, fears that had already been expressed in books like David A. Noebel's *Communism, Hypnotism and the Beatles* (1965). On the other hand, they represented the youthful quest for a meaningful spirituality that offered tran-scendence, beauty, love, freedom, and social justice. Their widely publicized experimentation with drugs (mainly cannabis and LSD) was not a mere search for kicks but an attempt to gain perceptions that would make sense of life. Timothy Leary, the Harvard professor turned acid guru, said in his book *The Politics of Ecstasy* that they were "philosopher-poets of the new religion" and that their songs were "delicate hymns of glory to God."

In 1968, at the urging of George Harrison, who had fallen in love with all things Indian, the Beatles went to Rishikesh to study Transcendental Meditation under the personal tutelage of Maharishi Mahesh Yogi. It was during this period of study that they wrote much of the double album *The Beatles* (better known as *The White Album*), which was appropriately more simple than their recent creations and had a plain, white cover that suggested the blankness of a mind cleared of the sort of thoughts that Maharishi said kept us bound to the "gross level" of existence.

If the Beatles had a core message, it was that we need to rise above the petty issues that bog us down by enlarging our field of consciousness. As John put it in "Revolution," we've got to free our minds. Yet such a message manifests itself only after careful scrutiny, because the band members' instinct was to write from the perspective of the altered state of mind rather than to command others to achieve it. The magical realism of "Penny Lane," which turned a mundane area of Liverpool into a blue-sky paradise, practiced the freed mind whereas "Rain" and "Tomorrow Never Knows" preached it.

Christians were ill-equipped to deal with the Beatles' phenomenon. Rather than judging them by their artistic achievements, integrity, and handling of truth, many Christians dismissed them as unworthy idols and misguided heathens. Rather than sensitively evaluating their records, they burned them. The Beatles' view that salvation was possible through an expanded consciousness may have been wrong, but it was a view worth countering intelligently rather than flinging it to the flames.

The Beatles are an object lesson to anyone endeavouring to incorporate his or her worldview into art. Most of the time they were unaware that this was what they were doing, but it's probably this lack of self-consciousness that made them so effective. The ideas that were poured into their minds just came out naturally through their lips and fingertips. They didn't make a statement; they became a statement.

STEVE TURNER

# Miles Davis

Virtuoso trumpeter Miles Davis ushered in virtually every major shift in jazz during the latter half of the twentieth century: from bebop and cool jazz to fusion and funk. His 1949 and 1950 recordings with the Miles Davis Nonet were hailed as *The Birth of the Cool* (1957). A wave of laid-back, West Coast-style jazz followed. Ten years later, Miles gathered a sextet that included saxophonists John Coltrane and Cannonball Adderley, and pianist Bill Evans to create the best-selling jazz album of all time, *Kind of Blue* (1959). While jazz pioneers like Louis Armstrong played a flurry of notes to create "hot" sounds, Miles was revered for what he *didn't* play. Bebop musicians "burned," but Miles floated above his accompanists in a lyrical manner. He reveled in the spaces between the notes in his modal jazz. Miles retained an air of mystery in his persona and playing, epitomizing "cool jazz."

But what happened when cool jazz became a cliché, and imitators followed Miles's spare innovations with arrangements that veered toward innocuous elevator music? Amid the turbulence of the late 1960s, he went electric, incorporating elements of rock, funk, and world music. His trumpet was now plugged in, with cool sounds replaced by hot flashes. Album titles that had promised *Seven Steps to Heaven* (1963) eventually invoked the power of a *Sorcerer* (1967) or *Dark Magus* (1977). What kind of spirits was Miles Davis exploring? *Bitches Brew* (1970) combined the psychedelic with Afrocentrism. The cool style was replaced by furious and elemental jams like "Miles Runs the Voodoo Down." Miles incorporated multiple drummers, percussionists, electric guitarists, bass players, and electric pianists to create a raucous and scary roar. The quiet, introspective Miles was swept from the stage. Yet Miles never lost his cool; he simply redefined it.

What is cool? Advertisers and brands covet it, yet fashions shift on a regular basis. Consumers know it when they see it. But how do you define cool and perhaps more importantly, how do you maintain it? In an article for *Adbusters,* Dick Poutain and David Robins defined cool as "a permanent state of private rebellion," but rebellion is difficult to maintain. While other musicians projected toward an audience to win approval, Miles aimed his trumpet down, hiding behind dark sunglasses. Toward the end of his career, Miles literally turned his back on his fans in concert, as if playing for an audience of one. His was a private rebellion. Despite radical shifts in his style, Miles maintained his cool throughout a long career. A decade after his death, his records still sell with gusto, and his iconic "cool" status remains secure.

Miles's compositions never announced themselves as traditionally spiritual in intent. They did not depend on gospel or black church traditions. He fused beauty with the blues. Like the biblical psalmist, a Miles Davis song might combine a blast against injustice for boxer Jack Johnson with a satisfying appreciation of the gift of life. Conflicting experiences could be poured into one evocative improvisation. But Miles never needed words to communicate a message. He ushered in style as substance—the birth of the cool.

Miles Davis consistently defied acceptable standards, launching new initiatives that defied conventional wisdom. He did the unexpected and heard things differently. He gave his band members limited instructions, trusting them to improvise. They were required to listen carefully to each other, to respond in the moment, spontaneously, creatively, authentically. There were plenty of mistakes and misfires along the way. But when the elements came together, the results were glorious—so fresh, so innovative, so heartfelt that they became permanently cool.

Why does Jesus seem so timely across eras and yet the institutionalized church is so often uncool? Perhaps we have failed to listen to Jesus' music, to notice the notes he isn't playing, the things he emphasizes by not underlining them. When the religious authorities tried to pin Jesus down, he responded with a creative riff on existing laws. When his popularity grew, he often turned his back on the crowds, withdrawing to a quiet place. He only got hot and bothered when he saw the free gifts of God's love turned into a power play. He turned the tables on the commodification of religion. While Roman governors tried to rattle him, Jesus kept his cool, answering their question with his own question. The rebel Jesus died on the cross as an outsider, his private rebellion seemingly a public failure. Yet, he left behind a complex body of work that has demanded attention and reinterpretation with each generation. He has remained permanently cool.

Jazz is the art of improvisation. It may be cool or hot, sad, mad, or glad. Miles Davis reminds us all that life is lived without a script. We can practice, rehearse, and do our scales. But when the bandleader counts off, "A one and a two," we have to start blowing.

CRAIG DETWEILER

---

## Doctor Who

For roughly fifty years, "the Doctor" has made house calls in living rooms all over the world. One of the top five grossing properties for the BBC, *Doctor Who* has made its mark. The show has been parodied in *Family Guy,*

*Saturday Night Live,* and *The Simpsons;* it was also referenced in *Star Trek: The Next Generation,* as well as the video game *Rock Band.* It is the longest running sci-fi program of all time, running for thirty-four seasons and still going strong (twenty-seven from its original run and seven in its modern continuation). There is no question that *Doctor Who* has been a dominant force in shaping global popular culture.

The sci-fi series revolves around the Doctor, an enigmatic figure who is believed to be the last of the Time Lords, a race of beings from the planet Gallifrey, which was destroyed during the Great Time War. This being—this Time Lord—has saved humanity on many occasions, sometimes fatally injuring himself to the point where he must "regenerate" and take on a new look (and somewhat of a new personality). Lord over time and space, he travels the universe with a human companion in his "spaceship," disguised as a blue 1950s police box named the TARDIS (Time and Relative Dimension[s] in Space). Together, the Doctor and his companion explore the universe in all its vast history, present, and future.

The show premiered on November 23, 1963—the day after President Kennedy was assassinated—and continued until 1984, when it took a two-year hiatus. Picking back up in 1986, the show ran until 1989 when it was canceled. It was revamped in 2005 and is once again picking up steam, enjoying several spin-offs, including *Torchwood, K-9,* and *The Sarah Jane Adventures.*

*Doctor Who* presents a world exploring the sociological nature of humanity, as an infant race still learning its place in the universe. Our time/space-traveling hero moves about humbly, working behind the scenes, abhorring violence as a solution to problems, and never claiming praise or credit for saving the day.

The show exhibits an undertone that religion is harmful to society's growth. Russel T. Davies, the producer from season twenty-eight through thirty-one, added even more of an antireligious aspect than the show's predecessors. From the Doctor's confrontation with a being that claimed to be the "Satan" of every culture, to one-liners claiming to visit the first Christmas (later described by a narrator as a "celebration of the pagan rite to banish the cold and the dark") and the first Easter, Davies makes no secret to his belief that there is nothing beyond the natural order.

But an antireligious undercurrent had been present in the series even before Davies became the producer. In Davis's second episode, "The End of the World," as the Doctor and Rose Tyler arrive on Platform One (of a tourist space station) to witness the end of Earth, an announcement is heard, "Guests are reminded that Platform One forbids the use of weapons, teleportation, and religion." Davies later stated in an interview, "If they haven't reached that point by the year Five Billion, then I give up!"

For a broader look at the show, however, it is tough to nail down an over-arching viewpoint, since there have been many producers and writers over the years, as well as eleven different actors portraying the Doctor, represent-ing each time he has gone through the process of regeneration. But at the heart of the show's message the viewer is asked to live life to the fullest, discovering the social mores of other cultures and ways of life.

While the series may be a bit down on the religious aspect of life, the Doc-tor puts a heavy emphasis on not interfering with the people and places he visits, to allow time to take its course, and to allow people (and alien races) to make their own discoveries and mistakes. In the same manner, through free will, the true Creator of space, time, and matter gives all individuals the ability to build or destroy, to love or hate.

ERIC BUMPUS

---

# Bob Dylan

In a hit single of 1993 titled "Mr. Jones," Adam Duritz of Counting Crows intones a wide range of seemingly universal longings—wanting to believe, wanting to be believed in, wanting to be a big star though he doesn't know how or why, wanting to be loved and therefore never lonely. He finally lands at the feet of the figure from whose opus the song title is drawn: he asserts that he, like the rest of us, wants to be Bob Dylan. Anyone who's dabbled the tiniest bit in that impossibly broad field we call popular music will know exactly what he's alluding to—the feeling that whatever road we choose, whatever avenue of authenticity we try to travel down, we meet the image of Dylan making his way back from wherever we hope we're headed.

Like Shakespeare, Dylan, it seems, has always been there before us. And even apart from his comprehensive lyrical wit, there's his abiding presence in history: sitting at the bedside of an ailing Woody Guthrie; performing in Greenwood, Mississippi, at a voter registration rally in 1963; appearing with Martin Luther King Jr. for the March on Washington; notably skipping Woodstock around the time he recorded an all-country album in Nashville; conducting a traveling carnival campaign for the release of the wrongly imprisoned Rubin "Hurricane" Carter; founding Farm Aid with an offhand remark onstage at Live Aid; releasing an album that describes a landscape of doom, gloom, and myriad forms of mixed-up confusion *on* September 11, 2001. All paths converge in the imagination of His Royal Bobness.

But Dylan the man, as opposed to the principality, power, or brand, will not suffer such sycophantic talk. Even as he navigates commercial waters in an expert fashion, he will countenance no title save that of song and dance man. "I'm only Bob Dylan when I have to be," he remarked in 1986. In an age of image and illusion production, he avoids becoming a walking antique by remaining an elusive, hypnotist collector of songs, phrases, and styles. Keeping his imagination alive is the job as he sees it.

Consider the opening scene of the second part of Martin Scorsese's Dylan documentary, *No Direction Home*. Dylan stands staring, smoking a cigarette while taking in the words of signs that advertise the buying and selling opportunities that await passersby inside a pet store. He personalizes aloud the standing offer to "collect, clip, bathe, and return" his dog to reasonably humorous effect, as if he's a confused and weary pilgrim processing a surrealist promise. But he then employs the cut-up technique often associated with William S. Burroughs (and later made available via letters and words on refrigerator magnets) in a meaning-making move that renders possible an awakening to associations ridiculous, provocative, and inescapably political—"commission my bath," "collect my will," "animal my soul." Passive submission to the con artistry of advertising signs, we know only too well, is the rule of the day, but it need not be this way. Anyone with pen, paper, or voice can begin to cobble together a counter-environment, a redeeming way of rearranging the words and images that will otherwise colonize our imaginations.

It is with this kind of work that Dylan, according to Robert Shelton, became a mass media poet; poetry not in the highfalutin sense, but as the expression that makes things new, as the living newspaper. In any case, we need not worry too much over labels or definitive meanings. In fact, we must not. If we "boundary it all up," as Dylan once warned, we mistake our own categories—our own grasp—for a living voice. When it comes to *living* traditions (whether religious, lyrical, or poetic) the only way to practice and partake of them is to hold to them loosely, to occasionally deny them, and to borrow from them shamelessly. In sync with this spirit, Dylan once remarked that traditional music "is too unreal to die." Concerning its open source powers, he observed, "I think its meaninglessness is holy."

When Dylan positions himself as a true believer in the songs that remain ("Those old songs are my lexicon and my prayer book") and the Bible ("That's the only instrument I know"), he reminds us that it's in the movement—the soul—of these ever ancient, ever-new broadcasts that we might yet find wisdom and sanity. "No man gains immortality thru public acclaim," he tells us. But in an illuminatingly public and paradoxical fashion, Dylan loses his life to find it again and again. His prophetic witness, should we choose to "boundary it up" that way, is a source of constant counsel.

DAVID DARK

# Aretha Franklin

In 1956, Chess Records released a live recording of a fourteen-year-old Aretha Franklin singing "Precious Lord" in Detroit's New Bethel Baptist Church where her father, Reverend C. L. Franklin, was pastor. As if offering instruction concerning the manner in which the beauty and spirit of what would become her lifelong witness might be most effectively received, a man within the congregation can be heard crying out, "Listen *at* her! Listen *at* her!" Having ushered her toward her place as a global fixture within the popular imagination years later, producer Jerry Wexler would say of this recording, "The voice was not that of a child but rather of an ecstatic hierophant."

Hierophant (someone who elevates a group of people to an experience of holiness) is an especially apt characterization of Franklin's performances as invigorating calls to a more lively discernment of what's going on between people. This is always a showing business, one might say, to the extent that we're made to pay heed to the holy as the fact of it having been recognized, forsaken, or denied. Recall the way a crowd of people is immediately roused by the sound of Aretha's version of the Otis Redding's "Respect." Almost despite their nervous system's sense of decorum, bystanders young and old will often put on a furrowed brow and enjoin their voices and postures to Franklin's enunciations. What should and could have been between women and men has gone horribly awry and requires our attention. Aretha can set it all straight, and we might as well get in on the act. This very kind of cultivating work occurred in 1967 when Franklin performed a ju-jitsu number on Redding's song, deploying its demands in the direction of a specifically feminist, ethical insistence on decency, care, and demonstrable affection. And if its call for sexual attentiveness wasn't already sufficiently explicit, Franklin and her sisters sealed the deal in the studio with their insertion of the famous "Sock it to me" line. The hierophant's space-making enterprise knows no borders.

"Everything Aretha does is gospel," the pioneering choir director, composer, and arranger James Cleveland once observed. And while her credentials as a gospel *genre* performer are unassailable, we do well to allow her work to expand our view of *good news*. It must include inescapably *social* tidings of blessing and admonition lest we miss her not-to-be-negotiated emphasis on embodiment. The word, properly understood, is *made* flesh—not protected from it. There's a place for talk of love, certainly, but love's proof is in the pudding or nowhere at all. Whether shining a light to celebrate sensual ecstasy or to expose disrespect and dysfunction, the very fact of illumination is already gospel. The hopes of a "do-right-all-day woman" can't be easily distinguished from those of "a do-right-all-night man." All is connected. In Aretha, these hopes are given voice.

And in her lifting of every beleaguered voice within view, this Queen of Soul knows whereof she speaks. She remains the most famous current (and inspiringly active) resident of Detroit where her mother left her at six, where she became the mother of two at seventeen, and where she has long-suffered, on occasion, a chain of myriad male fools. After she struggled to find her own path between jazz and gospel as conventionally understood in the late fifties and early sixties, Jerry Wexler encouraged her to be more steadily herself. At Atlantic Records she continued what Ray Charles started in the mass popularizing of black gospel music. By way of her musical persona ("plugged into the main circuit of Holy Ghost power" according to Wexler), she largely cobbled together personally the form now occupied by countless female singers.

Whether making the connection between practical mindfulness and the possibility of living freedom as she does in the song "Think" (made famous in her appearance in *The Blues Brothers*) or moving between lamentation and a hopeful resolution to gather up the gifts that remain in spite of broken promises and devastating abuse in her collaboration with Lauryn Hill, "A Rose Is Still a Rose," Franklin engages us with the work of *re*-membering that which all too often suffers *dis*-memberment. When we note the latter song's inclusion of Hill intoning Edie Brickell's phrase, "What I am is what I am," we begin to see the ways in which Franklin's own soul work invites recognition of its place within a larger project of human interest that transcends genre, a radically catholic and ecumenical work of what Martin Luther King Jr. called the Beloved Community. Franklin fittingly brought her witness alongside King's when she performed his favorite song "Precious Lord" at his memorial service in 1968. This is how the work of witness, receiving, bearing, and giving gets done. Franklin's music enriches our understanding of our own relationships if we let it, if we have ears to hear. Listen *at* her.

DAVID DARK

# John F. Kennedy

He was the youngest president ever elected, the first president born in the twentieth century, and the first (and still only) Roman Catholic president. His razor-thin victory over Richard Nixon in the 1960 election was attributed to the power of television. In the first presidential debate broadcast over fledgling black-and-white TVs, Nixon looked nervous, sweaty, and tired. He refused makeup that would have covered his five o'clock shadow. Those tuned into the debate via radio declared Nixon a clear, compelling winner. But the 70 million Americans watching on TV saw Kennedy as young, tan, fit, and electable. John F. Kennedy became our first fully mediated, electronic president.

His inauguration was another triumph of style. From his decision to eschew an overcoat on a freezing January day to the soaring sound bites, "Ask not what your country can do for you . . . ," Kennedy's appearance suggested a new frontier. The style of First Lady Jacqueline Lee Bouvier Kennedy burnished comparisons to Camelot in the White House. Their young children playing in the Oval Office gave *Life* photographers countless classic photo ops. Comedian Vaughn Meador sold millions of records by satirizing the First Family, their Boston accents thick with humorous possibilities.

Some voters feared that a Kennedy White House would take orders from the Pope. But Kennedy campaigned as a president who happened to be Catholic, rather than as a Catholic president. His election seemingly erased a hundred years of prejudice against immigrants, especially Irish and Italians, who did not trace their heritage to pilgrims on the *Mayflower*. Kennedy's presidency served as an affirmation of the American dream, a shining symbol that religious prejudice may not prevail on the national stage. His championing of civil rights suggested that racial prejudice could not be defended in federal courts or in the court of public opinion. The new frontier affirmed freedom to worship, freedom to assemble, and voting rights for all.

The burgeoning media machine swept up in JFK's iconographic power magnified his legend amid collective grief. The 1963 assassination of John F. Kennedy on a Friday afternoon in Dallas interrupted the otherwise mundane soap operas being broadcast on CBS. Walter Cronkite reported on the shooting as the sketchy rumors of a priest administering last rites emerged. As Cronkite struggled to keep up with shifting accounts from the hospital, the nation shared his sense of confusion. Millions mourned via live coverage of Monday's funeral procession from a Requiem Mass at St. Matthew's Roman

Catholic Cathedral to Arlington National Cemetery. The poignant image of three-year-old John Jr. saluting his fallen father still elicits tears.

The bloody tragedy generated by Lee Harvey Oswald's rifle could not be salved by network newscasts. But who could have guessed that two days after the assassination, Jack Ruby would shoot Oswald to death on live TV? Back-to-back murders sent America into a psychological tailspin that spiraled across the sixties.

The desperate quest to make sense of the horrific events led us only further down the rabbit hole. Twenty-six seconds of eight-millimeter film shot by Abraham Zapruder allegedly held the key. But frame-by-frame analysis left us only more confounded. The Warren Commission failed to assuage conspiracy theorists. Pop culture had a new national narrative to hang their hat on. Suspicion of the CIA and shady oil cabals has continued unabated.

How could a far-out film like 1962's *The Manchurian Candidate* have anticipated the rise of a trained murderer like Oswald? *Executive Action* (1973) and *The Parallax View* (1974) exploited lingering questions surrounding the grassy knoll. Oliver Stone amped up the skepticism with the startling biopic *JFK* (1991). The controversy around the movie's fuzzy historicity almost overwhelmed the legitimate loss it aspired to revive. By the time Nicholas Cage survived *The Rock* (1996), "Who really killed JFK?" had become a punchline.

Those seeking to feel the depth of the tragedy are advised to turn to another pop cultural source. Kennedy's death was the first of a trio of murders. In 1968, assassins' bullets also brought down Martin Luther King Jr. and Robert F. Kennedy. Doo-wop singer, Dion Dimucci, resurrected his career by recording a tribute song to fallen statesmen, "Abraham, Martin, and John." Dion sings that though they each freed a lot of people, it still seems, "the good they die young." The hope and promise of an inclusive America with room for Catholics and Protestants, for black and whites, was foreshadowed under John F. Kennedy. But he would not live to see it realized.

CRAIG DETWEILER

---

# Corita Kent

Corita Kent is the poster girl for the intersection of popular art and theology. Her colorful serigraphs merged art and activism amid the backdrop of the Vietnam War. Corita created over six hundred original silk screens, many of which are displayed in major museums. At a 2008 Berlin exhibit of Kent's work titled *Passion for the Possible*, curator Aaron Rose remarked, "Corita repurposed pop culture's vernacular into spirituality. Although she's been dead thirty years, she's coming up again with this [present] generation of twenty-year-olds. I consider her work more modern than those who call their work contemporary."

Born Frances Kent in 1918 in Fort Dodge, Iowa, the artist grew up in Hollywood, studied at parochial schools, and at age seventeen joined the Order of the Immaculate Heart of Mary, taking the religious name Sister Mary Corita. Corita graduated from Immaculate Heart College in 1941, began to teach art, and soon headed the Art Department there. Former students and members of the order recounted stories of her vigor and challenge—forcing them to use pop culture in ways that broke down barriers and communicated God's love in fresh and life-giving ways.

In 1951, Kent earned a master's degree in art history from the University of Southern California. As a nun in full habit, she worked prodigiously in making thousands of prints, gaining international fame as a designer and printmaker. For many, her signature "rainbow-thinking" colored serigraphs epitomize the zeitgeist of the 1960s and 70s.

Corita believed that "art is a common experience open to everybody and anybody." In response to people calling her a great artist, Corita would demur with the Balinese saying: "We have no art, we do everything as well as we can." Corita had a sense of placing words and images together in ways that would move people. Her work challenged us to "Power Up," "Open Wide," and "Stop the Bombing." Like Andy Warhol, she repurposed logos for her own artistic messages, suggesting that the big "G" in "General Mills" should stand for "goodness" or emphasizing the "Wonder" of "enriched bread." She anticipated the protest art of Barbara Kruger with phrases like *Damn Everything but the Circus*. However, in pushing to clarify her political agenda, she said simply, "Our job is to make the flowers grow."

Corita's passionate creativity magnetized John Cage, Charles Eames, Alfred Hitchcock, and Henry Miller, among others. Many celebrities joined her in both the classroom and for "instant celebrations," which were Corita's own version of group performance art. Her verve and talent galvanized creativity in community. Corita's discipline matched her mirth as she revolutionized traditional ceremonies. In 1966, what had been a somber procession in honor of the Blessed Virgin Mary was transformed into a joyous democratic celebration. Sixties students, society doyennes, and religious women—all garlanded with fruit and flowers—danced the Hava Nagila together. Placards proclaimed, "God likes you," and "Let us break bread together." She and other members of the Sisters of the Immaculate Heart of Mary were eager to incorporate the spirit of Vatican II. While many adored Corita, the magisterium did not. Although a 1967 *Newsweek* cover story honored her as an artist and an activist, tension mounted.

Exhausted from the cardinal's pressure to conform, Corita left her teaching load of six classes, and eventually the Order. Moving to Boston, she designed posters and billboards, created ads, and continued to work on her own serigraphs. In 1971, Corita designed a 150-foot rainbow wash painting on a natural gas tank that remains a vibrant landmark on Highway I-95. Religion scholar Harvey Cox speaks of this largest of public paintings as "a humorous prank," one that reflects Corita's value of "art as a common experience." Corita believed in taking the common objects of one's environment and using them, playing with them, living with them. She spoke out against racism and the Vietnam War and became even more involved with the antinuclear movement. "I'd like to think my work is some small help in helping people reexamine things that they thought were okay."

After being diagnosed with cancer in 1976, Corita outlived the prognosis by a decade. "You've got to grab life wherever you find it," she said. In 1985, she designed the LOVE stamp for the U.S. Postal Service, a creation so popular that it required a printing of 700 million stamps, the largest to that date. In 1986, the year of her death, Corita wrote to her friends asking for their prayers "to help me in the new life I begin now . . . [one] I feel is just the next step and that I will still be knowing and caring for all of you forever."

LEAH BUTURAIN SCHNEIDER

## Stan Lee and Marvel Comics

Where would adolescents be without the distraction and comfort of the Fantastic Four, Spider-Man, and the Incredible Hulk? Stan Lee was born Stanley Martin Lieber on December 28, 1922, in New York City. Starting at the age of eighteen, Lee worked for Marvel Comics in such roles as writer, art director, editor-in-chief, publisher, and president. Although during the 1940s and 1950s he wrote comic books in whatever genre was popular at the time, Lee is best known for his superheroes.

By the early 1960s, other superhero comics were still being written according to the age-old model of the rugged individualist who never had doubts or struggled with real-life issues like love, family, money, or health. In 1961, Lee, along with artist Jack Kirby, changed all this with the introduction of the

Fantastic Four, a superhero team that was created to compete with DC Comics' Justice League of America. The success of the first issue was overwhelming and unexpected, and led Lee and his artists to create such other well-known heroes as the Incredible Hulk, Spider-Man, Iron Man, Daredevil, and the X-Men.

The basic feature that Lee wanted to introduce into the genre was realism. He could never relate to the perfect heroes like Superman or Batman, but instead wanted to write the kind of stories that he himself would want to read. For him, this meant creating heroes who would have the same sort of problems and shortcomings as real people. Thus, the Fantastic Four sometimes can't pay their bills, Spider-Man has problems concentrating in school, and the Thing suffers from low self-esteem.

Lee's Marvel was also the first in superhero comics to consistently tackle controversial issues like war, sexism, and racism. In every one of Marvel's series, at one time or another, Lee's liberal ethic of tolerance shone forth. Sometimes this was done subtly, as in the inclusion of traditionally underrepresented persons as background and supporting characters. Sometimes it was done explicitly, as in the Silver Surfer's frequent ruminations on the misery of war and his self-reflections on the fear that humans have of things and people they don't understand.

Lee's ethics, moreover, are anything but passive. He is a firm believer that all of us have a duty to fight evil and injustice wherever we find it, and to whatever extent we are able. This is quintessentially shown in Spider-Man's introductory story from 1962, in which Peter Parker uses his new powers only for himself, refusing to stop a thief who has escaped with stolen money. After discovering that this same thief later murders his Uncle Ben, Peter is devastated by guilt and learns a hard lesson that "with great power there must also come great responsibility!"

Although the Marvel Comics writers after Lee have added to and changed many of his original ideas, most scholars agree that the recent Marvel superhero films are faithful to Lee's conceptions, particularly his turn to realism and his focus on ethical responsibility. *X2: X-Men United* and *Spider-Man 2* especially not only are critically acclaimed but emphasize the issues of self-sacrifice, community, tolerance, and human love that have always been close to Lee's heart. Moreover, the fact that directors like Bryan Singer and Sam Raimi make it a point to stay true to Lee's innovations—even fifty years later—speaks loudly about his place in the pop cultural pantheon.

Lee himself is Jewish, but not observant. It is difficult, therefore, to judge the extent to which his tradition informs his ethical and political views. Nevertheless whenever God comes up in his comics, it is always a positive representation. For him God is both all-powerful and benevolent, even if unarticulated.

Refreshingly, this does not in any way diminish human choice and responsibility. Rather, Lee might say that in loving our neighbors we are in fact doing the will of God. In numerous interviews he has stated that he accepts the Golden Rule of "Do unto others as you would have others do unto you," which has resonance in both early Christianity and Second Temple Judaism.

Lee's spiritual worldview can be seen in an exchange he penned for a 1968 issue of the *Fantastic Four* in which the Silver Surfer attacks Earth in an attempt to teach humanity a lesson. This is arguably the best example of Lee's ethics and theology, all rolled into one.

*Invisible Girl:*    "But what . . . can [Reed] do . . . against the all-powerful Silver Surfer??"

*The Watcher:*    "All-powerful? There is only one who deserves that name! And his only weapon . . . is love!"

ANTHONY R. MILLS

# Malcolm X

The message of controversial civil rights leader Malcolm X (1925–1965) was clear: equality and a connection to God. His passion was unmatched and he could be explosive at times. His capacity to critically assess situations in a matter of seconds was remarkable, as was his connection to not only the black community but to all people of color. Although his methods were controversial, Malcolm X helped create a new groove in American pop culture and aided in ushering in the postmodern/post-soul era. His unique ability to question authority, recover empty answers from a system that had lied countless times to African Americans, and resist the dominant culture paved the way for people like César Chávez, movements like women's liberation, and a global culture called hip-hop.

The iconic leader was born Malcolm Little on May 19, 1925, in Omaha, Nebraska. According to his best-selling *Autobiography*, the Ku Klux Klan drove his family out of Omaha while he was still a baby. Malcolm's early childhood experiences deeply influenced his constant and unapologetic stance against white racism. When Malcolm was six, his father was crushed by a streetcar and killed. The loss devastated his family, and their economic situation went from bad to worse. As a boy and then a teenager in foster care, Malcolm took to street hustling and eventually was arrested.

During his years in prison Malcolm read—a lot. His mind opened to a new sense of consciousness and awareness both for life and for the struggle that many people of color—especially blacks—had during the 1950s. In prison, Malcolm unexpectedly joined the Nation of Islam (NOI), led into the movement by his brothers' letters and visits. Within a year of his release, he was a minister with the NOI, openly denouncing the power structures of his day and proclaiming founder Elijah Muhammad's message of black superiority and separation from white people. After years as a prominent leader of the NOI movement, however, Malcolm aligned himself with the teachings of Sunni Islam and went on a life-changing pilgrimage to Mecca. He began to see Islam as a unifying force in race relations around the world, a message that was not popular with his former NOI colleagues. The following year, he was assassinated in New York City, with three NOI members being convicted of the shootings.

Malcolm helped reshape the American pop culture scene in three major ways. First, he used the media outlets of his day to question and criticize the white structures that oppressed many minorities. He debated and argued his positions on radio and television. This created a sense of hope, giving African Americans a vision for their community, for their families, and for their personal lives. This, in turn, translated into other social movements.

Second, Malcolm created a culture of questioning authority, rooted in knowledge of law, American history, and the self. Malcolm also debunked the utopian representation of American life by arguing that whole sections of the United States had not been invited to the "American Dream" party.

Third, Malcolm affirmed faith and a daily connection to God. While he did not believe in the westernized white version of Jesus, he did acknowledge Jesus as an important spiritual figure and sought a connection to God. After his departure from the NOI, Malcolm saw a new future and vision for life, for all people of God, and for marginalized people. His extensive travel gave him new perspectives and interpretations on life and humanity.

Long after his assassination in 1965, Malcolm shows up on T-shirts, watches, medallions, and blankets. His philosophy was a key part of shaping hip-hops's Golden era (1988–1995). Many rap artists adopted his message of "by any means necessary," setting forth a new ethos not just for Black people but all the oppressed and marginalized. Hip-hoppers adopting Malcolm's image and message include Public Enemy, Tupac Shakur, Brand Nubian, Nas, and Mos Def. Filmmaker Spike Lee has drawn on Malcolm's legacy in *Do the Right Thing*, *School Daze*, *Bamboozled*, and the biopic *Malcolm X*. Even television shows like *Rosanne*, *Fresh Prince of Bel-Air*, and *The Boondocks* have alluded to Malcolm.

Malcolm was a child of God who questioned white power structures at a time when it was dangerous to do so. His spiritual journey inspired millions of people during his lifetime and continues to do so after his death.

DANIEL WHITE HODGE

---

# Marshall McLuhan

In the 1960s, Marshall McLuhan's telling cultural predictions and reflections on media and communication earned him covers on *Newsweek* and *Life* magazines. In *Communication Habits for the Pilgrim Church*, Warren Anthony Kappeler said that McLuhan's "theory of communications offers nothing less than an explanation of all human culture, past, present, and future." Not bad accolades for a Canadian-born professor of English literature. McLuhan was a frequent guest on television shows in the 1960s, discussing his theories about the emerging electronic culture and the effect of the new communication technologies of radio and television on society. He coined the familiar phrase "the medium is the message" and the term "global village," as well as intimating the emergence of the World Wide Web thirty years before it appeared. His views on media, though influential, were often misunderstood, as the film director Woody Allen demonstrated to comedic effect when he gave McLuhan a cameo role in his film *Annie Hall*. In the scene, an academic is arguing about McLuhan with Allen in a cinema line when McLuhan walks up to them and tells the academic, "You know nothing of my work." McLuhan might just be one of the most significant and least understood thinkers of the twentieth century.

McLuhan held two important views about technology. First, he viewed culture as a result of technological change rather than as an independent element. "We shape our tools and thereafter our tools shape us," was his interpretation of the way technology reshapes a society. Second, he saw technologies—particularly media technologies—as an extension of self, something that extends our natural human abilities. Television extends our sight, for instance, allowing us to see ourselves and the world around us in ways not possible independent of that technology. Media technologies change how we think, feel, and act, and they even shift the information we process. In other words, a move from text to visual media will change the content we look for and manage. McLuhan believed that new media technologies had physical, mental, and social effects. He offered up four laws of media that helped to describe his views on the various properties and actions of media and technology:

*Extend*—When we employ a technology, it extends the reach of our body and mind. For example, a car could be seen as an extension of the feet. This raises the question: what does the technology extend or make possible?

*Reverse*—Every technological advancement has the potential to push its target audience to desire what was left behind. An over-extended car culture stressed by traffic jams and high gas prices longs for a pedestrian society.

*Retrieve*—Humans have a limited set of sense and motor skills, and the technologies we use only stimulate and reinforce some of them. Digital culture enhances the visual over the aural, for example. When a new technology is embraced it will retrieve and enhance senses or skills that are not stimulated by the current technologies—the new brings back the old, if you will.

*Obsolesce*—New technologies and media subsume older forms; older technologies are not eliminated, but they are subsumed. Image culture did not abolish textual culture, but print media has lost its effectiveness and place within society.

McLuhan argued that communication culture had gone full circle in the 1960s—from oral culture to written culture, and then back to oral culture. But the new oral culture, which has emerged via the new media technologies of television and radio, reached much larger audiences at far greater distances. This range was the foundation of his view that these connections would lead to a new tribal consciousness and to the idea of becoming a "global village," in which the world would be connected by a common oral culture. In McLuhan's day this was via the medium of radio and television, and currently it is via the language of digital culture.

In McLuhan's terminology, we could understand Christianity as a communication technology. As Shane Hipps wrote in *Flickering Pixels*, "any serious study of God is a study of communication, and any effort to understand God is shaped by our understanding—or misunderstanding—of the media and technology we use to communicate." McLuhan tells us that media helps us understand who we are, but it also changes who we are. It is no different with God—different technologies will *extend* God in different directions, and the message that reaches a global village united by a language of visual technology will need to hear something very different than a world fragmented by textuality.

BARRY TAYLOR

## Star Trek

In an accidentally significant, televised conversation with Conan O'Brien, William Shatner once lost the thread of the tale he was telling when he struggled to recall a particular name: "I went over to the producer and I said 'I got an idea . . . Captain . . . uh . . .'" After instinctively supplying the implied "Kirk" (the role of Shatner's lifetime) out of politeness, O'Brien nervously raised a hand and slowly backed away as if to pay due reverence concerning the holiness—or the profanation of the holy—at work in this strange moment. Had Shatner really forgotten his place at the helm of Gene Roddenberry's cultural touchstone? Does he live with the knowledge, for instance, that he and Nichelle Nichols's Lieutenant Uhura exchanged the first interracial kiss between characters in a television series? Or that NASA's first Space Shuttle Orbiter was named after Kirk's very own *USS Enterprise*? Probably not on a daily basis. And in any case, committed adherents of the *Star Trek* tradition have come to expect, and perhaps even regard with affection, the levity and nonchalance with which Shatner occasionally disburdens himself of the weight of his presumed significance. Perhaps a sanity worthy of the tradition requires it. "Get a life," he once advised a crowd of avid Trekkies in a famous *Saturday Night Live* skit (1986), which served to promote one more film (there would be others) in which he returned to the role of Kirk. The imaginative economy of *Star Trek* could handle the ridicule and even assimilate it into itself, reenvisioning the tale thus far, as traditions do, and making it all new.

For many fans, the best stories and the most provocative ideas only really got off the ground in 1987 with *Star Trek: The Next Generation*. Over seven seasons, three spin-off series, feature films, and numerous novels, audiences were accorded the thrill of watching wise, serious, good-looking crew members have to delay their own judgment again and again in their encounters with strange new worlds. The power of the stories and the deep character development was not lost on actor Patrick Stewart. As Captain Jean-Luc Picard, Stewart survived violent assimilation by the machine-human hybrid race called the Borg *and* experienced an entire lifetime in just under twenty-six minutes via a probe that contained the memories of a long-extinct alien civilization. When asked to compare his work as a Shakespearean actor to his years with *Star Trek*, Stewart refused popular distinctions: "All those years of working for the Royal Shakespeare Company . . . was nothing but a preparation for sitting in the Captain's chair on the *Enterprise*."

Stewart might have had in mind what seems to be the rich, signifying trope of the *Star Trek* tradition: the endlessly generative idea of a future intergalactic communion that seeks—and at least occasionally realizes—a kind of just, righteous wholeness. In this case, it's the United Federation of Planets that unites all of *Star Trek*'s protagonists as they seek out new life forms while generally holding to a rule of noninterference called the Prime Directive. Avery Brooks's Commander Benjamin Sisko of the *Deep Space Nine* series offered an apt account of the Federation's ethos: "We are constantly searching not just for answers to our questions but for *new* questions. . . . We explore the galaxy trying to expand the boundaries of our knowledge . . . [and] that is why I am here—not to conquer you with weapons or with ideas but to coexist and to learn."

When we consider this moral vision, we might recall that most beloved representative of the Vulcan and human races: Leonard Nimoy's Spock. Having sought to put the character to rest with a memoir titled *I Am Not Spock* in the 1970s, Nimoy later became more reconciled to his fate in another volume—*I Am Spock*—and would recall that "live long and prosper" (with the accompanying hand gesture) was a variation of the Jewish Priestly blessing, *Nesiat Kapayim.* He also stated that Spock as a beleaguered, outsider pilgrim is "a diasporic character if there ever was one."

Spock's understanding of what it means to be a bringer and a mystic practitioner of peace, a redemptive agent among fellow life forms, haunts the heart of *Star Trek* even when his character is absent (or residing in another dimension). And even when its offerings strike us as overly mixed with the silly, the inane, or the gratuitous, its appeal to the human conscience, should we choose to take it seriously, is a summons to mindfulness. *Star Trek*'s call to consider unforeseen possibilities beyond present social imaginings—the ethical imperative to do so—resonates still.

DAVID DARK

# The Super Bowl

The 1966 merger of the National Football League (NFL) with the upstart American Football League (AFL) resulted in a new championship match, christened by Kansas City Chiefs' owner Lamar Hunt as "the Super Bowl." Such bigger-is-better bonhomie made older college contests like the Rose Bowl and the Orange Bowl sound modest in comparison. The addition of a Roman numeral to demarcate the NFL finale added to the epic promise. The Green Bay Packers won the first two Super Bowls, and when Coach Vince Lombardi lost a battle to cancer, the championship prize was christened the Lombardi Trophy.

The comparatively new franchises from the AFL, like the Chiefs and the Oakland Raiders, couldn't contend with the long-standing powerhouses from the NFL like the Packers. The winner seemed like a forgone conclusion until Joe Namath and the New York Jets swaggered into Super Bowl III in 1969. "Broadway Joe" even dared to promise an upset victory over the Baltimore Colts. And when Namath and the Jets delivered on his boast, the Super Bowl finally looked like a battle of equals up for grabs on any given Sunday.

The Super Bowl has consistently delivered massive ratings for television networks, so advertisers line up to spend piles of money on a thirty-second burst of glory. Special commercial spots are commissioned just for the game. Apple's stylized "1984" Macintosh ad premiered at Super Bowl XVIII, never to appear on television again—a brash statement. Animated beer bottles brought "The Bud Bowl" to life in 1989. During the dotcom boom, upstarts like Monster.com and GoDaddy.com stepped up to make their presence known. The Budweiser Clydesdales famously bowed in respect to honor those who died on 9/11/01. A Doritos spot led to a million-dollar contest, with thousands of amateurs investing their time and creativity to make Doritos look even tastier. Viewer interest in the commercial contest rivaled and maybe even exceeded the outcome of the game. The event became the Super Bowl of Advertising.

So many people now tune in to the broadcast that Super Bowl Sunday approaches the scale of a national American holiday. The countdown begins weeks in advance, with the preshow starting up to twenty-four hours before kickoff. Menus are planned and millions of dollars are wagered on the game's outcome.

Churches have struggled to respond to the Super Bowl's media onslaught. Sermons may tilt toward gladiators like Samson or underdog stories like David versus Goliath. Ministers wrestle with whether to cancel Sunday evening services. A few have fought back with outreach programs built around the halftime break when legendary Dallas Cowboys' coach Tom Landry offered his Christian testimony via videotape. Occasionally, an unlikely football hero like Kurt Warner has arisen. He credited God with raising him up from a grocery store clerk to the Arena Football League to Super Bowl MVP. When he guided the St. Louis Rams to victory, Warner gave God the glory with a postgame testimony heard by millions. Such promises fueled the dreams of faith-fueled quarterbacks everywhere.

With a few notable exceptions, the game itself rarely lived up to "super" standards. Perhaps all the superlatives swirling around the Super Bowl destined it for disappointment. What game could live up to such outsized hype?

Pressured to satisfy massive expectations, the NFL has invested millions in cranking up the halftime show. Michael Jackson appeared in 1983, and U2 offered a salve after the pain of September 11, 2001. During the Super Bowl halftime in 2004, Janet Jackson seized the opportunity to promote her comeback album, but an infamous "wardrobe malfunction" turned into a scandal that tarnished her star power while the one doing the ripping (Justin Timberlake) received little blame or blowback. The flash of nudity made a nervous nation blush. Stung by viewers' outrage, the NFL punted. Thereafter, "safe" rock legends like Paul McCartney, Bruce Springsteen, The Who, and Prince were tapped to deliver their hits (without surprises). With a medley of songs scheduled down to the second, The Black Eyed Peas hit a new low in perfunctory performances for Super Bowl XLV in 2011.

Perhaps the Super Bowl can best be understood as the Big Letdown: the moment when American sport and commerce overpromises and underdelivers. By the end of the game, the chips and beer are stale and the disappointment usually palpable. So why do we keep gathering on the couch, in front of the biggest TV screens possible? Because the Super Bowl remains a rare opportunity to come together with people we may disagree with, to boo and cheer in a civilized, even familial way. It is a communal Sunday, when we wear our allegiances but refuse to let them separate us. We understand that the sharing of Doritos is more important than winning or losing. Such community building is something our churches and synagogues can root for.

CRAIG DETWEILER

# John Updike

It is difficult to imagine great American fiction and pop culture in the same sentence. The best novelists of our day are seldom on the bestseller list, and Stephenie Meyer or John Grisham will never win the National Book Award for Fiction. Yet John Updike was both a best-selling author and a literary giant. When he died in 2009 at the age of seventy-six, he left behind a corpus of twenty-eight novels; fourteen collections of short stories, many of which first appeared in the *New Yorker*; and nine volumes of poetry, essays, and criticism.

Though one of a handful of great American novelists during the last half of the twentieth century, Updike spoke even in his last year of needing to publish a book a year to justify his existence. Writing was, for him, a self-affirmation that his life had meaning and purpose. His grandfather had been a minister; his father, a teacher. For Updike, his "vocation" would come through the arts. Yet, Updike never felt fully at peace with this. As his young character Peter

Caldwell tells his mistress in the semi-autobiographical *The Centaur* (1963), "Priest, teacher, artist: The classical degeneration."

Updike's focus was on the common and ordinary, yet his brilliance with words and expression caused some critics to wonder if he was actually more about style than substance. That is, he wrote beautifully, but about precious little. Such a judgment is a mistake, however. Updike sought to discover in the sterility of modernity a spiritual significance, and the beauty of his language was the means. Particularly in his four novels that followed the life of Harry "Rabbit" Angstrom (*Rabbit Run, Rabbit Redux, Rabbit Is Rich,* and *Rabbit at Rest*), Updike chronicled the restlessness and spiritual yearning of America over three decades. In the process, Rabbit's angst was seared into a whole generation of Americans who lived from Eisenhower through Reagan.

Not all of Updike's writings worked, particularly as culture turned in the nineties. But 1968's *Couples* (which explored the sexual revolution amid suburbia), 1984's *The Witches of Eastwick* (which explored women's liberation and was made into a hit film starring Jack Nicholson, Cher, Susan Sarandon, and Michelle Pfeiffer), and 1962's *Pigeon Feathers* (a collection of short stories that explored the possibility of divine presence within the banality of modern life) match the Rabbit books for their incisive portrayals of everyday Americans struggling to find significance and spirituality.

Through his writing, Updike sought to unpack, both for himself and for his readers, Pascal's "Penseé 507" (which he used as the epigraph for *Rabbit Run*): "The motions of Grace, the hardness of heart; external circumstances." This triptych expressed Updike's lifelong quest for belief, however marginal, given the passing of small-town, Protestant America. Realizing it's a fraud, but making it likable, such was the vacuousness of much of modern life. Wife-swapping in suburbia, impersonal old people's homes, concrete cities, clergy rehabilitation centers—such externalities almost guaranteed a loss of faith. In his novels, the old stories that conveyed meaning are seen more as hollow than hallowed—Tonto is now having an affair with the Lone Ranger's wife; the old church with its spire burns and must be torn down, to be replaced with a concrete, parabolic roof that lacks transcendence; like Coke, churches promote thirst without quenching it.

And yet, Updike could not help but examine everything for God's fingerprints. Modernity might be ready to forsake God, but was God ready to forsake us? However marginal, however indistinct, God's blessing remained foundational. As the protagonist David Kern described it in one of Updike's short stories ("Packed Dirt, Churchgoing, a Dying Cat, a Traded Car"), after this young father experienced on the same evening both a dying cat and the birth of his daughter, it was "supernatural mail." It "had the signature: decisive but illegible."

Such experiences could happen anywhere, and in the corpus of Updike's vast fiction, they do. But particularly important for Updike was the role of sexuality. Here was not a panacea. Sexuality could destroy, and often did in Updike's stories; it could never be manipulated to produce God. But sexuality also could reveal something of the divine mystery. It was inherently sacramental.

In his creation of beauty, his focus on bodily sexuality, his recognition of the everyday and commonplace spirituality, and his quest for the sacramental, Updike prepared a new generation for its move into postmodernity. The angst in his fiction presaged a postsecular return to a spiritually charged world made alive through beauty. As a white male member of the establishment, he felt that his influence was waning in later life. But his instincts and creations were formative, continuing to give shape to spiritually charged cultural expressions today.

ROBERT K. JOHNSTON

# Volkswagen Ads

In the early twentieth century, German automakers concentrated on producing luxury vehicles, making it very difficult for ordinary German citizens to own anything more than a motorcycle. All that changed in the 1930s with the introduction of the Volkswagen, a "people's car" developed by the German Labour Front, a Nazi trade union. The idea for the car came directly from Adolf Hitler, who wanted a basic vehicle capable of carrying two adults and three children at 62 miles per hour. The car was to cost about the same as the price of a small motorcycle. The car, officially named Volkswagen Type 1, debuted in 1938 just before the beginning of the Second World War. After the war, the car became a symbol of German economic regeneration and the automakers added more models to complement what, by then, had come to be known as the "Beetle."

The car was introduced to the American market in 1949, briefly sold as a "Victory Wagon." Initial response to the car was lukewarm and only two models were sold in its first year of availability. A combination of factors contributed to this poor reception, not the least of which was the car's association with Germany, Hitler, and the Nazis. But eventually the practicality and reliability of the vehicle won out, and by the time Volkswagen of America was formed in 1955, the Beetle's presence in America was cemented and over one million cars had been produced.

It could be argued that soaring Volkswagen sales were in large part the result of the famous advertising campaigns created for the company by New York ad agency Doyle Dane Bernbach (DDB). The campaigns were led by art director Helmut Krone, considered by many to be a pioneer of modern advertising. Krone is famous for creating a number of seminal ad campaigns, including Juan Valdez the Colombian Coffee persona and the Avis "We Try Harder" series. But it was his work for Volkswagen in the late 1950s and 1960s that cemented his reputation and helped the company appeal to younger consumers.

Two print campaigns in particular carved a niche for Volkswagen in the public eye: "Think Small" and "Lemon." Automobile ads at the time tended to focus on providing potential customers with as much information as possible about the vehicle in question. They were also intent on appealing to fantasy rather than reality by creating visual images of cars and owners in chic or modern environs, enjoying the high life. Krone and his working partner, Julian Koenig, went for something different. Instead of print ads loaded down with copy and images, they opted for mostly white space with a small image. This was meant to emphasize both simplicity and minimalism of the vehicle itself (Volkswagens were not loaded down with many of the features that were expected in U.S. vehicles, such as electric windows, automatic locks and air-conditioning). The text, extolling the virtues of owning a small car, appeared at the bottom of the ads in fine print. The ads were instant hits. The trade magazine, *Advertising Age,* named the 1959 "Think Small" campaign as the number one campaign of the twentieth century.

The other major campaign presented just the car with "Lemon" in bold type. Ad copy explained that the chrome strip on the glove compartment was blemished and had to be replaced. The take-away was obvious: If this was Volkswagen's idea of a lemon, the Beetle must be a well-built car.

The Beetle ad campaign also stands out for its use of television, which was in 90 percent of U.S. homes by the mid-1960s. It may have been a grainy, black-and-white image, but the emotional connection between car and consumer was picture-perfect in Beetle commercials. In fact, it was the emotional connection between product and consumer that the campaigns truly pioneered; this element boosted sales and created a lifetime of brand loyalty. For years the Beetle ads conveyed a message of economy and sensibility with a clarity and emotion that had not been seen before.

DDB opted for campaigns that changed the way advertising itself was created (for example, it was the first agency to put art directors and copy writers in the same room working together). They also changed how consumers see products—the emotional connection DDB pioneered replaced advertising's prior emphasis on information and relentless repetition.

The Volkswagen ad campaign allowed the company to remain true to its historic roots and intentions and yet connect with a new, emerging cultural shift that prized a different set of values. The company, with the help of DDB, defied the conventional wisdom and, in doing so, found new life. It found ways to address the new market by recognizing that the past was a legacy to build on, not an anchor to hold them. Here is a lesson for the church as well.

BARRY TAYLOR

# Andy Warhol

It is difficult to overestimate the influence of Andy Warhol on modern American life, or anywhere else in the world that America has exerted any cultural influence in the last fifty years. This leader of the pop art movement of the 1960s and 1970s helped to level the sharp distinction between fine and commercial art and brought popular culture into the rarefied air of art museums.

Born Andrew Warhola in Pittsburgh in 1928 to Czech parents, Warhol was a sickly child who spent long periods in bed, drawing. His father was a construction worker who died in an accident when Warhol was thirteen years old. After high school, Warhol studied commercial art at the Carnegie Institute of Technology in Pittsburgh. He then went to New York where he worked as a magazine illustrator and as a designer for album covers. By 1956 he was earning a six-figure annual salary and was one of New York's most sought after and successful commercial illustrators.

In 1960, Warhol began creating paintings based on newspaper advertisements, soup cans, soda bottles, and dollar bills. Underscoring the artistic value of ubiquitous images as well as questioning and parodying American consumerism, he made the everyday, ho-hum object epic and worthy of artistic consideration.

Warhol seemed to celebrate what others thought of as slightly distasteful, including the cult of the celebrity and film star. He painted many portraits of the rich and powerful—from Elizabeth Taylor to Chairman Mao. At the same time, he uncovered American society's voyeuristic tendencies by creating large disaster paintings—replicating reportage of car crashes or paintings that dealt with the instruments of death, including the gun, the atomic bomb, and the electric chair.

Warhol's paintings were shown for the first time in 1962, first in Los Angeles and later that year in New York. He became an instant sensation and a celebrity star of the pop art movement. The following year he started the Factory, employing a number of assistants to produce a range of silkscreen paintings for purchase, including sculptures of boxes of Brillo soap pads and Heinz ketchup.

In 1965, Warhol announced his retirement as a painter (only adding to the desirability of his product) to concentrate on filmmaking. He made more than sixty films featuring his own cast of appointed "superstars" from the Factory. They are differentiated by their do-it-yourself aesthetic, reveling in the low-fi, the amateur, and the voyeuristic. Warhol's films anticipate the moment when YouTube invited us to "Broadcast Yourself."

In July 1968, Warhol was shot three times in the chest by a woman who had a minor role in one of his films, explaining that "he had too much control over my life." It made only minor headlines due to Robert Kennedy's assassination two days later, but Warhol never recovered completely, having to wear a bandage around his torso for the rest of his life.

In the early 1970s he began painting again, focusing on portrait art and working on his celebrity status in the New York party and club scene. He commanded huge fees for painting the faces of wealthy patrons: John Lennon, Mick Jagger, Brigitte Bardot, Michael Jackson, even the Shah of Iran. By 1986, the Neiman-Marcus Christmas catalog was advertising portrait sittings with Andy Warhol for $35,000. Warhol died unexpectedly in 1987 from complications following a routine gall bladder surgery, leaving behind an estate estimated at $100 million.

Unbeknownst to most, Warhol regularly attended mass throughout his life, holding on to the Orthodox Christian faith of his childhood. Were all those larger-than-life images of celebrities connected to the icons of saints that surrounded him in church? He elevated his subjects to a higher plane. Warhol saw no difference between a beautiful ad, a beautiful painting, or a beautiful face. He celebrated them all and refused to believe that art was just for the lucky few. As he famously said, "When you think about it, department stores are kind of like museums."

GABRIEL FERRER

# The Seventies

*T*hose who came of age during the seventies might rather forget their year-book pictures—polyester, leisure suits, long hair, bell-bottoms, and even hot pants. Certainly their kids would! Yet thanks to John Travolta and *Saturday Night Fever*, disco triumphed for a brief, delirious moment. Such mindless dancing was a reaction to a tumultuous era, a longing for "Happy Days."

Author Tom Wolfe dubbed the seventies as "The 'Me' Decade." A turn inward, a movement toward finding one's self, proved pervasive. Christopher Lasch's book *The Culture of Narcissism* captured the spirit of the times as people attempted to find and further themselves amid growing social upheaval. Many turned toward the East for inspiration. The Beatles went to India, and Eastern religious thought became popular on college campuses and in the West. George Harrison topped the charts singing "My Sweet Lord," as Hare Krishna communities and vegetarian restaurants proliferated.

Resistance to the Vietnam War peaked in the seventies. The National Guard gunned down student protestors at Kent State, memorialized by Neil Young in the poignant song, "Ohio." John Lennon asked listeners to "give peace a chance" and to "imagine there's no heaven . . . and no religion, too." Yet countless hippies were baptized as "Jesus Freaks," including musicians like Larry Norman, Phil Keaggy, and Keith Green. After Led Zeppelin climbed a "Stairway to Heaven," AC/DC invited their fans to join them on the "Highway to Hell."

The Watergate scandal cast a pall over Richard Nixon's presidency. All the President's men looked like crooks. The 1972 Olympic Games—intended to promote world peace—were marred by terrorists' murder of Israeli athletes. Volatile oil prices sparked economic malaise and tamped down America's bicentennial celebration. Jimmy Carter made headlines as America's first "born-again" president.

Norman Lear's television series' reflected the complexities of the era, with comedies like *All in the Family*, *Good Times,* and *Maude* firmly rooted in the headlines of the era. *Little House on the Prairie* snapped audiences back to an earlier, simpler era. *Sesame Street* and *The Muppet Show* introduced children to a contemporary world in which people who looked and thought differently needed to be embraced.

The seventies also saw the rise of divorce and the Supreme Court case of *Roe vs. Wade*, a landmark decision that legalized abortion and the right of women to have a choice. Many found these new directions liberating and fulfilling. But others wondered, in the words of American psychiatrist Karl Menninger's best-selling book, *Whatever Became of Sin?* The decade ended with dueling sounds of defiance. Gloria Gaynor triumphantly declared "I Will Survive" for women, for homosexuals, for all who previously felt disempowered. And the Sex Pistols were snarling, "Anarchy in the UK" for punks eager to undermine the old world order. Whose vision would prevail?

# Hank Aaron

Most people don't think of Hank Aaron when they think of home runs, yet he held the career record for thirty-three years. Aaron's running total was always thought to be a product of consistency, and consistency has never been "sexy." Instead, we remember the towering blasts of Barry Bonds and Alex Rodriguez. We glorify Mark McGwire and Sammy Sosa for "saving" baseball in 1998 and mythologize Mickey Mantle's one-armed bomb back in '61. We question how well Babe Ruth would have done against Satchel Paige and whether Ken Griffey Jr.'s body held him back from hitting eight hundred home runs. And we marvel at players' ability to hit home runs, literally, out of the ballpark. It's a skill nothing short of godlike in the eyes of fans.

Of course, Aaron could hit the cover off a ball. They didn't call him "Hammerin' Hank" or shout, "Oh, Henry!" for nothing. But Aaron is an anomaly compared to most modern athletes. His nickname never really suited him. "Hammer" is fit for someone brash and bold like Reggie Jackson, someone who says what's on his mind and speaks in headlines. Aaron was a quiet great. A home-run hitter by trade, he often called triples the most exciting play in baseball. He was reserved and humble, two things not often rewarded in the media-driven world of professional sports.

Aaron made his noise on the field. As the last Negro League ballplayer to make the jump to the majors, he lived the civil rights movement between the lines, playing twenty-plus seasons of all-star-caliber baseball throughout the 1950s, '60s, and into the '70s, averaging more than thirty home runs a year.

The tag line for Michael Tolin's Oscar-nominated documentary *Hank Aaron: Chasing the Dream* was apt: "He hit everything life threw at him." Growing up poor and black in 1940's Alabama gave Aaron the right to be callous. Waiting on the team bus outside a diner for white teammates to bring back food should have made him bitter. Death threats during his race to pass Babe Ruth as the home-run king could have put him over the edge. He ended the 1973 season one shy of Ruth's record of 714 home runs. Over the course of a long winter off season, Aaron endured taunts and threats from people who didn't want to see a black man break the Babe's mark. But come April 1974, Aaron confronted bigotry with dignity. Legendary broadcaster Vin Scully remarked on the setting for Aaron's 715th homerun, "What a marvelous moment for Atlanta and the state of Georgia; what a marvelous moment for the country and the world. A black man is getting a standing ovation in the Deep South for breaking a record of an all-time baseball idol. And it is a great moment for all of us, and particularly for Henry Aaron."

With his home runs behind him, a retired Aaron became baseball's ambassador. And the steroid era made him the game's last ethical icon. McGwire and Sosa chased home-run records empowered by chemical enhancements, skewing a game that had always been measured in numbers across eras. Photos demonstrated the change in Barry Bonds's head and body size since his early playing days. Rumors abounded throughout Bonds's assault on Aaron's record. When Bonds finally crushed his 756th career homerun, Aaron's image flashed on the Jumbotron at Pac Bell Park in San Francisco moments later. Aaron congratulated Bonds and baseball despite the allegedly tainted record. He took the high road, connecting Bonds's moment to his own, "My hope today, as it was on that April evening in 1974, is that the achievement of this record will inspire others to chase their own dreams."

As much as he loved playing baseball, he now loves being its benevolent representative. He loves the ballpark and once said it made him feel, "like I was surrounded by angels and I had God's hand on my shoulder." A rumor among baseball writers was that Hank kept a copy of the 500-year-old text *The Imitation of Christ* in his locker, reading it regularly throughout his career. The words of Thomas à Kempis helped—his emulation of Christ's forbearance in the racially tense city of Atlanta was nothing short of miraculous. Hank is a throwback to a bygone era when hard work exceeded short cuts, and consistency trumped controversy.

MATTHEW KITCHEN

## *Adventure*

If any game designer enjoys eternal security in video game history, it must be Warren Robinett. Taking his inspiration from Don Woods and Willy Crowther's text-based game *Adventure*, Robinett labored for six months to redesign that game as the image-based Atari *Adventure*. In so doing, he ushered in a new genre that directly paved the way for landmark series such as *Ultima, The Legend of Zelda,* and even *World of Warcraft*.

In 1979, *Adventure* introduced the gaming experience of a persistent, expansive, and fully navigable off-screen world, populated by creatures with lives and personalities of their own. Although this world encompassed thirty screens, the player—represented by an on-screen cursor—could see and explore only one screen at a time. Restlessly searching for the elusive

Enchanted Chalice, the player traversed far and wide through a series of castles, labyrinths, catacombs, and dungeons. Along the way, the player alternately hunted and fled from a family of three strangely duck-like dragons named Yorgle, Grundle, and Rhindle. The kingdom also hid a handy assortment of magical items—an arrow-shaped sword, a u-shaped magnet, a large purple bridge, and three castle keys. However, the player could carry only one item at a time. In order to unlock a castle drawbridge, the player had to leave the sword behind in order to fetch the key from a remote location. Making matters worse, a chaotic bat tended to swoop in to steal away a useful item or drop off a dragon at the most inopportune time. No video-game player had ever before conceived of anything so mythical and magical as *Adventure*.

Perhaps *Adventure*'s most enduring story is the tale of the mysterious "Easter Egg" phenomenon. Receiving an annual salary of $22,000, Robinett single-handedly designed and coded the *Adventure* cartridge for the original Atari VCS. *Adventure* went on to sell a million copies at $25 each. However, Atari refused to pay Robinett even one penny of royalties for his contribution. Adding insult to injury, Atari also refused to give Robinett any credit for his work on the box art or game manual. All of this was company policy. Thus, Robinett was moved to sneak an undocumented secret room into his game world. Within that secret room, a marquee read, "Created by Warren Robinett." Only the cleverest players would ever find the hidden "Grey Dot" that unlocked the entrance to this secret message.

For its day, myth and magic infused Robinett's *Adventure* with an almost transcendent sense of mystery, awe, and wonder. Players spent dozens—even hundreds—of hours mapping terrain, plumbing the depths of its lamp-lit dungeons, searching for hidden rooms, testing the properties of each magical item, and poring over the secrets of the kingdom. *Adventure* was a timer-less game as well, allowing for welcome moments of careful contemplation and reflection.

The transcendence of *Adventure* was also experienced within the "non-Euclidean structure" of its pathways, as Mark Wolf suggested in *The Meaning of the Video Game*. Screens that seemed to connect east and west also connected north and south, inexplicably. Although walls and borders constrained player movement, the dragons and bat broke those rules through their own form of "god movement." Their special powers enabled them to phase through all walls and borders in order to pounce on the player at any moment. Perhaps the most wondrous of all *Adventure* experiences occurred after the player's death. Once eaten, the player sat in the dragon's belly until the bat swooped in, picked up the dragon, and flew around the kingdom on a carefree tour that afforded a bird's eye view otherwise inaccessible. Playing

*Adventure* was an immersive encounter with anticipation, imagination, nervousness, dread, and delight.

Likewise, the life of faith is a transcendent journey into mystery, awe, and wonder. In the midst of an increasingly mechanized and modern world, we need enchantment more than ever before. We too often try to turn the faith journey into something that we master and, in so doing, fail to honor its essential nature as something that masters *us*. This journey is less a technical problem to be solved than a transcendent potentiality to be savored. To paraphrase that great mythmaker, C. S. Lewis, transcendence is a faith-enriching gift that "stirs and troubles" us "with the dim sense of something beyond our reach and, far from dulling or emptying the actual world, gives it a new dimension of depth."

MARK HAYSE

# Woody Allen

Woody Allen is not simply a filmmaker. In the truest sense of the word, he is an *auteur*. He has written, directed, starred in, and even produced nearly a film per year over the course of a career that dates back to the 1960s. From critically acclaimed, genre-defining romantic comedies like *Annie Hall* (1977), to darker comedies such as *Crimes and Misdemeanors* (1989), or dramatic thrillers such as *Match Point* (2005), Allen has repeatedly shaped his films according to his unique and discernable cinematic vision. In a certain sense, Woody Allen films are a genre unto themselves. Although often comedic, his work is concomitantly distinguished by its somber, philosophical undercurrents, inspired by the likes of European filmmakers Ingmar Bergman and Federico Fellini. Allen frequently casts himself as a quirky, neurotic, and relatively successful writer or producer of film who, along with a number of other upper-class intellectuals and academics, not only struggles with his own Jewish identity and tradition but also deconstructs the value and role of religious faith, questioning the meaning of life amid the world's apparent absurdities and contradictions.

The son of Jewish parents, Allen was raised in New York City and attended Hebrew school on the lower east side of Manhattan. At the age of fifteen he began writing jokes for a local New York publication, and by nineteen he was writing for both *The Ed Sullivan Show* and *The Tonight Show*. Discouraged by the ways in which his jokes were being "wasted" in these venues, Allen tried his hand at stand-up comedy, where he developed the neurotic persona that eventually became another mark of a "Woody Allen" film. Indeed, it was this comedic orientation that Allen first brought to his filmmaking. Yet, as his work matured, Allen increasingly turned from purely comedic material toward more sober and dark dramas, exploring time and again the explicitly existential themes of the indifference of the universe and humanity's naive pursuit of meaning in a world without God.

Consequently, Allen's films do not simply invite theological dialogue; they demand it. They press audiences to consider whether there is a moral structure to the universe and whether, by extension, there is any meaning in life that is not of our own creation. As he makes explicit through films like *Crimes and Misdemeanors*, *Match Point*, and *Vicky Cristina Barcelona* (2008), in the face of an indifferent world, we have but two choices. We can either make an existential "leap of faith" and accept the reality of God in spite of and in contradiction to reason, or we can honestly face the utter meaninglessness of life and construct our own meaning according to "whatever works" for each individual—an epithet that happens to not only be a particularly salient line of dialogue in *Vicky* but also serves as the title and main theme of Allen's later film *Whatever Works* (2009). It seems reasonable to suggest that, given his entire oeuvre, Allen leans toward the latter. That is, in the end, it is the self-determining agent who is solely responsible for imbuing life with meaning.

To be sure, Allen is first and foremost a filmmaker. Yet, as he rails not only against the absurdity of an apparently godforsaken, meaningless universe, but also against the very notion of a just Deity who rules the world in love, Allen is also a theologian—one whose post-Holocaust understanding of God cannot be ignored. For Allen, like Job, the person who has never contended with the God who permits such arbitrary randomness and meaningless suffering does not, in fact, truly know God. In the form of his atheistic, Jewish existentialism, Allen's vehement protest is not antithetical to theological reflection; rather, it resides at the very heart of both the Jewish and Christian faiths.

At the same time, Allen's existential vision—the choice between a simple theism and a rational atheism—rings somewhat hollow. Perhaps it is for this reason that audiences have received his twenty-first century films less warmly than his earlier work, especially in America. In a certain sense, contemporary culture has moved beyond existentialism and embraces a more tempered spirituality. Rather than suppressing contradictions through false dichotomies, it admits contradiction, paradox, and even mystery into the inner recesses of our deep-lived experiences. Thus, the question we are left with is not-so-much whether Allen's past films successfully captured the existential angst of the twentieth century, but whether his upcoming work will reflect, resist, or embrace a postmodern spirituality that takes up within itself both unbelief and belief, both protest and devotion, both absurdity and meaning.

KUTTER CALLAWAY

## Neil Diamond

Where did Neil Diamond come from? And where is he going? The temporal answers are, respectively, Brooklyn in the 1940s and Los Angeles today. To which prosaic statement of demography Mr. Diamond would most likely respond that you can build a life in a place that isn't home, yet find that what used to be home doesn't belong to you anymore either. In giving voice to just that sentiment in his 1971 song "I Am, I Said," he would locate himself in the tradition of musical poets from the Psalmists onward, projecting the hope for rootedness as an archetypal dimension of what it means to be human. His career encompasses 1960's Brill Building songwriter magic-for-hire, to seeing his work recorded by Elvis and the Monkees, and eventually making one of the great live albums on a *Hot August Night* at Los Angeles's Greek Theatre—a 1972 performance in which the audience and the singer achieve a kind of rare symbiosis, one in which he really does seem to be speaking *for* them as much as *to* them.

An appearance at 1976's the Last Waltz, the astonishing all-night-long career valedictory for Bob Dylan's former backup The Band, consolidated his position as someone who could belong anywhere. It was no surprise then that he later followed the most clichéd work of his career—a series of cinematic love songs, lushly scored as *The Movie Album*—with two pared-back declarations of masculine spirituality, *12 Songs* (2005) and *Home Before Dawn* (2008), produced by Rick Rubin, the man who helped Johnny Cash come around at the end of his life. At age sixty-seven, Diamond experienced his first chart-topping album with *Home Before Dawn*.

But Diamond has always been more impressive as a live performer than when studio bound: what he does is to incarnate people's hopes. In concert he becomes the projection of our desires—for love, for friendship, ultimately for community, and with a specifically Jewish American ability to laugh at himself. The live shows—massive endeavors, in which a huge band turns

Madison Square Garden and the Sydney Opera House alike into macro-level, pub-singing sessions—actually *become* the kinds of community he mourns in songs like "Be," or "America," which is an ode to nationalistic pride that manages not to be xenophobic precisely because it's written by the child of immigrants.

Not long ago, when a recently deposed Irish Prime Minister walked into a Dublin rugby stadium before a Diamond concert, the crowd of 70,000 strong jumped to their feet and cheered, not because he represented their politics, but because his appearance at a Diamond concert granted him entrée to a world in which politics doesn't matter. Diamond fans don't care whether you're left or right. They just want to fall in love; to dance in a bar; to drink some red, red wine; and to enjoy the traveling salvation show that his songs evoke as nothing less than the purpose of life itself: To keep going, to be kind to people along the way, to allow yourself to be changed, and to find home.

After missteps like the *Hollywood* album (not to mention the 1980 cult classic of so-bad-it's-good filmmaking in his remake of the Al Jolson movie *The Jazz Singer*), he seems to have found an authentic voice again with the Rubin albums. The turning point may have been his "Girl, You'll Be a Woman Soon" being covered for the *Pulp Fiction* soundtrack—appropriate enough, because his writing has become that of a man who has grown into himself. He writes as someone who knows that life is hard but that the trick is not minding. He gives the audience a magnificent show to make their lives just a little bit brighter. The career is emblematic of a certain kind of artistic maturing—while he used to take himself too seriously, he seems to have changed in front of our eyes. He's allowed himself to permit genuine collaboration, to have his music partly shaped by the visions of others, which is no easy task when the trappings of ego and celebrity are readily available.

"Did you ever read about a frog who dreamed of becoming a king, and then became one?" begins the climactic bridge of "I Am, I Said"; the way you respond to those words will depend on whether or not you like ice cream full or low-fat, I suppose. Let it suffice to say, whether you like his music or not, Neil Diamond speaks to profoundly human emotions, and he may be the last of the performers who achieved fame in the 1970s who's still getting better at it.

GARETH HIGGINS

# Clint Eastwood

Pauline Kael, the dominant American film critic of the second half of the twentieth century, could not contain her excitement at the 1971 release of *Dirty Harry*, Don Siegel's film, which had Clint Eastwood, star of TV's *Rawhide* and half a dozen stark westerns, projecting the public's fear of judicial impotence in the face of violent crime by simply blowing away the perpetrators, asking questions later. For Kael, *Harry* was "the first American film that is a fascist work of art," writing large the Nixon era's fear of threats within and without, and reverse projecting the imperialist aggression of the Vietnam War onto the streets of San Francisco. It was easy to see Eastwood's protagonist as a progenitor for Ronald Reagan, who himself used Harry's famous "Go ahead, make my day" line to threaten elected representatives who wanted to raise taxes. The use of violent metaphors in politics is nothing new, of course, but what was startling about Reagan's invocation of Dirty Harry was that mainstream culture did not perceive it as distasteful for a President to imply that the best way to govern is to kill your opponents. Clint Eastwood had helped make horror the acceptable way to do business.

Twenty years later, after Eastwood had made at least a film a year, most as actor *and* director (including two ill-advised attempts at buddy comedy with a monkey); served a two-year stint as a city mayor in Carmel-by-the-Sea, California; and been anointed by the French government as a Knight of Arts and Letters, something unusual happened. The Man with No Name, who could smirk as he left a hanging man to die; Officer Callaghan, who could kill suspects with impunity; and Mitchell Gant, the unthinking patriot who could steal a Soviet plane to keep America strong, not particularly minding who gets killed along the way, started making films in which the consequences of violence were not only the subtext, but the *point*.

It began with *Unforgiven*, his 1992 Best Picture Oscar winner, about a hired killer who chisels off part of his soul every time he goes to work. It continued with 1993's *In the Line of Fire*, a thriller in which the legacy of a murder three decades in the past foregrounds the life of its protagonist—a man who can't pretend that killing doesn't really mean anything. It reached its peak in 2003 with *Mystic River*, an astonishing drama in which the sins of the fathers do what they always do—they continue, until they are confronted. By this stage, Eastwood was clearly saying that he knew bullets didn't stop anything: they merely perpetuate the cycle of violence. Two of the most nuanced films about war ever made—*Flags of Our Fathers* and *Letters from Iwo Jima* (both 2006)—followed, and there could be observed the startling sight of a conservative white American demanding that his culture face up to the role that deceptive propaganda had played in the Iraq war, and to stop dehumanizing the enemy. At seventy-eight, he wasn't finished yet, producing in *Gran Torino* (2009) an acting swan song that aimed for nothing less than the naming of ageism, racism, and urban blight in America. It felt like atonement for the sins of his earlier films; he acknowledged as much, even speaking of regret for some of the messages he had endorsed in the past.

That expression of regret might itself be seen as regrettable, for in reality he had always been a nuanced filmmaker and performer. Read between the lines of the 1966 film *The Good, the Bad, and the Ugly*, and you see a central character who doesn't trust authority—not because rules are themselves bad, but because the kind of authority available in the Old West was repressing people; 1973's *High Plains Drifter* was as sympathetic and respectful to the plight of Native Americans as any of the so-called "revisionist" Westerns such as *Dances with Wolves* that emerged years later. Eastwood's magnificent 1988 biopic of saxophonist Charlie Parker, *Bird*, was only one example of his passion for aesthetic beauty and understanding the demons that often plague artists And in 1995's *The Bridges of Madison County* he turned a sentimental novel into one of the screen's great depictions of the enormous risk that always constitutes real love between two people. It may therefore be more accurate to say that Clint Eastwood's vision of masculinity matured with age, but the grace notes of humor, humility, and humanness were always there, if you looked beyond the 44 Magnum.

GARETH HIGGINS

# Marvin Gaye

*"What's Going On?"*

Marvin Pentz Gay Jr. (1939–1984), better known by his stage name Marvin Gaye, was a singer-songwriter and part of the Detroit-based Motown Records roster of musicians who changed the face of popular music. In spite of intense family pressure to follow his father into ministry, Gaye began his career as a drummer and part-time doo-wop singer, but he soon transitioned into a new path as a solo R&B artist. He had a string of popular hits, including "Can I Get a Witness" (1963), "How Sweet It Is (To Be Loved by You)" (1964), "Ain't That Peculiar" (1965), and "I Heard It through the Grapevine" (1968). These songs, as well as some duets with female artists such as Mary

Wells and Tammi Terrell, established him as one of his record company's brightest stars and its best-selling solo artist in the 1960s, earning him the title, "The Prince of Motown."

Motown Records had a stable of well-known artists who churned out seminal pop songs in the 1960s and '70s. Gaye's future looked set to follow a very well-trodden path as a sort of smooth, sophisticated ladies' man, but he had other desires. He wanted to explore other kinds of music, particularly jazz and classical, which caused a number of clashes with his record company, which wanted to continue capitalizing on his established formula for success.

But it was an album released on May 21, 1971, that changed everything. *What's Going On* was his eleventh studio release, but it was unlike any other he had recorded thus far. One of his singing partners, Tammi Terrell, had died quite suddenly the year before. Gaye, already prone to depression and other anxieties, said that he would not sing duets with any other female artists and went on a sort of enforced review of his future. *What's Going On* was the result of that introspection. It was a politically charged and yet deeply personal work, a unique and potent combination of his own troubled relationship with the world inside and out.

Gaye produced the album himself and created a nine-song concept piece, told through the eyes of a Vietnam War veteran returning home and asking questions of the country he had fought so hard for. The album became a huge crossover hit (it was later voted number six on *Rolling Stone* magazine's list of the 500 greatest albums of all time) and gained Gaye an audience among white rock fans.

The album was the first to reflect a burgeoning socially conscious trend in popular black music and featured introspective lyrics about the haves and the have-nots, the generous and the selfish. It tackled the larger issues of environment, poverty, war, drug addiction, and a whole host of other social themes that had seldom been mentioned in R&B music up until then. But these were changing times. The hippie movement had run out of steam; the Vietnam War had sapped the life out of the national psyche; and urban areas were encountering waves of unemployment, unrest, and racial tension. All these elements came together in Gaye's mind and eventually were released out through his music.

The title song was a collaborative effort with two other Motown songwriters, Al Cleveland and Obie Benson. Benson came up with the original idea for the song after seeing antiwar protesters treated brutally by the police. Gaye drew much of his inspiration from the experiences of his younger brother Frankie, a Vietnam War veteran.

Gaye grew up in an extremely strict and repressive religious environment, which can be seen in *What's Going On*. The album is filled with biblical imagery and Christian ideas, but it is also veers far from traditional paths in its handling of life's meaning and purpose. Gaye was a deeply conflicted person whose life was marked by struggle. The strictness of his upbringing and his volatile relationship with his preacher father gave him a distaste for organized religion, but he never lost his interest in the spiritual, saying more than once that he considered giving up music to become a monk. This struggle is what manifests in Gaye's music and is what gives it its continued appeal. This is music that explores the whole person—it is sensual, sexual, spiritual, and conflicted. Gaye said at the time that he wanted to reevaluate his whole concept of what his music would say, addressing social realities and inviting people to look at what was going on in the world. Gaye spoke about God in the reality of life's complexity rather than in the safety of old assumptions, and the world is better for it.

BARRY TAYLOR

## *The Godfather*

"I'm going to make him an offer he can't refuse," Marlon Brando's Don Corleone tells his movie-star-wannabe godson Johnny Fontaine (Al Martino) in *The Godfather,* Francis Ford Coppola's 1972 Academy Award-winning film. The American Film Institute lists this line as the number two movie quote of all time, second only to "Frankly my dear, I don't give a damn" from *Gone with the Wind. The Godfather* was based on the novel written by Mario Puzo in 1969, which was on the *New York Times* bestseller list for sixty-seven weeks and sold over twenty-one million copies. Puzo and Coppola cowrote this film script, as well as the scripts for *The Godfather Part II* (1974) and *The Godfather Part III* (1990).

*The Godfather* tells the story of one Sicilian mafia family within a confederation of five other families in New York between the years 1945–1955. Don Vito Corleone (the surname means "lion heart"; there is an actual village in Sicily with this name) heads the family with his eldest son Sonny (James Caan) and his consigliere Tom Hagan (Robert Duvall). A less-talented son, Fredo (John Cazale), is apprenticed to a casino owner in Las Vegas, while youngest son Michael (Al Pacino) insists that he does not want to join the family business. All this changes through power grabs, assassinations, and two attempts on the life of Don Vito.

*The Godfather* is a crime opera of the first order; it vies among critics with *Citizen Kane* as the best film of all time. It was nominated for eleven

Academy Awards and received three. With its two sequels, the movie has made an indelible mark on the world of popular culture, as well as on the craft of filmmaking. The films have also provided a narrative landscape to consider faith and family, particularly the Sicilian family and the Catholic religion. (*The Godfather* is perhaps the only film to explicitly depict all seven sacraments of the Catholic Church.)

Godparents are all-important in Catholic sacramental theology. They make solemn promises to God in the name of the child, until the child can make them for him- or herself. This role actually carries great spiritual responsibility, though in modern times it is considered more of an honor than a commitment to follow the spiritual welfare of a child, and to sometimes step in with material care. In one sense, a Mafia godfather cared for and punished his "godchildren" in this way. But it was a relationship based in a feudal honor system parading under the guise of Catholicism rather than sincere religious sentiment.

Overarching the first two films are the consequences of the moral degradation of the once golden boy of the Corleone dynasty, Michael. Coppola juxtaposes American Protestant individualistic, nonsacramental culture with the Sicilian Catholic family or communitarian, sacramental culture. Michael is the one who becomes mainstream American by getting an Ivy League education, serving in the military, and choosing to go his own way rather than the family's. After his first wife is killed in Sicily, he returns home to marry his original girlfriend, Kay (Diane Keaton), who is a nominal Protestant. He promises Kay that he will stop participating in the murderous ways of the family, but he is drawn in despite this promise. In *The Godfather II*, as Kay realizes he has no intention of changing, she has an abortion, refusing to bring another male into such a family. Although it is all right for Michael to murder, it is not acceptable for Kay to do so. They divorce, and any bond between the two cultures is irreparably ruptured.

The contrasts in *The Godfather* pile up in the first film's final sequence, one of the most memorable in all of cinema. The Corleone family is celebrating a baptism; Michael is the child's godfather. With the family, Michael affirms his rejection of Satan as the organist plays Bach's "Passacaglia & Fugue in C Minor." But while the priest asks his questions and speaks the words of the ritual in Latin, scenes of Michael's lieutenants' killing his enemies are cross-cut relentlessly with those of the ceremony. If the sacraments are outward signs of divine invisible realities, *The Godfather* is sacramental, but it also signifies a sacrilegious parading under the signs of grace.

*The Godfather* is considered an undeniable masterpiece because of the way Coppola interprets the narrative into a complex concert of sight and sound. It will live on in other films, whether referenced in its dialogue or in its filmmaking style.

ROSE PACATTE

# Billie Jean King

To many, Billie Jean King was a tennis player, famous for her thirty-nine Grand Slam championships, including twenty Wimbledon titles. However, since the 1970s, she has been building an irreplaceable legacy that has influenced the lives of women and girls in America and across the globe. Born into an era when American girls were discouraged from playing sports and women had no opportunities to be professional athletes, King paved the way for every professional female competitor, including Chris Evert, Lisa Leslie, Misty May Treanor, Mia Hamm, Serena Williams, and Bethany Hamilton. Without Billie Jean King, there would certainly be no Women's Tennis Association (WTA), but there might also be no AYSO girls' soccer leagues, no NCAA women's softball, no WNBA or LPGA, and no FIFA Women's World Cup. She provided opportunities and changed the lives of all ordinary girls who like to throw, run, dive, swing, jump, climb, kick, and swim.

A child of working-class Methodists, King began breaking down barriers for girls and women when she started winning on the tennis court in the late 1950s. Before her, professional women's tennis did not exist. In 1971, King was the first female athlete in any sport to earn more than $100,000 in one season. Because of her threats to boycott tournaments due to unequal pay, the U.S. Open was the first tournament to pay men and women champions equally in 1973.

The defining moment in King's pop cultural influence came in September 1973, when she became a pillar in the women's movement by beating self-proclaimed male chauvinist Bobby Riggs in a controversial, nationally televised battle of the sexes tennis match watched by forty million viewers. King contributed to the media spectacle by arriving in the Houston Astrodome aloft in a chair held up by four hunky muscle men. Earlier that year, Riggs had beaten tennis champion Margaret Court in a less-publicized battle of the sexes on Mother's Day. But King, who had turned down Riggs's previous request to play him, beat Riggs easily in three straight sets. The psychological battle King won in Houston helped improve the public's mood toward women in sports and justified passage of Title IX legislation, the contentious policy requiring gender equity in education and athletics, signed into law a year earlier by President Nixon.

At the same time that Billie was taking on Bobby, denominations were opening up the ordination process to women in Methodist, Presbyterian, Lutheran, and Episcopal churches. Not all churches have followed (most notably the Roman Catholics, the Orthodox, and the Southern Baptists). Although salary disparity remains both in tennis and the church, significant changes occurred in the seventies. Thanks to Billie Jean King, no longer can we assume woman to be the weaker or dependent sex. Old prejudices are now seen for what they are—prejudices.

King founded the Women's Sports Foundation in 1974 to advance the lives of women and girls through physical activity and athletics. Today, it has an operating budget of more than $10 million per year with offices in four states. The Foundation gives scholarships, travel, and training awards; funds research; and advocates for women and girls. To ensure that generations of tennis fans and professionals honor her legacy, in 2006 the U.S. Tennis Association renamed the National Tennis Center, home of the U.S. Open, the Billie Jean King National Tennis Center. King's influence spans the globe, as the United Nations Educational, Scientific, and Cultural Organization (UNESCO) named her a Global Mentor for Gender Equality in 2008.

Perhaps King's greatest battles occurred off the court. A palimony suit filed by King's female lover forced her out of the closet in 1981. Thirty years before the majority of the American public exhibited a cultural shift in its attitudes toward the civil rights of homosexuals, the revelation that King was a lesbian cost her many lucrative endorsements. She told *The Times* of London, "I wanted to tell the truth but my parents were homophobic and I was in the closet. As well as that, I had people tell me that if I talked about what I was going through, it would be the end of the women's tour." After twenty-two years of marriage, King and her husband, Larry, were divorced in 1987. Yet, King recalls how long it took her to acknowledge her sexuality to her parents: "At the age of fifty-one, I was finally able to talk about it properly with my parents and no longer did I have to measure my words with them. That was a turning point for me as it meant I didn't have regrets any more." In 2009, President Obama awarded Billie Jean King the Presidential Medal of Freedom for breaking down barriers and being an agent of change, first for women and later for lesbian, gay, bisexual, and transgender people.

CAROLINE CICERO

# Bruce Lee

Bruce Lee was born in San Francisco on November 27, during the hour of the Dragon (7 to 9 a.m.) in the year of the Dragon (1940). Thirty-two years later, he died in Hong Kong three weeks before the release of his first American film, the now-classic martial arts epic *Enter the Dragon* (1972). The official cause of death was acute cerebral edema, or swelling of the brain, brought about by hypersensitivity to a painkiller that a mistress had given him. Befitting a rising star of his stature and complex personal associations, many believed he died under more sinister circumstances.

Like James Dean and Buddy Holly before him, Bruce Lee's extraordinary charisma and groundbreaking talents, coupled with a sudden, still-controversial early death at a critical point in his career, established him as a pop icon for the ages. An actor, martial artist, teacher, and philosopher when he was alive, in his death Lee became a myth, an endlessly influential and lingering presence in our collective consciousness.

Having trained under the legendary Wing Chun practitioner, Yip Man, in his youth Lee fought his way through the streets of Hong Kong and, at eighteen years old, was sent to America by his concerned parents to avoid trouble with the law. With only one hundred dollars in his pocket, he navigated his way through San Francisco and Seattle with uncommon resilience and toughness, working at a Chinese restaurant, winning kung fu matches, and studying philosophy in school. During this period, he married an American woman, had children, established his own system of free-style martial arts called "Jeet Kune Do"—defined by its nonclassical employment of body movement and lack of rigid formalism—and taught martial arts to eager and curious westerners, which, at the time, was an unheard-of practice that drew the ire of his fellow martial artists in the Chinese community.

In the process, Lee became an actor, having drawn notice for his dynamism, strength, and lightning-fast speed as a martial arts demonstrator in Southern California. In the Hollywood of the 1960s, he starred as Kato in the short-lived series *The Green Hornet*; made appearances on *Batman*, *Ironside*, *Here Comes the Bride*, and *Longstreet*; did action choreography for movies; and taught a cohort of famous students that included Steve McQueen, Lee Marvin, and Roman Polanski. Dissatisfied with his career progress in America, Lee went back to Hong Kong and made a string of box office hits. Movies like *The Big Boss*, *Fist of Fury*, and *Way of the Dragon* catapulted him to stardom in his native Asia. When Hollywood started to pay attention, Warner Brothers offered him the starring role in *Enter the Dragon*, a joint venture between the East and the West that was supposed to finally make him a global superstar. It did, but Bruce Lee's sudden passing three weeks before the film's release meant that he would not live to see his international celebrity realized. Ironically, the tragedy also guaranteed lasting fame and cemented his now-legendary status.

As a teacher, Lee popularized kung fu, Eastern philosophy, and physical fitness and self-improvement through martial arts, familiarizing them with a global audience that once regarded Eastern ideas and practices as an exotic curiosity. As a martial artist, he distinguished himself from other world-class fighters by making memorable animal sounds and incorporating fluid, intricate body movements and instruments like nunchuck into fighting. As a performer and filmmaker, he revolutionized action cinema and brought about ethnic diversity in American popular culture, paving the way for the likes of Jackie Chan and Jet Li.

Bruce Lee's image lives on today in the form of endless imitations, classic movies, hip merchandise and memorabilia, and in the martial arts and Eastern philosophy taught around the world. To many, he signifies perseverance, optimism, rebellion, and cool; he is an icon of strength in the face of adversity. He famously urged his followers to "be like water"—fluid and resilient, not bound by any particular shape or form. Indeed, in his life and career, Bruce Lee exhibited an impulse for liberation, self-determination, and the defiance of rules and convention to which the public continues to respond.

Bruce Lee's enduring popularity hints at our innate attraction to symbols that signify the overcoming of defined social and cultural expectations, as well as a hope to keep on fighting, to stare down opponents in the presence of unlikely victory. The mythology of Bruce Lee points to a longing for such ultimate victory.

EUGENE SUEN

## Bob Marley

*"The one good thing about music,*
*When it hits you feel no pain."*

*Bob Marley, "Trenchtown Rock"*

Bob Marley (1945–1981) didn't invent reggae—that infectious mix of American R&B and Caribbean folk music—but he put it firmly on the world map, becoming not only its ambassador but the first global pop star from a third-world country and one of the most important figures in twentieth-century popular music.

For Marley, as for many of his peers, music became a way of coping with, and hopefully exiting, the poverty in Trenchtown, the township in Jamaica where he lived. Jamaica's vibrant music culture was a magnet for young people eager to find fame and fortune. Reggae music emerged in the early 1960s as more and more American music was embraced by the local population and merged with other styles of Caribbean music—calypso, ska, and rock-steady. What "reggae" means is somewhat contested. Some say it comes from the Jamaican-English word *rege-rege*, which can mean either ragged clothing or a quarrel (either definition seems appropriate). But no matter where the word came from, the music itself is a unique genre that has become part of the fabric of popular music. Its rhythmic style makes even the heaviest feet feel like dancing.

For millions of listeners, Marley's music, with its hypnotic rhythms and grooves, is a perfect complement to the frenetic nature of life in the modern world. It is a release, an escape, and something to be danced to. But for others he is much more than a pop star; he is a prophet, a herald, and a messenger. These followers view his songs as parables. He is revered as a mystic and a messenger whose songs offer hope and inspiration to disenfranchised peoples around the globe.

Marley's music articulated the challenges and fears of the Jamaican people in a postcolonial age, and echoed the challenges and fears being experienced by many people around the world in the waning days of European colonialism. His social conscience, political courage (he suffered an assassination attempt due to his outspoken political views), and spiritual hunger made him a unique voice in pop culture.

Even Marley's religion was postcolonial. He was a Rastafarian—a blend of Afro-centrism and Christianity, viewed with disdain by traditionalists but embraced by young Jamaicans with a hunger for a spiritual expression of their own, free from colonial oversight. Rastafarianism is a critique of traditional modes of Western Christianity, which had chiefly been experienced as a means of domination and oppression in Jamaica.

"Most people think / Great God will come from the skies / Take Away Everything / And make everybody feel high / But if you know what life is worth / You will look for yours on earth." So sang Marley in "Get Up, Stand Up," one of his most famous songs. The song is a militant call to action and a rejection of a faith that urges people to accept the dire conditions of life on earth. Its anthem-like title is a literal call to uprising against any and all who seek to oppress.

This fusion of biblical metaphors and local folk traditions gave Marley's music a deeply spiritual focus. The magic in his music is how he used Christian symbolism in new ways. He articulated Rastafarian theology in a compelling way. Rastafarians believed that they, as descendants of slaves and oppressed by racial and economic inequalities, could find great meaning and hope in the Bible by making it their own. In particular, they identified with and adapted stories of the Israelites in captivity and exile. They saw themselves as children of Yahweh, *jah* as they call him, taken into captivity from their African homeland and put into slavery. Their religion was a call to action, to get the justice they deserved. They sought release from slavery, in mind and body, to get liberation from Babylon (their name for the oppressive social and political systems they had been forced to live under). This was the backbone of Marley's music and with it he found a global audience—people hungry to be freed from whatever it was that they felt was oppressing or inhibiting them.

Bob Marley's tunes might be dance music, but the dance was for God. Its hypnotic and ecstatic delivery echoes the emotional intensity of mystical music through the ages. His message was compelling: "my message is the message of humanity—love and peace." When that music hits, listeners feel nothing but hope.

BARRY TAYLOR

# Mary Tyler Moore

Mary Tyler Moore, born in 1936, danced her way onto television in the 1950s as the prancing elf from the Happy Hotpoint commercials sponsoring *The Adventures of Ozzie and Harriet.* When the telltale signs of pregnancy forced her to surrender her leotard, who would have guessed Mary Tyler Moore would go on to eventually embody two iconic portrayals of women in the twentieth century?

The first of those iconic roles was as Laura Petrie, the charming but slightly neurotic wife and mother of the Petrie family in *The Dick Van Dyke Show* (1961–1966). It seems impossible to recall the 1960s classic sitcom without a vision of her signature Capri pants and flats, but Laura Petrie was actually the last and most difficult part to cast on *The Dick Van Dyke Show.* Producers Carl Reiner and Danny Thomas auditioned more than sixty actresses before casting Moore in the role.

The semi-autobiographical creation of Carl Reiner, *The Dick Van Dyke Show* explored both the work life and home life of Rob Petrie (Dick Van Dyke) as the head writer of *The Alan Brady Show*. The work life played out in a fast, furious ba-dump-ch rhythm, keeping time with the vaudeville talents of Buddy (Morey Amsterdam) and Sally (Rose Marie) as Rob's writing staff. But as a show straddling the conservatism of the 1950s with the socially progressive 1960s, Rob's home life called for a subtler, more nuanced approach.

Laura was more than a mere straight woman to trigger her husband's pratfalls. In contrast to previous sitcom housewives, she had a career before she married Rob. The former USO dancer's talents often surfaced, reminding us she might have been something other than a housewife. She often chafed at the expected submission of her position and resented being excluded from Rob's work life. Also unlike other sitcom couples, Laura had a chemistry with Rob that belied the twin beds in their bedroom. Motherhood had not diminished her sex appeal.

Ultimately, however, regardless of all Laura's strengths, her oft and nervously repeated "Oh, Rob" signaled a continuing dependence on her husband. Her loveable-but-loopy performances echoed the uncertainty of women across America, caught between the failed expectations of times past and the untested promises of the future.

The 1970s would launch the second of Mary Tyler Moore's iconic female images, Mary Richards from *The Mary Tyler Moore Show*—an image so successful that she would literally be bronzed. The city of Minneapolis, home to the show, would eventually raise a statue commemorating Richards's famous tam toss in the opening credits. The burgeoning women's movement, along with an increased willingness from the networks to create programming for smaller, niche audiences, produced the first television show to feature a never-married, independent career woman striving to "make it after all."

While hopeful for marriage, Mary was never defined by her search for Mr. Right. The original storyline indicated Mary was fleeing a recent divorce, but networks were afraid the television audience would associate Mary's off-screen ex-husband with Rob Petrie from *The Dick Van Dyke Show* and withhold their sympathy. The revised backstory found Mary driving into the heartland following a broken engagement.

The *Mary Tyler Moore Show* set precedents for the sitcom genre in more than just its choice of a lead. Instead of remaining morally static, characters were allowed to evolve. The real strength of Mary's life, and of the sitcom itself, came from the depth of relationships Mary had with her "work family" at WJM-TV and her "friend family" at home. The crusty boss, Lou (Ed Asner); the cynical reporter, Murray (Gavin MacLeod); the foolish anchor,

Ted (Ted Knight); the loud friend, Rhoda (Valerie Harper); and the snobby landlord, Phyllis (Cloris Leachman) all orbited Mary in familial fashion as she navigated the waters of being a single woman. While Mary's character never married, the success of her "family" relationships reassured the collective zeitgeist of 1970s' women that making it on their own was not such a lonely business after all.

Perhaps the reason that Mary Tyler Moore's iconic women characters are so memorable is that they do not preach to us, but instead speak to us from their vulnerability. The nervous, charming Laura Petrie and the subtly funny, self-deprecating Mary Richards were both dependent on the relationships around them while still pressing to express their independence. They were also relentlessly hopeful. Their dogged determination despite the disappointment of reality inspired others to keep faith.

LISA SWAIN

# Mother Teresa

Mother Teresa of Calcutta (1910–1997) is an iconic figure. Her name is used often in film, television, and popular fiction as a behavioral standard, with dialogue such as "Who do you think you are? Mother Teresa?" In fact, she was even satirized in a 1998 episode of Comedy Central's *South Park*. But for the most part, popular culture is quietly in awe of her.

Born Agnesë Gonxhe Bojaxhiu in 1910 in Skopje, Yugoslavia (today in Macedonia) to Albanian Catholic parents, she was a devout girl. After hearing about the needs of people in India, she applied to the Sisters of Loretto, who operated schools there. At age eighteen she left for their motherhouse in Ireland to learn English, and two months later she sailed for Darjeeling, India, to begin the novitiate.

On entering the novitiate, Agnes took a new name, Sister Teresa, in honor of St. Therese of Lisieux. She was assigned to teach geography and history at a school for middle-class Bengali children in Calcutta. In those fifteen years, the growing slums of the city outside the school walls impressed on her deeply. During a train trip to Darjeeling for her annual retreat, Mother Teresa heard God's second call: "You must leave the convent to help the poor by living among them."

It was 1946 when Teresa received permission to leave Loretto and begin a new life. The newly independent India was in political turmoil. What distinguished the new work of Mother Teresa was her desire to intimately share in the plight of those she served. She and those who joined her would not work among the poor by day and go home to a nice convent at night, but would live as the poor, among the poor.

On August 16, 1948, she exchanged her religious habit for a white sari with a blue band. She learned basic nursing skills in Patna and then returned to Calcutta and began to visit the poor. With the help of teachers and friends she bought a two-room hut with a broken door to open a dispensary. The people called her "the Slum Sister." The new congregation, Missionaries of Charity, would be dedicated to the poorest of the poor. In 1950, when the group had twelve members, Pope Pius XII gave his approval. Today, the congregation has about 4,500 members with sisters living and working in 133 countries. Mother Teresa also inspired the foundation of orders of priests, brothers, and lay missionaries.

Mother Teresa's place in popular culture was launched in 1971 with the publication of Malcolm Muggeridge's bestseller *Something Beautiful for God*, which interprets Mother Teresa's life "as a light that could never be extinguished." Her work in providing food, medicine, and education to the poor earned her the Nobel Peace Prize in 1979. Mother Teresa also had a few critics. In 1994, for example, British atheist and social pundit Christopher Hitchens produced a documentary, *Hell's Angel*, that not only questioned her integrity in accepting donations from dubious sources but mocked her for meeting only the daily needs of the poor rather than working to change the system that kept them poor. But this tiny woman proved bigger than these criticisms.

Mother Teresa's health started to fail in the late 1980s. In 1997 she stepped down as the Superior General of her congregation. Back in Calcutta, on September 5, as she was preparing to attend a memorial service for her friend Princess Diana, who had been buried only a week previously, Mother Teresa collapsed and died. She was 87 years old.

Two years after her death, Pope John Paul II waived the five-year waiting period for beatification of a person deemed to have lived a life of heroic charity, and opened the investigative process for Mother Teresa. A miracle was attributed to her intercession, and she was beatified on October 19, 2003.

Even in death, the iconic Mother Teresa continues to surprise many. The 2007 publication of her letters, *Mother Teresa: Come Be My Light – The Private Writings of the "Saint of Calcutta"* reveals her as having lived a crisis of faith for almost fifty years (better known in the Christian tradition as a dark night of the soul). She wrote, "I want to speak—yet nothing comes—I find no words to express the depths of darkness." And later, "If I ever become a saint—I will surely be one of 'darkness.' I will continually be absent from Heaven—to light the light of those in darkness on earth."

Her darkness is our light.

ROSE PACATTE

# Pelé

Born in 1940, Edison Arantes do Nascimento, better known to the world as Pelé, is purported to be one of the greatest football players to ever live. "Football" here refers to what Americans call soccer—the Beautiful Game—the most popular sport on the planet, played by over 250 million people in over 200 countries. Pelé, who grew up in poverty in Bauru, São Paolo, Brazil, is the all-time leading scorer of Brazil's national football team, was declared Footballer of the Century in 1999, and is one of the sport's first truly international stars.

Like many of Pelé's peers, football became his passport out of a life of drudgery and struggle. Growing up, he was so poor that he was unable to afford a soccer ball to practice with and used instead a sock filled with newspaper or a grapefruit. At fifteen, he was spotted by a coach and was taken to Santos, the port city in the state of São Paolo, and signed with the local team, Santos Futebol Clube. His career took off, and he quickly became a national star. His amazing skills, electrifying play, and ability to score spectacular goals captured the national and, eventually, the international imagination. He was of average size and height, but he possessed tremendous balance and vision and was able to control the ball superbly and shoot accurately with both feet.

He played national and club football from 1956 until 1972, when he retired from Brazilian club football. Along the way he became a global football star, playing in a record three World Cup Championships. In 1958, he stunned the world in his first international appearance playing for Brazil. Pelé scored six goals in the tournament, including two against Sweden in the final, helping Brazil to win its first World Cup. He was only seventeen at the time. He scored an average of one goal in every international game he played in, something akin to a baseball player hitting a home run in every World Series game over fifteen years. Pelé still holds the world record for hat tricks (92) and for international goals scored (97). He ended his career with a record of 1,281 goals in 1,363 games. In 1975, Pelé emerged from semi-retirement and joined the New York Cosmos of the fairly new North American

Soccer League. His reputed three-year, $7-million contract cemented him as the highest paid player in the North American League. This move gave the American League instant credibility and made millions of Americans aware of a sport it had largely ignored. Football (or soccer as it came to be known in the United States in order to distinguish it from America's own game) finally found a fragile foothold in America because of the Brazilian star. After his career ended, Pelé became an ambassador for the sport and also an advocate for children's concerns through UNICEF. He was also featured in a number of advertising campaigns.

Nowadays most of our favorite celebrities come from the world of sports, but it was Pele who launched the concept of the global sports figure, the sports superstar who transcended his own particular sport to become an icon. He was the de facto leader of the most influential sport in history (it is estimated that 2.2 billion people tuned in to watch the 2002 World Cup).

There have been many associations made between soccer and religion: fervent congregations (fans); the rules and rituals (the rules on and off the pitch); the hymnody (like most sports, soccer has its own canon of songs); the tribes (teams); and, of course, the pain, exhilaration, loyalties, and the stars. Soccer even has its own high priests, those god-like figures who transcend their humanness, rising to dizzying heights, and captivating us with their other-worldly abilities. And like many sports, part of the function of soccer seems linked to the idea of ritualizing and sanctifying aggression and competition. But Pelé offered up an entirely new way of understanding soccer. "The Beautiful Game" has become the descriptor of soccer, and Pelé was one of the first to use it. His autobiography, published in 1977, was titled *My Life and the Beautiful Game*. To him, soccer was not simply about competition or the sanctification of aggression. It was about beauty and grace, skill and sportsmanship. Soccer provided a way to bring the world together in a celebration of global connectivity and national pride.

BARRY TAYLOR

# Mister Rogers

In the Gospel of Luke, when Jesus entertained the question, "Who is my neighbor?" it is quite possible that his hope was to engender the behavior circumscribed by pop culture's most iconic neighbor, the host of *Mister Rogers' Neighborhood*, Fred McFeely Rogers.

In a retrospective interview for the Archive of American Television in 1999, Rogers said, "I'd like to be remembered for being a compassionate human being who happened to be fortunate enough to be born at a time when there was a fabulous thing called television that could allow me to use all the talents that I had been given." Hosts of grateful fans of *Mister Rogers' Neighborhood* (1968–2001) could testify to the heroic success of such a modest aspiration. While other children's shows competed for attention with slick animation, elaborate sets, and fast-paced editing, Fred Rogers used simple tunes, quiet conversation, and a zippered sweater to convince the least of these in society that they were loved, valued, and safe.

Graduating with an undergraduate degree in music composition in 1951, Rogers postponed plans to enter seminary when his curiosity was piqued by the emerging medium of television. Intrigued by the educational potential of the medium, Rogers worked as a floor manager for NBC on *NBC Opera Theater, The Gabby Hayes Show,* and *The Kate Smith Show*. But by 1953, he left the network, discouraged over the rising influence of advertisers that undermined the ability of programmers to educate.

Rogers traced his repugnance for commercialism back to the charitable wisdom his father, James Rogers, had passed along. A devout Christian, his father would admonish, "The church should always be a little bit in the red," implying that the needs of those served should take precedent over the cathedral coffers.

Following his two years at NBC, Fred Rogers moved to Pittsburgh and returned to seminary, completing his degree at the Pittsburgh Theological Seminary and becoming an ordained Presbyterian minister. Following his ordination, however, Rogers did not want to preach, at least not in the traditional way. While in seminary, Rogers had migrated from network to public television, working as the program director for WQED in Pittsburgh. When no one else could be found for the job, Rogers stepped up to produce the station's first children's program, *The Children's Hour*. By doing so, he stumbled upon the genre by which he would demonstrate the generosity of his Good Samaritan heart to generations of children.

Rogers had a brief but important sojourn away from Pittsburgh in 1963 when the CBC (Canadian Broadcasting Corporation) in Toronto offered him an opportunity to create *MisteRogers*, a fifteen-minute children's program featuring Rogers on camera. After a year developing his signature gentle persona, he purchased the rights to the show and returned to Pittsburgh. By 1967, the show had morphed into *Mister Rogers' Neighborhood* and was nationally distributed by the NET (National Educational Television).

Like the certainty of a church service, ritual played an important role in *Mister Rogers' Neighborhood*. Every episode began with a trolley meandering through a neighborhood and stopping at Rogers's house. The camera cut inside as Rogers returned home from work, shed his coat and loafers, and donned his iconic sweater and canvas sneakers, all the while singing his warm invitation straight to the camera, "Won't You Be My Neighbor?"

The comfort of ritual and the leisurely conversation belied the gravitas of the material encountered on *Mister Rogers' Neighborhood*. Rogers never condescended to children but respectfully identified and addressed their concerns. The significance of their emotions was explored regardless of how large or small the precipitating event. He talked about death when his pet goldfish died, then again with the assassination of Senator Robert Kennedy, then again with the onset of the Gulf War. He discussed fears of abandonment resulting from the birth of a sibling or from the tragedy of divorce. He even took the show to the former Soviet Union to alleviate fears of nuclear annihilation. With little songs about big ideas and quiet words about loud problems, Rogers provided children with tools to cope in an increasingly scary world.

Among his many awards, Rogers received four Emmys; two Peabodys; thirty honorary doctorates from various colleges and universities; and the highest U.S. civilian honor, the Presidential Medal of Freedom. But more than all of his conspicuous recognition, Fred McFeely Rogers is perhaps best memorialized as one whose attentive care for his neighbor always found him a little in the red.

LISA SWAIN

## *Star Wars*

In a lengthy public conversation concerning how a young person might hope to operate sanely, creatively, and redemptively in the twenty-first century, the philosopher Cornel West put a couple of questions to the hip-hop artist Lupe Fiasco: "How would you characterize your spirituality? Where does it come from?" The questions came on the heels of considerable back-and-forth on the topic of vocation, getting called out, and having a heart that will sense and pay heed to subtle forms of *in*vocation. Fiasco began by noting that while he was born Muslim, he also passed much of his childhood in Baptist churches. From there he began to catalog the living traditions he spied within his late father's library, "the Bushido code and Taoism and Buddhism and pieces of Judaica and *Star Wars* . . . all these artifacts and things that came from—that were created—for religious purposes."

While the inclusion of *Star Wars* (1977) elicited giggles from the audience, it was clear that hardly anyone found it far-fetched. Instead, the laughter seemed to register the strange realization that someone like Fiasco (born in Chicago in 1982) could hardly *avoid* being formed, in some fashion, by this particular space opera franchise. *Religiously* formed? But of course. Is there a better word for social formation? Consider the catechisms on file in the minds of younglings, true believers all, who don Jedi robes, brandish plastic light sabers, and stand on couches with one leg perched on the armrest imagining how Luke Skywalker might have felt as he gazed longingly upon a Tatooine sunset.

"You've taken your first step into a larger world," says Alec Guinness's Obi-Wan Kenobi to Luke Skywalker after he's successfully deflected the attacks of a remote training device with his light saber while deprived of eyesight, using the Force alone. And this wide, resonant world of meaning (strong enough, we might add, to have survived such painful missteps as Ewoks, Jar Jar Binks, and every unconvincing romantic scene between Hayden Christensen's Anakin and Natalie Portman's Padmé) might be rightly decreed a candidate for the primary functioning myth of American mainstream culture. It is the de facto religious tradition of popular appeal in many a national census (Religious preference: Jedi) and in its music and mantras ("May the Force be with you" as benediction). Such sentiments are featured in symphony performances, fireworks displays, and what are often otherwise secular weddings, birthdays, and even funerals.

This isn't to say that all are equally well-versed within the *Star Wars* lexicon (not everyone deploys "nerf-herder" as a put-down), but its imprint on our cultural fabric, largely transcending ethnicity and class, is undeniable. And when we contemplate its vision of the interdependence of all of life and a cosmos in which there are no *un*related phenomena, we could do a lot worse. "Luminous beings are we, not this crude matter," observes Jedi Master Yoda as he strikes Luke with a stick. And while some might complain of a dualistic, *dis*incarnate view of the body and soul at work, it is haste, anxiety, and small-mindedness he means to rebuke in young Skywalker, as he did in Luke's father before him. We receive life by holding it loosely and lose life when we cling to it fearfully. "Fear is the path to the dark side. Fear leads to anger. Anger leads to hate. Hate leads to suffering," Yoda had intoned years previously. In playing out this cycle, a gifted but murderous Anakin Skywalker will resist Obi-Wan's efforts to draw him away from the path of evil and declare a threat wherever there's a questioning of his will: "If you're not with me, you're with my enemy!" In Anakin's refusal of reasoned nuance, Obi-Wan recognizes the ideology of the Jedi's ancient foe: "Only a Sith deals in absolutes."

If we can forgive George Lucas for his occasional strangling of his own creation (like the insertion of midi-chlorian counts that foreclose the possibility that those with the wrong microbes in their bloodstream might be Force-sensitive), we can note how the story's powers of applicability reside in Lucas's own determination to be nourished and enriched by the religious traditions from which *Star Wars* draws even as it surpasses them in popularity. A rarely noted instance of such openings occurs in Episode I when we observe the presence of the ancestors of E.T. (Spielberg's extraterrestrial) in a Galactic Senate scene. If we're prone to connect the dots, as any faithful recipient of the *Star Wars* tradition is compelled to do, we'll be forced to recognize that a representative of that life from long, long ago, in a galaxy far, far away, eventually makes it to our own century where he gestures plaintively at a child in a Yoda costume on a Halloween night and even demonstrates powers of Force sensitivity.

DAVID DARK

# The Eighties

$A$t the dawn of the decade, fifty-two Americans were held captive by Iranian revolutionaries at the American Embassy in Tehran. After almost twenty years of social upheaval, voters longed for stability, a turning back of the clock. With the elections of Ronald Reagan and Margaret Thatcher, the Americans and Brits embraced a conservative promise of peace through strength and prosperity. While Oliver Stone intended Gordon Gekko's *Wall Street* mantra, "greed is good," as satire, yuppies embraced the power of investing. Donald Trump became a celebrity and J. R. Ewing, scion of the television drama *Dallas*, became the oil baron viewers loved to hate. While some prospered, rappers like Run DMC chronicled the "Hard Times" that followed the explosion of crack cocaine in urban communities.

While Steven Spielberg and George Lucas dominated the box office with *Raiders of the Lost Ark*, an unheralded story of Christian conviction, *Chariots of Fire* won the 1981 Oscar as Best Picture. Cable television exploded in the 1980s with the birth of CNN and MTV. Michael Jackson became the first video icon, moonwalking to "Billie Jean" and "Thriller." Prince topped the charts with "Purple Rain" but piled too much sexual provocation into "Darling Nikki." Both Jackson and Prince were very different kinds of Jehovah's Witnesses. Bruce Springsteen belted out "Born in the U.S.A." with a pride that Vietnam veterans hadn't felt in years, and Madonna sported spandex and a crucifix in videos for "Like a Virgin" and "Material Girl." Both Springsteen and Madonna channeled their Catholic upbringings into populist sentiments. Televangelist scandals undermined confidence in religious authorities. Spike Lee merged the sensibilities of Martin Luther King and Malcolm X in challenging filmgoers to *Do the Right Thing*.

Computers crossed over into personal use. In the early eighties, IBM's PC premiered, followed in1982 when *Time* magazine named the home computer the "person of the year," which was the first time in its history that an inanimate object had been given the award. In 1984, Steve Jobs introduced the Mac, replete with windows, icons, menus, and pointers, and the information age was born. The days of the typewriter were numbered.

While America thrived, the eighties was also a period of political volatility. Lech Walesa led the Solidarity union movement that undermined communism in Poland, and the Velvet Revolution brought democracy to the Czech Republic. Perestroika and the dismantling of the Berlin Wall sparked a celebration to end the Cold War. Disasters at Three Mile Island, Chernobyl, and Bhopal demonstrated the dark side of technology. The deaths of Rock Hudson and Liberace created a public panic around the threat of AIDS. Bob Geldof organized a massive Live Aid concert to benefit Ethiopians victimized by famine. Calls to end apartheid in South Africa rose. Iran and Iraq engaged in a bitter border war and the Soviet Union gave up its debilitating fight in Afghanistan. The Cold War might have ended, but what would replace it was less certain. As the decade concluded, thousands of Chinese students occupied Tiananmen Square until tanks from the People's Liberation Army crushed the peaceful resistance. Would freedom still ring?

# Jean-Michel Basquiat

Jean-Michel Basquiat (1960–1988) was a New York painter, graffiti artist, and musician who collaborated with Andy Warhol and was influential in depicting the African American experience in various media of modern art. He rose quickly from obscurity to fame, with his legend still growing a decade after his death. Born in Brooklyn to a Puerto Rican mother and Haitian father, Basquiat studied art first at Edward R. Murrow High School in Brooklyn and then at City-As-School in Manhattan. He eventually dropped out, choosing to be homeless and living in abandoned buildings or with friends. Basquiat performed music and worked off and on as a DJ, while also selling home-made postcards and T-shirts outside the Museum of Modern Art to support himself.

Toward the end of the 1970s, Basquiat, along with high school friend Al Diaz, began to create graffiti art and aphorisms to which he signed the name SAMO (Same Old Shit). As SAMO©, Basquiat took on the role of charlatan, selling a false religion and thereby satirizing our search for instant answers and quick fixes. His witty and biting gibes at consumer culture became so ubiquitous that SAMO© became a popular brand (co-opted by the system it was created to critique). Basquiat eventually declared "SAMO© is Dead." In 1980, his work began to attract attention from the art world, particularly after a group of artists from the punk and graffiti underground held the "Times Square Show" in an abandoned massage parlor, in part to challenge the closed doors and sanctity of art and the city's museums.

In 1981, Basquiat was introduced to the artist Andy Warhol, who would become a mentor and confidant. Soon, Basquiat's social life (he was romantically involved with Madonna) garnered as many headlines as his art. In 1983, he became the youngest artist ever featured in the Whitney Museum's Biennial Exhibition, showing alongside other emerging graffiti artists such as Keith Haring and Kenny Scharf. Basquiat continued to show throughout the decade, garnering many awards and accolades.

Tragically, Basquiat died of a heroin overdose on August 12, 1988. A film of his life, *Basquiat*, directed by artist Julian Schnabel, was released seven years after the painter's death. Basquiat's star was still rising, with celebrities lining up to play celebrities in his life story. Rock star David Bowie portrayed Andy Warhol, with Dennis Hopper and Parker Posey playing influential gallery owners.

To a degree, Basquiat's shabby life (including his homelessness) was self-imposed and performative. At the same time, unlike many of his contemporaries, he used painting to push the use of symbols and images, fusing together a language that melds together street, literary, intellectual, and spiritual life into a powerful art form.

Basquiat's short artistic career also occurred during the 1980s, a time of economic boom both for the New York art scene and for top corporate and business leaders in America during the Reagan years. As such, he became both prophet and witness to issues of race, gender, sexuality, AIDS, and the economic discrepancies that all come rushing to the forefront during this decade. Basquiat gave voice to it all, and (as his critics will quickly point out) he himself prospered greatly because of it. Nevertheless, Basquiat was at heart a black artist within an almost exclusively white art world, and therefore a unique voice of a marginalized body politic. He utilized found materials of a decaying New York and the realities of urban culture to make public his inner thoughts and other bursts of expression.

Halos, crowns of thorns, skeletal faces, and words and phrases became his code of imagery and language. His 1981 painting *Per Capita* places a black boxer under the words, *E Pluribus* (out of many). But what of *unum* (one)? A halo floats above the boxer's head, and he holds a torch echoing the Statue of Liberty. *Per Capita* questions the promises of America; is there really liberty and justice for all? His massive 1983 painting *The Nile* reaches back to ancient Egypt and connects the ancient city of Memphis to contemporary Tennessee. Didn't slaves inhabit both worlds? A word like "Sickle" alludes to an Egyptian boat, a slave's tool, and sickle cell anemia, which plagues the African American community. Basquiat juxtaposes the Egyptian god Amun with the Negro spirituals that sing, "Amen." In Basquiat's world, distinctions between private spaces and public places quickly dissolved; the past and present became interwoven, and levels of reality were multiplied and scrambled.

In all of this he foretold the postmodern notion of plural and relative realities. The combination of rough, urban materials, ethereal concepts, angst of imagery, and multiplicity of elements evoked prophets from all ages. This one just left this world too soon.

GABRIEL FERRER

---

# Tom Cruise

Tom Cruise lit up big screens with his megawatt smile. During the 1980s and '90s, he embodied America's speed and swagger, whether soaring through the sky in *Top Gun* (1986) or racing around a NASCAR track in *Days of*

*Thunder* (1990). He was the most powerful movie star on the planet, drawing audiences to multiple *Mission Impossible* movies. Yet his meteoric rise was accompanied by an unexpected fall when he fired his longtime publicist and made his private beliefs public.

Born Thomas Cruise Mapother IV, he was raised in a poor Roman Catholic family dominated by an abusive father. The family moved often, with Tom attending fifteen different schools. As a teenager attending a Franciscan seminary on a church scholarship, Cruise considered the priesthood. But positive affirmations for his acting pulled him toward drama.

Before soaring to fame in *Top Gun*, Cruise made *All the Right Moves* (1983) as a high school wrestler, conveying decency and determination. He engaged in *Risky Business* (1983), sliding into our living rooms in his skivvies. Cruise made Ray Bans and a button-down shirt look incredibly cool; "Old Time Rock and Roll" had never seemed more contemporary. Cruise served as Americans' collective stand-in, a maverick who piloted American power back to international prominence during the Reagan era.

The Cruise persona was honed and protected by Pat Kingsley, through her public relations firm, PMK. Kingsley wielded remarkable power over Cruise's appearances, offering interviews only in exchange for cover stories. Journalists who did not conform to a predetermined set of questions were cut off from future coverage of Cruise and Kingsley's growing list of clients. While rumors of Cruise's involvement in Scientology spread, Kingsley and company kept the star's private life under considerable wraps.

The Church of Scientology had actively courted stars like Cruise since establishing a Hollywood Celebrity Centre in 1969. Scientology was founded by L. Ron Hubbard, a sci-fi writer whose self-help book, *Dianetics*, became a bestseller in 1950. He advocated "auditing," in which people would confront earlier pains and disappointments. When adherents spoke of past lives, Hubbard described them as thetans, souls that had existed for millions of years. Scientologists affirm that there is a godlike possibility residing within each of us. Upon death, a thetan will return to Venus and eventually be plunged back to earth in search of a new body to inhabit. Hubbard invented an Electropsychometer (E-Meter) to aid people's process of clearing themselves of bad body thetans and reaching their full potential. Hubbard incorporated the Church of Scientology as a religion in 1953.

Cruise credited Scientology with helping him overcome dyslexia. He assumed the highest profile amid fellow celebrity Scientologists John Travolta, Kirstie Alley, and Jenna Elfman of the sitcom *Dharma & Greg*. Their collective success was held up as confirmation of the power of Hubbard's teaching and practices. This new religious movement expanded its influence despite accusations that it was a cult. After a twenty-five-year legal battle in the United States, Scientology was granted tax-exempt status in 1993.

While Cruise ascended greater box office heights in *The Firm* (1993) and *Mission Impossible* (1996), his role as sports agent *Jerry Maguire* (1996) garnered an Academy Award nomination for best actor. His commitment to the craft of acting expanded with an unsympathetic role as a master manipulator in *Magnolia* (1999). Cruise and his second wife, Australian actress Nicole Kidman, explored their id with director Stanley Kubrick in *Eyes Wide Shut* (1999). Their marriage unraveled soon afterward.

The altered states and competing personas of *Vanilla Sky* (2001) hinted at the upheavals to come. The press linked Cruise with Cruz, his Spanish costar, Penelope Cruz. In 2004, a newly independent Cruise fired the publicist who had built his Teflon persona, Pat Kingsley. With his sister now guiding his career, Cruise went on a media blitz to declare his newfound love for actress Katie Holmes. On Oprah Winfrey's couch, the cool Cruise persona began to crumble. On *The Today Show*, he criticized Brooke Shields for her postpartum depression, revealing Scientology's critique of psychiatry by suggesting that prescriptions were for weaklings. When a private interview recorded for a Scientology award ceremony leaked onto YouTube, the Cruise crack-up was complete. Millions saw Cruise talk in a cryptic language and laugh at odd moments. Having earned Paramount billions at the box office, Cruise was cut loose, a liability the studio no longer cared to subsidize.

Time will tell whether Scientology will turn more toward the mainstream or collapse under the weight of ongoing allegations. Cruise's initial comebacks were met with audience indifference, and his marriage to Katie Holmes is now over. He has hid behind mounds of makeup in *Tropic Thunder* and played a bare-chested idol in *Rock of Ages*. Yet the smile no longer sparkles as much. Restoring the luster on a celebrated career depended on one more *Mission Impossible*.

CRAIG DETWEILER

---

# Amy Grant

For fifteen-year-old Amy Grant, 1976 was a watershed year. She wrote her first song, "Mountain Man," largely inspired by the film *Jeremiah Johnson* (starring Robert Redford). She covered songs by Carole King, Elton John, and James Taylor in her first public performance at a Nashville high school. And she found herself squarely located—culturally and contractually—within an emergent, deeply problematic marketing phenomenon called "Contemporary Christian Music" when a demo tape she'd cobbled together with her youth group leader (budding producer/songwriter Brown Bannister) was overheard by a musician with the poignant name of Chris Christian. He went ahead and got Word Records in Waco on the line.

Grant's 1982 album *Age to Age* went platinum. The song "El Shaddai" blurred the lines between pop music and Christian worship. Four years later, she was atop the Billboard singles charts singing a duet with Peter Cetera, "Next Time I Fall." Her rapid ascent set unexpected precedence for a contemporary Christian artist. Could such success be sustained?

"I've never felt any demarcation between life and art, faith and day-to-day living," Grant remarked more than thirty years into a career as a popular icon. But certain commercial successes related to her own fame have often made it difficult to successfully communicate such nuance. Advertising language, in order to effectively perform its function, will differ radically from the more modest and artful task of telling one's story truthfully. From the outset, Grant chafed against such commercial limitations even as her brand image navigated these complicated waters successfully. This work became especially difficult following the 1999 dissolution of her seventeen-year marriage to songwriter Gary Chapman, which overlapped a burgeoning friendship and eventual second marriage to country musician Vince Gill. Such marital turmoil defied buyer expectations for many within her longtime audience.

But Grant's appreciation for the complexity of real life and her commitment to bearing witness to it had always moved far beyond the sphere of what could be successfully advertised and mass marketed as "Christian." Her song "Ask Me" (*Heart in Motion*, 1991), for instance, chronicles a friend's experience as a victim of child sexual abuse, and it eschews the all-too-conventional Christian appeal of tidied-up realities or easily reconciled tragedies. Concerning people she's known and voices she's attempted to lift lyrically, Grant observes, "I've tried to tell some of their stories through songs and poems in hopes that if light were brought into that deep darkness, we could see each other's faces, see the scars for what they are, and find a way out of the cycle."

In this way, Grant exercises a more theologically robust vocation than the casual listener of pop music might guess. She draws her convictions concerning the socio-political meaning of Jesus ("He revolutionized our accessibility to God") into close proximity with the joy, the dysfunction, and the insights she's experienced as a mother, a musician, and a friend. She also consistently challenges her listeners with a more honest and sometimes darker take on human life than is expected by a culture that demands easy explanations and quick reassurances. She's received instruction in this work from her late mentor Sarah Cannon (known to her Grand Ole Opry audience as Minnie Pearl). As recounted in Grant's memoir *Mosaic*, Cannon once told her that the most important color in an artist's palette is black: "Without black there is no depth. Without black everything appears flat. But mix black with any color and you can paint an object so real you want to reach out and touch it."

The hazards of believing and teaching that some aspects of our lives are somehow beyond the pale of God's loving interest are difficult to underestimate. And if Augustine of Hippo is correct in his assertion that singing words once means we've prayed them twice, our relationship to the songs that inhabit our existence can't be sectioned off if we're to live sane lives of wholeness and integrity. By challenging the definitions of the CCM market, a marketing category that probably never should have existed in the first place, Grant has served as a pioneering and redeeming force within (and beyond) what we might awkwardly term "advertised-as-Christian" culture, clearing a path later journeyed down by myriad others. And, in 2010, Grant could be said to take affectionate and nonchalant aim at the limitations of "Worship Music" as a category with the song "Better than a Hallelujah," which lyrically asserts, in continuity with Martin Luther, that the curses of an honest voice are perhaps more pleasing in the ears of the Almighty than the praise of the pious. In Grant's view, we're called by God to speak what we feel, not what we ought to say, to sing truthfully, and to let the chips fall where they may. To artfully conjure a space for doing so, for seeing and speaking truly, is already gospel.

DAVID DARK

## Thomas Kinkade

It has been said that there is a Thomas Kinkade image in one out of twenty American homes—a conservative figure that does not even account for the painter's success in the international marketplace. Kinkade (1958-2012) accomplished this visual saturation through marketing savvy. His art comprised original paintings (which the artist always kept) that were reproduced as prints and then licensed on products such as lamps, figurines, greeting cards, calendars, bedsheets, and even as the logos on gated residential communities. His commercial success can also be attributed to his rejection of more traditional venues of promotion in the art world such as fine art galleries, auction houses, and museums. Kinkade appealed instead to a broader demographic by establishing his own galleries in malls, selling his work on television and through an expansive online presence, and distributing to evangelical Christian bookstores.

Yet, to merely consider Kinkade a marketing phenomenon does a disservice to his base product, his imagery. Trafficking in pastel-infused pictures that featured lighthouses, bridges, and homes emanating a soft glow, Kinkade's visual language struck a nerve with a population that sought comforting, familiar, and spiritual works to decorate their homes. While academic and art professionals were highly critical of his work, accusing Kinkade of producing reactionary kitsch, his success revealed the chasm between popular and elite taste.

Kinkade's life story was co-opted as part of his marketing campaign, framing the appeal and value of his art through his biography and narratives of individual salvation, success, and uplift. Raised in northern California in a broken home, Kinkade found solace in art as a young child. He was encouraged by a mentor to go to the University of California, Berkeley, but left after his first year, finding the politics of the art department too liberal and modern. He drifted around for a few years selling individual paintings, but he marked the true beginning of his career with being born-again and reorienting his focus explicitly on spreading Christian ideology through his art.

In keeping with this narrative, much of his publicity material emphasized Kinkade as a family man, married to his high school sweetheart, raising several children, producing art for the public, and attributing his financial success to his religious mission. Beyond his personal life, it was Kinkade's perfecting of a printing technology that allowed him to transfer his paintings with an effect of replicating brush strokes, and his technique of adding paint on top of the printed poster, that marked his transition from a successful local artist to a commercial force. With a method that allowed for infinite duplication of his original painting, Kinkade's business grew quickly, and in the mid-1990s he sold his company to a larger firm that pushed his imagery into numerous licensing deals. This relationship soured, however, and Kinkade bought back his company in 2004, claiming that he had lost focus and would devote himself more concretely to his mission. Numerous galleries closed, and he faced legal challenges to his business practices and licensing agreements. In subsequent years Kinkade reestablished his brand, attracting new partnerships with such clients as the Disney Corporation, NASCAR, and Major League Baseball. His 2012 death from a combination of alcohol and Valium cast a pall over his comeback.

Kinkade's business and art practice were built around the premise that he was an evangelical Christian artist and man who produced works that were family-friendly and religious. However, the religious imagery in his works is often subtle or oblique. Unlike other popular Christian artists, he seldom painted biblical scenes and would often make two versions of an image—one with Scripture, one without. His images of bridges, lighthouses, or churches nestled into green landscapes were meant to appeal to the most general audience possible; Christians read into the images concrete biblical allusions, while others saw more ambiguous spiritual serenity. In this way he was able to reap the rewards of Christian marketing networks, but was not limited by them. Yet this positioning also raised doubts among some critics on whether his relationship to Christianity was pious or profit-driven.

Regardless of what such criticisms might reveal about Kinkade the man, his success suggests a desire on the part of a large segment of the population for an art that, in both style and subject, is nostalgic, familiar, soothing, and even antithetical to the concerns of most contemporary art. In this way he embraced the elements of popular culture that sat comfortably with his evangelical faith and marketing ideals, and visually denied those parts of modern life that did not.

ALEXIS L. BOYLAN

# Stephen King

Perhaps horror innately traffics in the spiritual. But with Stephen King, born in 1947, there seems to be something more. Judging by the number of speculative Web sites promising answers, people have become increasingly fascinated by the religious beliefs of the world's best-selling novelist (350 million books sold). Maybe you've long appreciated his spiritual preoccupations. Or, maybe you've feared all your life to pick up a Stephen King book and rightly question what our most famous witness of the macabre would ever have to say about Jesus, God, or Christianity.

Consider some passages from King's writings:

1. "Jesus watches from the wall, but his face is cold as stone. And if he loves me—as she tells me—why do I feel so alone?" (*Carrie*, 1976)
2. "I don't want Church to be like all those dead pets! I don't want Church to ever be dead. He's my cat! He's not God's cat! Let God have his own cat!" (*Pet Sematary*, 1983)

3. "Do you know how cruel your God can be, David? How fantastically cruel? . . . Sometimes he makes us live." (*Desperation*, 1996)
4. "If it happens, God lets it happen, and when we say 'I don't understand,' God replies, 'I don't care.'" (*The Green Mile*, 1996)

Consider the works of King that turn on spiritual matters. He calls *Desperation* "a very Christian novel . . . it's going to make some people uncomfortable, I think." In *The Green Mile*, he writes a dream sequence directly linking John Coffey's sacrifice to Jesus on the cross (a scene that was not filmed for the movie). *The Stand* (1978) was his effort to give God his due, "to explore what that means to be able to rise above adversity by faith, because it's something most of us do every day." And that's only the beginning of a much longer list of spiritual questions in King's writings.

A critical consensus of his body of work highlights his belief in the supernatural or unnatural invading regular lives, a focus on the traditionally marginalized in society, and a preoccupation with the anxieties and challenges of adolescence. Reviewers agree that he has insightfully captured and recorded the fears, anxieties, and obsessions of the late twentieth and early twenty-first century. Does any of that make Stephen King a Christian?

It's a question King might appreciate, because his work has questioned Christianity all along. His Web site says he was raised in a Methodist church and grilled on doctrine. He still reads his Bible. In interviews, he's professed a belief in God but says he has "no use for organized religion." He calls the idea of God a mystery but makes it clear, "I don't see myself as God's stenographer."

Besides, he likes the idea of questions more than answers. He wants to make readers question. "If you have a real problem then I'm doing what a novel of suspense and horror is supposed to do, which is to just scratch below the surface and sort of rub your nerves the wrong way," he says.

Is Stephen King a Christian? In portraying the religious teachings of his childhood and confronting a suspenseful, horror-filled world where God often seems absent and cruel and the behavior of his followers puzzling if not downright evil, what if Stephen King is asking the same of us?

Is he affirming or decrying the Old Testament God in the prophetic rants of Mrs. Carmody in *The Mist* (1980)? Is he echoing or mocking Jesus in the death of John Coffey (*The Green Mile*) or the escape of Andy Richter (*Rita Hayworth and Shawshank Redemption*, 1982)? What kind of Jesus does Jim Rennie follow in *Under the Dome* (2009)? Is God as cruel as *Desperation* (1996) and *The Stand* argue? Does God really rain hardship (*Storm of the Century*, 1999) on us because we "piss him off"? Is there a "first cause" running things?

Does it matter if Stephen King's a Christian? Is it enough that he has filled more than two dozen novels with questions concerning the nature of God, the teachings of Christ, and the behaviors of those who follow him? Or that his six short-story collections have awakened several generations to the power and reality of the supernatural? Or that his movies and television miniseries have given viewers a scare, some hope, and a decent cry? His body of work prompts us to ask about his beliefs. "Is Stephen King a Christian?" we collectively chime, only to find he's turned the question on us. "Are you?" And more chillingly, "Does it matter?"

R. W. BONN

## Calvin Klein Ads

Dubbed the "supreme master of minimalism," Calvin Klein, born in 1942, is an American fashion designer whose company has become one of the most recognizable brand names in fashion. After receiving the Coty Award for best designer three years in a row (1971–1973), his fame and success as a designer grew rapidly. His name has been licensed for cosmetics, fragrances, jeans, and menswear, taking in revenues of over $100 million a year.

Klein's foray into designer jeans put him on the cultural map in an unforgettable and public way. Up through the 1970s, denim jeans had largely been consigned to the workwear end of the fashion industry. Brands like Lee, Wrangler, and Levi's essentially owned the majority market share. In the early days of emergent youth culture, denim jeans became part of the dress of teenagers and eventually crossed other fashion boundaries to become a regular part of casual style for most Americans. Klein capitalized on this new craze in fashion with the release of his designer jeans, putting his signature on the back pocket. His jeans were an immediate success, selling in excess of 200,000 pairs in the first week of sales. More than the jeans, it was the accompanying advertising campaign that cemented Calvin Klein in the public eye.

In 1980, his first advertising campaign for both print and television, shot by photographers Bruce Weber and Richard Avedon, featured fifteen-year-old actress Brooke Shields dressed in her Calvin Klein jeans and provocatively asking, "Do you want to know what comes between me and my Calvins? Nothing." The sexual innuendo, the suggestive manner in which the actress asked the question, and her youth made many television executives extremely nervous. Some of the ads were banned from television, which only fueled the perception that they were transgressive. This campaign established Klein as a provocateur as much as a designer, and his personal lifestyle—which was volatile and prone to decadence—only underscored the edgy nature of the products. Subsequently, Klein's designs became symbolic of modern sexuality and the exploitation of sexuality to sell products. He added to this aura with the release of a series of successful fragrances beginning with Obsession in 1985. With its slogan, "Between love and madness lies obsession," and a succession of naked models photographed in highly sexual positions, Klein's fragrances were directly linked to sexuality. Klein also entered into more cultural hot water in the early 1990s when he launched a series of billboards advertising his men's underwear and featuring hip-hop star Marky Mark (now actor Mark Wahlberg) clad in nothing but his Calvin Klein underwear. This was not an anonymous male model but a burgeoning celebrity, stripping for fame and fortune. Klein's provocation was the sexualizing of both women and men.

Not all the campaigns were successful. A series of ads for his children's underwear line were pulled after a public outcry with claims of child exploitation and pornography. Moreover, an ad featuring an underage teenager stripping for a photographer was investigated by the FBI.

Calvin Klein not only shaped fashion trends but precipitated larger shifts in popular culture. Feminist author Linda Hirshman offered a lecture at the School of Law at Washington & Lee University in 1996 titled, "Was There Sex before Calvin Klein?" Obviously sex existed before Klein came along, and he was certainly not the first manufacturer who tied it to selling a product, but Klein seems to have been a lightning rod for how we perceived ourselves physically and sexually in the latter part of the twentieth century. The work of Klein and others has ignited debate about the objectification of women, with critics saying that Klein's ads play into the idea that the singular goal of women is to make themselves attractive and sexually appealing to men. While there is certainly a strong case to be made there, Klein's male ads exhibit similar characteristics and would seem to make sexual objectification a gender-equal issue in his world. Throughout his career, Klein has tapped into changing views on gender and sexuality. Borders that were once clearly defined are now shifting—do the male ads appeal to women or men, or both? His work suggests that we are all sexual objects and are subject to both objectification and celebration.

BARRY TAYLOR

## *Les Miserables*, the Musical

Based on the classic novel by Victor Hugo, *Les Miserables* (the musical) began as a concept album produced by Alain Boublil and Claude-Michel Schönberg in 1980. After a limited staging in France, producer Cameron Mackintosh opened the show at the Barbican in London in 1985. Since then, it's become one of the most successful musicals of all time, spawning thirty-eight productions in twenty-one cities. Some 55 million people have attended its 43,000 performances. The original London cast recording sold one million copies in London the first year it was released. Since then, thirty-one cast recordings have been made. When the Broadway production closed in 2003, it had become Broadway's third-longest running show. Today, productions continue worldwide.

Some of its appeal lay in the music itself. Boublil and Schönberg brought opera-lite to the masses with a score that was part rock and roll. Repeating musical motifs deepened story themes, like writing Valjean's journey in a major key and using the same music in a minor key for Javert. Though both characters had a common journey—musically and personally—their end, like the key, was very different. In some of the larger chorus numbers, the writers blended character arcs and story lines into different lines of verse but united them in chorus. The disparate identities, journeys, and needs threaded into the chorus of "One Day More" emphasized that no matter what stage of life the characters were in—falling in love, going to war, seeking redemption, entering retirement—they all sang the same song and, by larger implication, were part of the same story.

The musical gained recognition for its grand visual staging. The revolving stage-within-the-stage gave movement to the production, allowing characters to walk or run even as they remained in place (while thematically reinforcing the cyclical nature of life exemplified in the song "Turning"). And the famous transformation of the barricades routinely drew applause. The success of *Les Miserables* was heightened by a clever worldwide advertising campaign featuring a waif-like girl. Though her attire changed by the holiday (including a Santa cap) and the words around her changed by the country, she remained the same: our forlorn waif, a symbol of the world's vulnerable and forsaken.

The staging's grandeur was paired with the intimate, tactile nature of the theatrical performances themselves. Distinct from flickering images on a screen, these were real people in a real space (however artificial), the poignancy of which remains hard to duplicate cinematically. When Colm Wilkinson sang Valjean's signature standard, "Bring Him Home" in a Los

Angeles auditorium, his voice was so soft and tender that thousands of spectators held their breath and wept. Here, a private prayer was offered publicly, and a vast public space became intimate and holy.

Why did fifty-five million people worldwide flock to this musical? Was it the plethora of theological insights John E. Morrison evocatively explores in his book *To Love Another Person: A Spiritual Journey through* Les Miserables? Or its many themes debated on the Internet: legalism vs. grace, work vs. faith, despair vs. hope, condemnation vs. redemption? Was it, as some said, a convincing morality play or, as others claimed, a life-changing illustration of atonement? Yes, and more.

"What is to be our way on this earth?" Victor Hugo asked in his classic novel. Can a man change? Is freedom possible? How can we, the wretched (the literal translation of "les miserables") of the earth, touch the face of God?

*Les Miserables*, the musical, was revolutionary not just because it so effectively portrayed personal and political revolution but because through music, staging, and performance it incarnated the most revolutionary teaching of all time. Two thousand years ago, Jesus told his followers to "Love one another." And for more than twenty-five years, the martyred heroes of *Les Miserables* have sung the same. Marching forward with flags unfurled, they have brought down the curtain 43,000 times with the same words—"To love another person is to see the face of God."

R. W. Bonn

## *The Little Mermaid* and Fairy Tales

The early 1980s were marked by financial difficulties for the Walt Disney Company. In 1984, the studio brought in new directors, including Michael Eisner, who decided to return the company's attention back to adapting fairy tales. It was an intelligent move, as Disney was built on the success of its fairy tales and "make believe." *Snow White and the Seven Dwarfs* (1937) had marked the beginning of animated feature films. By the 1940s, the studio was facing bankruptcy due to the large costs that accompany animating films. Releasing *Cinderella* (1950) saved the company and launched an extremely successful run of films, culminating in *Sleeping Beauty* (1959).

With such a rich history of fairy tale adaptations, it made sense for Eisner to turn toward Hans Christian Anderson's *The Little Mermaid* in the 1980s. Although the original 1837 tale bears moderate resemblance to Disney's

1989 version, the power of pixie dust again saved the Disney Company from financial ruin and launched a run of memorable animated films, including *Beauty and the Beast* (1991) and *Aladdin* (1992). History has proven that many of Disney's most popular and successful films originated as fairy tales.

The origins of fairy tales can be traced back hundreds, sometimes thousands, of years. Every culture around the world has its own folktales and fairy tales. Many fairy tales, such as *Cinderella*, exist in multiple variants around the world, in almost every culture. These stories have continued to capture our imagination. This enchantment expands beyond time, place, and culture. Scholars such as J. R. R. Tolkien and C. S. Lewis argue that the reason these fairy tales are so intertwined in the fabric of culture is because they ultimately reveal truths about God. Tolkien notes that every fairy tale contains universal truths, such as unconditional love and good triumphing over evil, that are fulfilled in the gospel. The modern idea of "happily-ever-after" (or "eucatastrophe" as Tolkien likes to call it) is ultimately seen in the gospel story with Christ's resurrection. For this reason, Tolkien believes that Christ fulfills the desires of humankind, which have been written in our myths, folktales, and fairy tales. Tolkien used this line of reasoning to convince Lewis that all he loved in myth and fairy tale revealed glimpses of God.

Tolkien and Lewis believed that God intentionally introduced aspects of Himself through the imagination of humanity so that we would recognize Him when we encountered Him. For example, suppose one grew up reading the tale of Snow White, who, after eating a poisoned apple, is resurrected by true love. Hearing the Christian story of a God who became man, died, and was resurrected because of God's perfect and unconditional love would resonate and ring true. Similarly, watching *The Little Mermaid* would cause many God-truths to resonate with its viewers.

Like other tales, *The Little Mermaid* contains powerful messages that point toward religious themes such as sacrifice. Not only does Ariel sacrifice her voice to be with Eric, but more significantly, King Triton sacrifices his life to save his daughter. Triton's sacrifice calls to mind the Christian notion of a heavenly Father, who sends His son to die on a cross and rescue His children from evil.

Another interesting aspect of *The Little Mermaid*, which is not seen in Anderson's version, is the concept of free will. Ariel constantly defies her father, seeking independence. Despite Ariel's willfulness, her father loves her, even while needing to punish her. Again, this reflects the relationship between God and humankind. God has given us free will to exert our independence. We often openly defy God and are sometimes punished for our defiance. But God's unconditional love, the love a Father has for a child, remains the same.

One of the best-loved aspects of Disney's *Mermaid* is its music. Alan Menken and Howard Ashman's song "Part of Your World" reinforces the idea that we are all longing for something more, something beyond this world. It suggests that people are on a quest for the ultimate love story and the chance to live happily ever after. "Part of Your World" speaks to our longing for a relationship with God and a chance at experiencing the "eucatastrophic" joy for ourselves.

CAITLIN LAWRENCE

# Macintosh

*"Apple is like a strange drug that you just can't quite get enough of."*
*Barry Adamson*

Macintosh is a line of computers designed, developed, and marketed by Apple Inc., the Cupertino, California-based computer company. The computers were created in the early 1980s for personal use, in contrast to the general trend of creating business machines. They were the brainchild of Apple employee Jef Raskin, who envisioned an economical and easy-to-use computer for average consumers. He wanted to name the computer after his favorite apple, the McIntosh, but the company ran into copyright issues and opted for Macintosh instead.

The first Macintosh was introduced to the public via a now-famous $1.5 million television commercial in 1984, conceived by the advertising agency Chiat/Day and directed by filmmaker Ridley Scott. The ad aired only once on U.S. television, in the third quarter of the Super Bowl broadcast, and immediately became a classic. The Macintosh went on sale two days after the commercial aired. The computer had limitations and did not function very well, but it did corner a small portion of the market. Gradually the company expanded its product line and introduced innovations that humanized computing.

The Macintosh replaced the impersonality of computer code with the familiarity of file folders. Icons on the desktop allowed users to see their work. The organization resembled both our offices and our brains. We simply had to search through the files to find what we were looking for. Moreover, the search involved a "mouse," a new invention that helped users scroll across the screen. Our fingers could do the walking—no more cursors, pulsing for a prompt. Clicking and dragging made it feel like our whole body was involved in computing. We moved files (and ourselves) around the Macintosh. Apple also launched the desktop publishing era with its combination of the Mac computer, a new LaserWriter printer, and Mac-specific software that enabled users to design, preview, and print page layouts, with graphics and text—revolutionary at the time.

But it wasn't until virtually the end of the twentieth century that Mac the product became Mac the icon. In 1998, Steve Jobs, one of the company's original founders, returned to the company and was responsible for the introduction of the all-in-one Macintosh called the iMac (the "i" stood for Internet and also represented the product's focus as a personal rather than business device). He returned to the company with a simple philosophy of creating recognizable products with a simple but beautiful design. The iMac's brightly colored and translucent outer shell immediately became an industrial design landmark and established the Jobs philosophy of recognizability. It also set the stage for Apple's transition from being a company selling computers to an iconic symbol of creativity and the object of almost cult-like worship. Apple built on the consumer embrace of its brightly colored iMacs and in the 2000s introduced a stream of products that were innovative, user-friendly, and design-conscious. In addition to the iMac came a slew of other 'i' products—iPod, iPhone, and iPad, all of which caused a veritable feeding frenzy for consumers anxious to be among the first to possess, or perhaps be possessed by, the merchandise.

The Macintosh began it all. Steve Jobs spoke about the three phases of personal computing. The first phase was about utility—people using their machines to accomplish things like word processing and spreadsheets. The second phase was about connecting people and their computers to the Internet and getting them to talk to each other. The third phase involved getting consumers to use their computers to integrate all the other digital devices that have come into their lives. The personal computer has become the focal point; it is where we store our music, access photos, find information, discover entertainment, and connect with social networks. It has become a defining and central hub of life in contemporary society.

Apple wants to change the way we think about technology. Much has been made of the introduction of the iPad with its touch-screen technology. The only instruction that comes with the device is that users should connect it to their home computer to launch it; everything else is left up to them to discover. All they have to do is slide a finger across the screen and new worlds open up. The iPad can become whatever consumers desire it to be. At the announcement of the iPad 2, Steve Jobs said, "It's in Apple's DNA that technology alone is not enough. That it's technology married with liberal arts, married with humanities, that yields us the result that makes our heart sing."

BARRY TAYLOR

# Madonna

Madonna. The name itself can divide people into fans or foes. She seldom elicits a neutral opinion; you love her or you hate her. She is a provocateur or a heretic, an icon of promiscuity or female sexual empowerment, a herald of new spiritual horizons or simply a "material girl." But just when you think you have categorized her, she does something contrary to what she is believed to be communicating.

Madonna Louise Ciccone was born in 1958 in Bay City, Michigan, and moved to New York in 1977 to pursue a career in dance. But it was a recording career that brought Madonna to the world's attention. Utilizing relationships with some of New York's savviest record producers, mining her dance club connections, and using new recording technologies and instruments such as drum machines and a new generation of synthesizers, Madonna burst onto the dance music scene in the early 1980s with a string of pop hits that propelled her to international stardom.

It was her second album, *Like a Virgin* (1984), that cemented her position as a true pop star. The album's title track "Like a Virgin" topped the charts for six consecutive weeks in the United States and became a hit in many countries around the world. Along with her music she developed a distinct style of dress consisting of lace tops, skirts over Capri pants, fishnet stockings, and lots of jewelry, much of which was religious in nature—including crosses and crucifixes. She quickly became a style icon and a female fashion trendsetter. Her performances drew the ire of family organizations that accused her and her music of promoting promiscuity and undermining family values, and many groups sought to have her and her music videos banned. This entire furor only served to build her awareness in the public eye and fuel her own role as a cultural provocateur.

In January 1989, she signed an endorsement agreement with Pepsi, the soft drink manufacturer. In one of her commercials for Pepsi, she debuted the song "Like a Prayer" with an accompanying video that was rich in Catholic symbolism from saints to stigmata and burning crosses. Its central theme appeared to be the heroine dreaming of making love to a saint. Needless to say, religious groups sought to have the video banned and urged the boycott of Pepsi products. She lost her endorsement but kept the cash; *Rolling Stone* hailed the song as "as close to art as pop music gets."

Her subsequent Blond Ambition tour, designed to "break useless taboos," only exacerbated the growing distance between Madonna and her accusers. The more they complained and campaigned against her, the more resolutely she offered her interpretation of the meaning and purpose of life. Her career has been marked by a commitment to free expression, an interest in the empowerment and celebration of female sexuality, and a burgeoning interest in spirituality.

While much of the dialogue in religious circles at the end of the twentieth century was bemoaning the loss of religion within culture, Madonna and others were celebrating the emergence of a new enchantment of culture, much of it occurring through the vehicle of popular culture rather than through traditional religious mechanisms. Eastern and Jewish mysticism, particularly Kabbalah, captured her attention. Her seventh album, 1998's *Ray of Light*, reflected the dawn of a new era in Madonna's life and creative output. Gone were the sexual explorations that characterized much of her musical output in the 1980s and early '90s, and in its place a more reflective Madonna ruminated on the mystical aspects of life. Critics quickly dismissed the album as simply an embrace of new age spirituality, but a closer exploration reveals something much more substantive. Her embrace of Kabbalah, her appropriation of spiritual language drawn from Hinduism and Buddhism, and her Catholic rootedness focused on the connections that encompass spiritual enlightenment and sexual or carnal ecstasy. Madonna's music seemed intent on dissolving the distinction between the two—collapsing the spiritual and the physical into a more holistic understanding of both the human condition and spiritual practice.

Julie Taylor, in her book, *Eva Peron: The Myths of a Woman*, posits that women are put in highly symbolic positions where they are seen as either sources of culture and refinement or sources of pollution. Madonna has filled both of these roles. She may not be everyone's icon of spirituality. But for many, Madonna leads the way to a new understanding of personal enlightenment in the twenty-first century.

BARRY TAYLOR

# Nike Ads

Nike was the Greek goddess of victory, but that's also the name of one of the world's most familiar and easily recognized sportswear brands. So familiar is the company's brand presence that one need not even see its name on a product to know the product's origin—it's instantly recognizable by the "swoosh" created by Carolyn Davidson, a graphic design student at Portland State University.

Nike began life as Blue Ribbon Sports in 1964 but officially became Nike in 1978. Founders Phil Knight and Bill Bowerman initially formed the company to distribute products made by a Japanese footwear company, Onitsuka Tiger. Their venture into producing their own items came about after Bowerman, who like Knight was a University of Oregon track coach, began experimenting with soles for athletic shoes that would better grip the new track at the University. The "waffle" design, Nike's first venture, was created when Bowerman poured liquid urethane into his wife's iron, creating the design that would debut as the now-iconic waffle trainer in 1974.

By 1980, the company had reached a 50 percent market share in the U.S. athletic shoe department, and the company went public in that same year. It is now the world's leading supplier of athletic shoes and apparel and a major manufacturer of sports equipment. But Nike sells more than goods for consumers. It sells a philosophy, a way of life. Nike has become synonymous with particular attitudes and strengths that have become part of the fabric of what it means to be human in some sense in the modern world.

Advertising and marketing played a significant role in Nike's success, and its advertising slogans function as motivational tools not just for athletes but also for people from all walks of life. An advertising slogan is a short, intelligent phrase used to capture the attention of the target audience. Given that its company mission statement is "To bring inspiration and innovation to every athlete in the world," and that one of the company's cofounders has stated that "if you have a body, you are an athlete," Nike's slogan had a lot of work to do. It was not until the 1980s that Nike found its stride as a company, which was largely due to a successful ad campaign and slogan that enabled the company to position itself as the cool, premium athletic brand. The prominent advertising agency Wieden+Kennedy created one of the world's most familiar ad slogans, "Just Do It." The slogan, and its accompanying ad campaigns, not only captured the company's philosophy of passion and determination but also infused it with a sense of humor. The ads rarely focused on the product, but on the person wearing the product. This subtle distinction is what has allowed Nike to become a "lifestyle" brand—it sells products, but the products are vehicles toward becoming a certain kind of person in the world.

Nike's chief competitor, Reebok, was the champion of the aerobics craze of the 1980s and had garnered a huge share of the athletic shoe business. Nike's ad campaign approach was a tough, no-nonsense focus that virtually shamed consumers into exercising. "Just Do It" became a metaphor for commitment, endurance, singular focus, and a statement of quality for Nike. Celebrity endorsements (Bo Jackson, John McEnroe, Michael Jordan) strengthened the brand identity and added a new layer of meaning to the wearing of Nike products: Nike wearers were successful, hip, and, of course, incredible athletes. And if Michael Jordan could fly through the air game after game throughout a basketball season in his Nikes, then surely ordinary weekend warriors could trust in the durability of Nike shoes for themselves.

So successful were the campaigns that people not interested in athletics began to purchase the products, and before long athletic wear became default casual wear for millions of people worldwide. It has become a lifestyle brand, embodying values and aspirations that appeal to a wide group of consumers. The original slogan has been expanded; Nike was one of the first companies to utilize failure and endurance—failure is good, so long as you get up and get going again.

Nike's corporate values don't seem particularly revolutionary. Most of them—hard work, endurance, commitment, focus—have been around for a long time. But Nike has managed to reinvigorate them by tying them to what it means to be human in the twenty-first century—old values for a new world. Not a bad example for religion to follow.

BARRY TAYLOR

## Oprah Winfrey

On May 25, 2011, the final episode of *The Oprah Winfrey Show* aired on U.S. television, ending a hugely successful run in daytime television. The nationally syndicated show had its roots in "AM Chicago," a morning talk show on WLS-TV. Oprah Winfrey took over as host in January 1984 and within a short period of time took it from third place to first in the ratings. In September 1986 it was relaunched as *The Oprah Winfrey Show* and picked up nationally, beginning what would become a twenty-five-year run.

Winfrey was born in poverty in rural Mississippi in 1954 to a teenage single mother but has risen to become the richest African American woman of the late twentieth and early twenty-first century. She has also been called the greatest African American philanthropist in American history and was, for a time, the world's only black billionaire. But wealth is not the full extent of her influence; some have heralded her as the most powerful woman in the world. Her support of presidential candidate Barack Obama was estimated to have given him over a million extra votes in the 2008 election.

*The Oprah Winfrey Show* was highly influential and found its way into the heart of American, if not global, pop consciousness. The program initially followed the successful format of previous talk shows such as *The Phil Donahue Show* and others. These addressed social issues in a tabloid manner, taking a sensationalist approach. Winfrey developed her own, more confessional style and transformed the genre by creating a more positive, spiritually uplifting experience. Episodes incorporated celebrity interviews; segments on self-improvement (her show gave rise to a number of now-famous TV hosts such as Dr. Phil, Dr. Oz, Nate Berkus, and others, each of them experts in particular fields of self-improvement, from home decor to health); book clubs; and philanthropic ventures. Lee Payne of *Newsday* noted that "Oprah Winfrey is sharper than Donahue, wittier, more genuine, and far better attuned to her audience, if not the world." *The Wall Street Journal* wrote that, "It's a relief to see a gab-monger with a fond but realistic assessment of her own cultural and religious roots." This potent combination of self-awareness and cultural savvy created a revolution in television and garnered Winfrey a virtually unparalleled celebrity power.

She created an intimate, confessional form of communication, which the *Wall Street Journal* termed "Oprahfication"—public confession as a form of therapy. The approach has led some, including Yale professor Kathryn Lofton, to declare that she functions as the leader of a form of religion. In her book, *Oprah: Gospel of an Icon*, Lofton contends that Winfrey's message—which can be understood as "you don't have to be perfect but you should do the best that you can"—is best acknowledged as a working religion. Winfrey believes that self-discovery is at the heart of transformation and change for oneself and that the world is a kind of gospel.

Along with regular celebrity interviews conducted with movie stars and artists like Tom Cruise and Michael Jackson, Winfrey also introduced her audience to religious figures like new age writer Eckhart Tolle, opening up an avenue for public discourse about religion in popular network television. But it is her own brand of spirituality that Winfrey championed the most over the course of her career, and arguably every guest, book, venture, and adventure on her show was an extension of her own particular canon of the spiritual life.

Oprah's philosophy of life is that we are all human, subject to the strengths and frailties of what that means. This frailty was made visible to viewers through Oprah's own admitted battles with weight, her early life experiences with sexual trauma, and her willingness to admit her own shortcomings. Human suffering on personal and global levels was often the focus of her show. Her advocacy for a number of issues and her desire that her audience find ways to address human suffering is central to understanding her view. Other consistent values of the talk show were self-examination, gratitude, and generosity. In spite of Oprah's immense wealth and segments in her shows highlighting her "favorite" material things, philanthropy and a willingness to benefit others were frequently emphasized. Finally, perhaps her greatest gift and single most important value was listening. Winfrey's success as an interviewer was linked to her desire to hear others and learn about their lives. In twenty-five years of daytime television—and then in the programming she selected for her television network, OWN—Oprah offered a philosophy of life that included the deepest values of her religious roots but liberated people from form and structure.

BARRY TAYLOR

# Ronald Reagan

In a poem titled "An Explanation of America," Robert Pinsky observes that while something as big and problematic as a nation-state can't be known or summed up definitively, it might be accorded a faithful thumbnail sketch by way of a vision; America as "the things it wants to see." Given the all-too-human penchant for wishful thinking and ego-protecting denial concerning our actions, motivations, and personal histories, appeals to *national* identity will always be a little sketchy, ethically speaking. And while individuals seeking public office in any democracy doubtless steer their spirits toward the less-than-truthful craft of brand images and associations, giving oneself over to a campaign for the office of President of the United States might be fruitfully compared to reaching for Tolkien's One Ring. One can hardly traffic in such a world without risking the forfeiture of one's soul. After successfully wrestling the shifting spirit—or poltergeist—of America's perceived, collective self-interest to the point of aligning it with one's ambitions, what's been won and what lost? Does a living soul still lurk within the person-turned-principality?

Serving two terms and crafting a winning, positive, and kindly image to which career politicians would make perpetual and perfunctory appeal, Ronald Reagan (1911–2004) is often touted as the most naturally skilled player in this particular, high-stakes game. Having lost his bid for the Republican presidential nomination twice, he won in 1980 and found a perfect foil in his opponent, incumbent president Jimmy Carter, who arguably began to lose the presidency when he asked Americans to practice their alleged love of country by curbing their energy consumption.

Needless to say, this vision of the *possibility* of a common wealth and the personal sacrifices required was not what the American public was buying, and, necessarily, it wasn't what Reagan's campaign would sell. Reagan could discredit Carter's gloomy witness to the long view with his announcement of "Morning in America" and the seemingly straightforward suggestion that the only real question facing voters that year was a simple one: "Are you better off now than you were four years ago?" For Reagan, the story of America was one whereby brave citizens aggressively pursue the limitless growth of their own wealth while somehow inevitably bringing freedom to all of humankind. It is this very hallucination, America's civic religion, any winning campaign will have to harness. The candidate's mission is not just to conjure but to *be* the product of Americans' preferred imaginings. And in this way, Reagan hitched the idea of his own incontestable sense, sincerity, and sweetness to the animating myth of America. Did he believe his own publicity?

Here, we're confronted with the awkward notion that a skilled politician might have to believe whatever it appears necessary to believe from one moment to the next. Throughout his long career, Reagan made successful use of certain caricatures and exaggerations. He asserted that the advent of Medicare would lead to socialism, complained about John F. Kennedy ("Under the tousled boyish haircut is still old Karl Marx"), and generated the urban legend of "the welfare queen"—an African American woman in Chicago who, he recounted, routinely collects $150,000 a year in Social Security through various aliases and nonexistent dead husbands. Critics of Reagan's slashing of welfare programs observed that it was the woman herself who didn't exist. The politically expedient anecdote is always with us, but a dependence on it risks the transmogrification of the otherwise honest mind into a politically expedient personality. A hold on reality can prove disturbingly malleable. When forced by the 1987 Tower Commission report to revisit his public denial of involvement in the Iran-Contra affair, Reagan felt compelled to utter an odd statement that might illustrate the phenomenon: "I told the American people I did not trade arms for hostages. My heart and my best intentions still tell me that's true, but the facts and the evidence tell me it is not."

For Americans, a president's pattern of evasions often mimics their own inasmuch as they partake of a common culture that is, inspiringly and democratically, up for grabs. Reagan's epitaph includes the conviction that "there is purpose and worth to each and every life." This sensibility served the world well in his relationship with Soviet leader Mikhail Gorbachev. It wasn't the power of positive thinking that brought down the Berlin wall, but Reagan's surge of affability struck an effective note alongside the chorus of beleaguered activists, living and dead, already in the Soviet satellite nations. Perhaps the habit of seeing what one hopes to see, like the temporary power of a president, can be put to redemptive use.

DAVID DARK

# Salman Rushdie

Sir Ahmed Salman Rushdie may have been born in Mumbai, India, in 1947, but it was in 1989 that he was born in the imagination of the public at large. He was already an author of some repute, the recipient of many awards and a prolific writer of fiction, nonfiction, children's stories, and occasional essays. But it was Bradford—a largely working-class town in northern England with a large immigrant population—that put Rushdie in a public spotlight that eclipsed anything his literary career and accomplishments had brought him thus far.

A public and well-organized book burning took place in Bradford that day, with the focus of public outrage being *The Satanic Verses*, Rushdie's fourth novel. As reaction to the book caught on with Muslims around the world, protests and book burnings broke out in the streets of many cities. The protests culminated with the issuance of a fatwa (a religious ruling) by the Ayatollah Khomeini in Iran. It pronounced a capital punishment on Rushdie for blasphemy against Islam and the Prophet Muhammad, and called on faithful Muslims everywhere to participate in its execution. The fatwa forced Rushdie into hiding for a decade.

That a book, and a novel at that, could generate such vitriol in the late twentieth century came as a surprise to many. This event pulled the shades back on an issue that has come to define life in the twentieth century: radical religious fundamentalism of every stripe, often characterized by violence both verbal and physical.

Like most of his writing, *The Satanic Verses* was a work of fiction that blended real events or themes with invented tales of magic and mystery. Rushdie's second novel, *Midnight's Children*, had told the tale of a child born at the stroke of midnight on the night of Indian independence, who is endowed with special powers and a connection to other children born at the dawn of a new era. The novel won the Booker Prize for Fiction in 1981 and was awarded the Best of the Bookers in 1993 and 2008, as the best book to have received the prize during the first twenty-five and forty years of the prize's existence. The novel shaped Indian writing in English and is viewed as one of the great books of the last century.

The magical realist style that threads its way through most of his stories is a device Rushdie uses to get at truth through the path of untruth. The fantastical elements in his stories are devices to bring the reader into a world where new ideas and new realities can be explored. *The Satanic Verses* took a contested portion of the Qur'an and dragged it into the twentieth century. For many Muslims, the passages Rushdie referenced, which concern the Prophet Muhammad potentially being influenced by Satan, are challenging in the best of situations. For a newly emerging form of Islam, attempting to face the challenges of new global realities, it was too much that a writer would handle the sacred words of their faith with such apparent callousness.

Rushdie, according to many interviews, did not set out to blaspheme Islam; he was simply trying to address the instability and volatility of the postmodern world. The book challenges religious, cultural, and national identities as it tells of two men falling to earth after their plane has exploded in the sky. It is on some levels a reworking of Islamic thinking for the new realities. This may explain why the book caused such uproar among the faithful.

Quite understandably, Rushdie has become something of a symbol for a new generation of people for whom religion is a perceived threat and little more than a holdover from a less-enlightened age. After the attacks of 9/11, Rushdie's critics like Ayaan Hirsi Ali reversed their position on the fatwa, seeing Islam as the problem. In *The End of Faith* (2005), Sam Harris opposed all religious faiths but renounced Islam as the most evil. Rushdie became an unintentional lightning rod, emboldening both sides of the religious, political, and cultural divide.

Rushdie's gift is his use of imagination. He took portions of the Qur'an and Muslim traditions and married them to the real and imaginary worlds of modern Muslims living in the West. Many orthodox Muslims could not conceive of faith sprouting in this way or of it being made fruitful by the use of imagination; nor could they see their faith's stories as a starting point from which new iterations could be built rather than a destination in itself.

Imagination and religion make for dangerous bedfellows, but Rushdie has made a craft of such marriages and has given a model for reimaging faith—if we can get past the blasphemy.

BARRY TAYLOR

---

## *The Simpsons*

*The Simpsons* is a groundbreaking, irreverent television sitcom that has run for more than twenty years, reaching tens of millions of viewers in North America and around the world. By the 1990s there were more than a thousand *Simpsons* Web sites in cyberspace. In 2007 came a long-awaited feature film that grossed more than half a billion dollars worldwide. The show has exerted an ongoing influence on American culture, high and low. "D'oh!" Homer's expression of consternation, has been added to the Oxford English Dictionary. Over a billion dollars' worth of *Simpsons* merchandise has been sold, featuring catch phrases like, "Underachiever and proud of it," and "Don't have a cow, man." *Time* magazine called *The Simpsons* the twentieth century's best television show, and the show has made the cover of *TV Guide* a dozen times.

One of *The Simpsons'* major breakthroughs was to bring to prime time, and to network TV, a family that accurately reflected the faith lives of most Americans at the end of the twentieth century—and beyond. In so doing, *The Simpsons* swung wide the door to portraying faith for other television writers and artists, including the creators of *South Park*. During the same two-week period in early 2001, the Simpsons appeared on the covers of both *Christianity Today* and *The Christian Century*, two magazines at opposite ends of the Protestant theological spectrum. The Reverend Rowan Williams, Archbishop of Canterbury, a fan of the show, told the BBC in 2002 that "The *Simpsons* is one of the most subtle pieces of propaganda around in the cause of sense, humility and virtue."

While religion does not define *The Simpsons*, it richly informs the show's world. According to one study by a theologian (and fan), fully a third of all the episodes include at least one religious reference. The series is not a television show *about* religion; it is a situation comedy about modern life that includes a significant spiritual dimension. Here is a family that says grace at meals, goes to church on Sundays, reads and refers to the Bible, and prays aloud—if only when absolutely necessary. God often answers their prayers and intervenes in their world. The family's next-door neighbor, Ned Flanders, is a committed evangelical and a character so good-hearted that he became a popular culture mascot for many committed young Christians.

The gift of *The Simpsons* is that the characters' fundamental beliefs are animated but not caricatured. God is not mocked, nor is God's existence questioned. Within the Simpson family, different members represent different strands of belief. Homer, the hapless dad, is a borderline pagan whose grasp of theological complexity is, at best, fuzzy, often confusing magic with faith. Asked by his troublemaking son Bart what the family's religious beliefs are, his father answers, "You know, the one with all the well-meaning rules that don't work in real life. Uh, Christianity." For much of the show's run, brainy daughter Lisa spoke for socially conscious, mainline Protestantism; later, she gave up and became a Buddhist. Long-suffering mother Marge was a true believer; Bart, an occasional devil worshiper.

Springfield, where the family lives, possesses a rich spiritual life. Supporting characters and guest actors provide the opportunity to showcase faith traditions beyond mainline Protestantism, in episodes devoted to Catholics, Pentecostals, Jews, Buddhists, and Hindus. Often, these portrayals introduced these diverse beliefs to young viewers for the first time.

As a narrative, the show presents a complete (if inconsistent) cosmology—God, the devil, angels—and a fully realized universe of faith. Characters believe in a literal heaven and hell, and, like most Americans, ridicule cults. Christians and Christianity are more a part of *The Simpsons* than of any other prime-time network sitcom or drama. Although in the show, salvation is believed to come through works rather than grace.

Still, nowhere was the initial uproar about the show's debut season more vigorous than in America's pulpits. Upset by his child imitating Bart at the dinner table, an outraged member of Willow Creek Community Church near Chicago complained to one of the ministers, Lee Strobel, who in turn preached a widely reprinted sermon titled "What Jesus Would Say to Bart Simpson." A Baptist pastor, Dan Burrell, recorded an educational audiotape titled "Raising Beaver Cleaver Kids in a Bart Simpson World," instructing parents how to rear their children with "value and character." Yet other clergy and youth leaders have also used the show to teach faith-based morals and ethics.

MARK I. PINSKY

# Steven Spielberg

The most financially successful director in the history of the movies *and* the friendliest guy in Hollywood—Steven Spielberg is a study in contradictions. He's the Jewish American who created *Schindler's List* (1993), the most famous Holocaust film, and *Munich* (2005), one of the most trenchant critiques of Israeli security tactics. He's the man responsible for both the monster *Jaws* (1975) and the cute messianic alien *E.T.* (1982). He's a boy wonder who happens to be one of the world's most powerful men, an artist, a humanitarian, a lightning rod for criticism by those who confuse childlikeness with childishness, the painter of our collective dreams.

Growing up in Ohio, New Jersey, and Arizona, and in the immediate post-Second World War period, it's no wonder Spielberg locates most of his work in Middle America (in heart if not always geography) and returns time and again to the desolation caused by WWII. His personal experience of family breakdown and anti-Semitic harassment can be inferred from much of his work, too; but most of all there is the search for magic, the hope that something transcendent would break through the mundanity and struggle of everyday life.

In *Close Encounters of the Third Kind* (1977), we watch a man bored with his work as an electrician as he follows an impossible dream evoked by seeing what appear to be aliens guiding him; in *Jaws,* a rumpled cop shakes off the stress of his new job and confronts the locals who don't like an outsider telling them what to do by saving their lives. Spielberg's story for *The Goonies* (1985) had lower-middle-class kids literally finding pirate treasure, and in the *Indiana Jones* series that began in 1981, a potentially stuffy academic archaeologist exchanges lecterns for supernaturally inflected adventure. So Spielberg is a magician, conjuring up the kind of worlds most human beings usually only dream about—and it's on this count that he is most often criticized. "Too Spielberg-y" became a go-to synonym for saccharine plot resolution, or overly sentimental portrayals of family, in which hope always paves the way for love to conquer all. But this betrays a vast misreading of the Spielberg canon. Themes of marital discord and parent-child dysfunction (*E.T., Indiana Jones and the Last Crusade*) vie with the horror of what men do in war (*Schindler's List; Saving Private Ryan,* 1998), or the existential perdition of a man wandering around an airport (*The Terminal,* 2004), or of human beings giving way to synthetic approximations of our souls after environmental apocalypse has all but destroyed the earth (*A. I. Artificial Intelligence,* 2001). Steven Spielberg is as serious a thinker as his films are box office successes. It's his genius that he makes philosophical depth accessible in the guise of enormous entertainments.

In *Schindler's List*, Spielberg's grave intent was writ large—an attempt, more than fifty years after the fact, to memorialize the six million Jewish victims of Nazi genocide. It was uncompromising in its depiction of ghetto oppression and concentration camp horror. The French new wave director Jean-Luc Godard condemned the film for a scene in which tension derives from the audience not knowing if the naked characters on screen are about to be gassed or have a shower; others took up this theme by calling the film a theme-park ride version of the Holocaust. These were understandable, if not necessarily accurate, criticisms (a more nuanced challenge would highlight the fact that his films are usually uncritical of violence done by the "good guys," with the notable exceptions of *Saving Private Ryan* and *Munich*). Most viewers would have identified with the humanity of the victims, the sheer terror of their predicament. They would have been galvanized into doing what Holocaust memorials ask: that the audience would never forget. It is a sign of Spielberg's prodigious talent that he could shoot *Schindler's List* in Poland by day and edit *Jurassic Park* (1993) (a *genuine* thrill ride) at night. But he never exudes any public sense of egotism. When Oprah Winfrey asked him to speak about the trauma of making such a painful film as *Schindler's List,* he could have taken the opportunity to wax rhetorical about the suffering of artists. Instead, he stated simply that the struggle to make the movie was nothing compared to that faced by its subjects, who, like all Spielberg's characters, are more interesting to him than he is in talking about himself.

"How much in life is lost through waiting?" asks a character in the fourth *Indiana Jones* film. There may be no better summation of Spielberg's philosophical demeanor. His movies are about people who learn, sometimes too late, that life needs to be seized; that love will not come to you unless you look for it; that adventure is behind the next door, if only we would open it. To engage with his work is, for some, to push at just that kind of door.

GARETH HIGGINS

# U2

The band—Bono (vocals and guitar), the Edge (guitar, keyboards, and vocals), Adam Clayton (bass guitar), and Larry Mullen Jr. (drums)—formed in 1976, while the members were teenagers at Mount Temple Comprehensive School. They have gone on to play over 1,249 concerts in at least thirty-two countries. Ten of their twelve studio albums have reached number one on the charts, while their music has garnered twenty-two Grammy awards. With album sales of over 150 million units, they are among the best-selling music artists of all time.

One way to analyze U2's theological contribution is to use a lens provided by prizewinning cultural historian John O'Malley, who suggests that Western thought has flowed as four streams:

1. the prophetic, which proclaims the need for radical change
2. the philosophical, in which the inquisitive mind seeks to understand
3. the poetic, which addresses fundamental human issues and works for the common good of society
4. the performance, in which society, whether in liturgy or ceremony, expresses itself

With regard to the **prophetic,** U2's musicians have proved adept at trading their profile for advocacy. At a personal level, Agnes Nyamayarwo, a Ugandan nurse and AIDS activist, has spoken of Bono as her Good Samaritan, given the way that his personal visit to her village gave her hope to live. At a public level, Bono has given leadership in the One campaign's fight against extreme poverty and preventable diseases. That this work is driven by a clear theology is evident in the keynote address Bono gave at the 54th National Prayer Breakfast in February 2006. He offered a theology in which "God is in the slums, in the cardboard boxes where the poor play house. God is in the silence of a mother who has infected her child with a virus that will end both their lives. God is in the cries heard under the rubble of war. God is in the debris of wasted opportunity and lives, and God is with us if we are with them."

Referencing the **philosophic,** the band members over time have appeared reticent to talk about faith. In a 2011 radio interview, Bono commented, "I'm a believer. I have a deep faith, but I am deeply suspicious of people who talk about their faith all the time." Nevertheless, books such as *Bono on Bono: Conversations with Michka Assayas* (2005) show evidence of a mind reflecting deeply on the implications of being human in the world today.

The **poetic** can involve analysis of the band's lyrics. This needs caution, given that Bono writes in a style that is suggestive rather than explicit. Nevertheless, Christian Scharen suggests that the musical catalog of U2 can be organized into categories of psalms as thanksgiving and lament; wisdom as desire and illusion; parables as offense and mercy; prophecy as judgment and hope; and apocalypse as ecstasy and healing.

Another approach has been to analyze the band's lyrics with regard to biblical references. Thus a song like "One Tree Hill" can be appreciated as a contemporary lament. The chorus about a river running to the sea carries echoes of the inevitability of death, as expressed in Ecclesiastes 1:7. The third verse has an eschatology that echoes Revelation 6:12–13, in which the world is changed at the end of time ("I'll see you again / When the stars fall from the sky / And the moon has turned red over One Tree Hill").

Regarding **performance**, people have often experienced a U2 concert as a spiritual encounter. Using liturgical language in the song "Mysterious Ways," Bono calls the gathered to worship. "Sunday, Bloody Sunday" becomes a lament over the repression of political and electoral freedom in Iran. "Walk On" becomes a prayer for others, while during "One" those gathered are invited to make an offering by texting their support to the One campaign. This can be viewed as a work of the Spirit, inviting all of creation, those inside and outside the church, to participate in a world in which people say yes to the divine, hear the cry of the oppressed, pray for those held captive, and offer themselves in the quest for justice.

STEVE TAYLOR

# Andrew Lloyd Webber

Could the Song of Solomon, that sensuously enigmatic love poem from the Old Testament, be the basis for the next Andrew Lloyd Webber musical?

There's been no talk of this, busy as he currently is with reality TV shows, a new musical production of *The Wizard of Oz* and *Love Never Dies,* the sequel to the highest grossing musical of all time (*Phantom of the Opera).* But it wouldn't surprise anyone, for Webber's best remembered songs echo the lush romanticism and barely restrained sensuality of the only surviving example of secular love poetry from ancient Israel.

In composing thirteen musicals, two film scores, and a Latin Requiem Mass, Andrew Lloyd Webber, born in 1948, has frequently used religious themes to become the richest musical composer of all time. His personal fortune is worth £715 million pounds. His list of awards is staggering—including forty Tony nominations (six wins), sixty Grammy nominations (three wins), 100 Olivier Awards nominations (seven wins), an Academy Award, and a Golden Globe. He's even been knighted.

Webber doesn't think of his work as religious. He says *Jesus Christ Superstar* "was never really intended to be anything more than a piece examining the story of Jesus from the point of view of Judas Iscariot. In that sense, it is a dramatic work and not specifically a religious work at all." But it was his radical choice to portray Jesus as an outspoken, rebellious spiritual leader that sparked the musical to unprecedented controversy and success. It may also have been the music, as it was the first rock-opera completely sung through. Ted Neely, who played Jesus in the film and is still performing the role in national tours thirty-six years later, said, "For me, all my childhood, Jesus was a stained glass window—unreachable, untouchable . . . this looks at Jesus as a friend."

There's no doubt that Webber influenced his generation by the religious subject of his works like *Jesus Christ Superstar, Requiem Mass, Whistle Down the Wind,* and *Joseph and the Amazing Technicolor Dreamcoat,* which is based in the story of the biblical character Joseph from Genesis. However, his greatest spiritual contribution may lie in what he's best known for: his simple, emotional, and easily remembered love songs. "It's what I call the emotional memory of these melodies that give them such dramatic potency," journalist Edward Seckerson says. "It stays with you because something about the ache within won't let go."

Andrew Lloyd Webber renews the language of sensuous romance through his songs. In books like Song of Solomon, we are given glimpses into God's sensuous love for us. A 1995 translation of that text by Ariel and Chana Bloch is cited by one reviewer "as an erotic, sensual love poem about two teenagers, unmarried yet reveling in the consummation of their love." In their translation, reviewers have seen parallels closer to Romeo and Juliet than the stodgy allegory of God's love for Israel often preached. For example, the Blochs translate Song of Solomon 1:4 as "My lover, my King, has brought me into his chambers. We will laugh, you and I, and count each kiss better than wine. Every one of them wants you."

In unabashedly writing songs of soaring love and romance, Andrew Lloyd Webber reminds us through the music of an emotional God's ardent love. Refugees from the war-torn fields of dogmatic debate and theological semantics may find hearts stirred anew to consider love of God and others. As the titular lyrics from Webber's 2010 musical *Love Never Dies* promise, "Love never dies, . . . once it has spoken, love is yours . . . as soon as you submit, . . . love takes on a life much bigger than its own. . . . you . . . feel more joy than you can bear."

Andrew Lloyd Webber will be remembered most for highly romantic, sensuous tunes. His music can remind us of the importance of music in our well-being, help us understand that music is also a language of the holy, and open our hearts wider to receive the message of Song of Solomon: that God is not unlike an ardent teenager wooing us with passion and might.

R. W. BONN

© Marka/SuperStock

# The Nineties

*T*he best adjective to describe the nineties might be "explosive." The decade got off to a rugged start with the Persian Gulf War, the Los Angeles riots over the Rodney King beating, the Rwandan genocide, the raiding of David Koresh's compound in Waco, Texas, and bombings at the World Trade Center and in Oklahoma City, all occurring within the first half of the decade. There were hints of a new world emerging, but from many angles, it didn't look positive. As the twentieth century lumbered to a close, a century of progress seemed set to implode.

With a blast of "Smells like Teen Spirit," the Seattle alternative rock band Nirvana redefined music much like the Sex Pistols did in the seventies. Kurt Cobain emerged as an iconic lightning rod for the expression of youthful frustration and anger at a world increasingly holding less promise. Cries of "Here we are now, entertain us," were extinguished in the resignation of "Oh well, whatever, nevermind." Cobain's 1994 suicide prompted an outpouring of grief. Add the Clinton sex scandal, the death of Princess Diana, the Columbine High School massacre, Britain's Mad Cow outbreak, the sarin gas attacks in Tokyo, the murder of Matthew Shepard, and Dolly the cloned sheep, and we can understand some of the fervor and apocalyptic fear surrounding Y2K as the decade, century, and millennium all came to a close.

But it wasn't all doom and gloom. The nineties was the decade when personal computers and cell phones became ubiquitous and the Internet began to transform how we communicate. America Online, Earthlink, and Yahoo became start-up successes by providing access to the World Wide Web. Amazon.com provided a convenient alternative to bookstores, allowing people to make purchases with a single click. Surfing the Internet made the world seem smaller and interconnected.

There were also shifts in media culture—everything old became new again via sampling and digital recording technologies. DJs like Moby mined the riches of classic rock, soul, blues, and gospel for fresh beats and rhymes. Forrest Gump was inserted into seminal historical moments. *Titanic* and *The Blair Witch Project* took filmmaking in divergent directions, from the grandiose to the ultra low budget. TV viewers hung out at the coffeehouse with *Friends*, but *Seinfeld* ended up embodying the era with a "show about nothing." Perhaps the decade's abiding interest was summarized by the unlikely rise of the game show, "Who Wants to Be a Millionaire?"

The millennium ended with a bit of a whimper—no Y2K collapse, no global economic meltdown. What would unfold as the twenty-first century took its first breaths?

# Deepak Chopra

Born in New Delhi, India, in October 1946, Deepak Chopra has become a leading figure in the world of alternative medicine and spirituality in the United States. He graduated from the All India Institute of Medical Sciences and immigrated to the United States in 1968, entering a clinical internship and residency training at Muhlenberg Hospital in Plainfield, New Jersey. After being granted his medical license in Massachusetts in 1973 he was on course for a career in medicine and teaching, with teaching jobs at both Tufts and Boston Universities and other opportunities before beginning his own private practice.

But it was an encounter with Transcendental Meditation that changed Chopra's life course. After learning the technique he embraced the practice more fully, eventually meeting with the Maharishi Mahesh Yogi, who invited Chopra to study Ayurveda. Ayurveda ("the complete knowledge for long life") is a system of traditional medicine native to India. In 1985, Chopra left his position and became the founding president of the American Association of Ayurvedic Medicine and head of the Maharishi's Health Center for Stress Management and Behavioral Medicine.

He quickly began to use his knowledge of both Eastern and Western medicine to full effect, writing a number of articles for journals and beginning his publishing career. His fifty-seven books, beginning with *Creating Health* in 1987, have combined sales in excess of ten million copies in English alone and have been translated into thirty-five different languages. His 1993 publication, *Ageless Body, Timeless Mind*, was his breakthrough book, bringing Chopra to the broader American public and establishing him as a key player in a society increasingly open to spirituality and alternative approaches to life and living. His writings cover all of life, from cooking to love poetry and everything in between. In the period since 9/11 he has published works on Christianity, Buddhism, Islam, Kabbalah, leadership, sex, and addictions.

Chopra's main areas of interest are at the intersections of Eastern and Western thinking—human potential, traditional versus alternative medicine, science and spirit, Eastern spirituality, and new age philosophy. These topics comprise much of the center of progressive spiritual thinking in the world today. Chopra is probably the most successful advocate of the synthesis of East/West thinking, enabling countless westerners, eager to push past what are considered the limits of Western thinking, to discover alternative ways of being. He is eminently capable of repackaging Eastern mysticism in credible Western forms. "Our brains are hardwired to know God," he writes in his typical blend of mysticism and tech-speak. He grants mystery and mysticism a central place in the modern world, which may be a key to understanding his success.

While proponents of more traditional approaches to faith, particularly Christians, bemoan the increasing secularity of society (pointing to moral decay, dwindling church attendance, and other issues), Chopra has championed the view that in spite of modernity, we no longer live in a society where God is unwelcome. The digital age is an era marked by a remarkable re-enchantment of society—a return to God, if you will. Chopra also understands that this return is not necessarily a reestablishment of old forms and practices. True to his synthesizing approach to life, he offers up wholly new approaches to understanding the idea of sacredness but also affirms ancient pathways, but always repackaged for the present moment. He will take a word like "soul" and replace it with "consciousness," or talk about the need for synthesis between religion and science, or argue that the insights of the religious traditions should transcend their traditional structures.

His 2008 publication *The Third Jesus: The Christ We Cannot Ignore* is an attempt to reintroduce Jesus to people who might be wary of a figure closely associated with a religion not known for its accommodation of alternative views. In the book he offers up three views of Jesus. He argues that we have met two Jesuses so far—the historical Jesus who walked the earth, and the institutional Jesus who is the property of the church and largely understood through doctrine and dogma. To these he adds his "third Jesus"—the mystical Jesus who comes to lead us out of the wilderness of doctrine, dogma, and history into a new path of what he calls "god consciousness," a transcendence of religious particularity or at least religious affiliation.

While we may take exception with Chopra's handling of Scripture and his somewhat reductionist views of how Jesus has been understood thus far, it must be said that tying Jesus to the resurgent interest in mysticism, and making room for Jesus in the world of alternative spirituality, is a remarkable accomplishment. He has given Jesus a voice in a world previously remote from his appeals.

BARRY TAYLOR

# Dalai Lama

Tenzin Gyatso, born in 1935 and better known as the fourteenth Dalai Lama, is the leader of the Gelupga (yellow hat) form of Tibetan Buddhism and the de facto spiritual leader of all Tibetan people. Tibetans believe Dalai Lamas to be the reincarnation of their predecessors, each of whom is believed to be an emanation of what in Tibetan Buddhism is known as bodhisattva Avalokitesvara (the enlightened Lord who looks down).

Tenzin Gyatso was selected for the role in November 1950 when he was only fifteen years old. Along with the spiritual position, he also inherited leadership of the government controlling the Tibetan Autonomous Region at a time when the People's Republic of China was attempting to assert central control over it. After a Tibetan uprising in 1959, the Chinese forced the Dalai Lama to flee to India, where he set up a government in exile in Dharamsala. He has lived there ever since.

His exile from his homeland launched the Dalai Lama on a new trajectory: he became a global figurehead for the rights and freedom of his people, appealing to the United Nations on behalf of Tibet. He also became a symbol for political refugees and oppressed people everywhere. He was awarded the Nobel Peace Prize in 1989 in recognition of his more than forty-year commitment to nonviolent resistance to China's domination of his homeland.

Unlike his predecessors, the fourteenth Dalai Lama has engaged with the world and its leaders, both political and religious, traveling the globe to spread his message of nonviolence, the plight of his own people, and the teachings of Buddhism. According to the Nobel Prize Web site, in 1981 the Dalai Lama declared at an interfaith service held in his honor, "I always believe that it is much better to have a variety of religions, a variety of philosophies, rather than one single religion or philosophy. This is necessary because of the different mental dispositions of each human being. Each religion has certain unique ideas or techniques, and learning about them can only enrich one's own faith."

This statement captures not only the generous view he personally holds with regard to the relationships between faiths and cultures but also hints at a significant part of his global appeal as a spiritual leader. The Dalai Lama's popularity is as much about what he is not, or perceived not to be, as what he is. For while he is obviously the spiritual leader of a particular religious group, he is widely viewed as being one of the few religious leaders who doesn't support killing or advocate hating people in the name of religion. Hollywood has rallied to his cause from introductions given by Richard Gere, to the Beasties Boys' Tibetan Freedom Concerts, through the 1997 films *Seven Years in Tibet* and *Kundun*.

The Dalai Lama also points to a growing embrace of both personalized spirituality and Eastern religiosity here in the West. Nondogmatic approaches to religious faith have increased in the West since the latter part of the twentieth century, and the Dalai Lama has become a major example of that move. He is a man who takes his own faith practice seriously but doesn't seek to impose his views on others. "This is my simple religion," he says. "There is no need for temples; no need for complicated philosophy. Our own brain, our own heart is our temple; the philosophy is kindness."

The second clue to the Dalai Lama's continuing popularity is connected to Western interest in Buddhism as a viable and meaningful spiritual path in contemporary times. The continuing decline of Christianity has been countered by the rise of alternative spiritualities and exponential growth of Western forms of Buddhism. There is a perception that Buddhism is better able to address the current state of affairs than other faiths, a perception the Dalai Lama has helped foster. He has frequently identified at least three crucial parallels between science and Buddhism that offer a way of expressing one's faith meaningfully in the twenty-first century: Both science and Buddhism share a deep suspicion of notions of absolutes; they both believe in universal laws of cause and effect (in popular parlance this is often understood as "karma"); and they both depend on empirical method. Buddhism, at least in popular perception and as it is expressed in and through the teachings and life of the Dalai Lama, is focused on practice over dogma, an appealing element in these times.

BARRY TAYLOR

# Ellen DeGeneres

Ellen DeGeneres, born in 1958, is a stand-up comedienne and actress who has become one of the most popular hosts of daytime television. Her daily show (initially called the *Ellen DeGeneres Show*, but later shortened to *Ellen*) debuted in September of 2003. Since that time it has garnered twelve Daytime Emmy Awards and remains a ratings powerhouse, averaging 2.74 million viewers per episode, making it one of the most highly viewed daytime shows. The show combines comedy, celebrity, musical guests, and often a human-interest story.

DeGeneres began her career in stand-up comedy, working her way through the club and coffeehouse circuits. She performed on the *Tonight Show* with Johnny Carson in 1986 and was the first comedienne to be invited to a post-performance chat with Carson. DeGeneres performs an observational style of comedy, not making jokes as much as making wry observations about life, much like the comedian Jerry Seinfeld to whom she has often been compared.

In 1994 her comedy routine and material became the basis for what was to become a successful television comedy sitcom. *Ellen* (called *These Friends of Mine* in its first season) aired on the ABC television network. The show reached peak popularity in early 1997 when DeGeneres appeared on the *Oprah Winfrey Show* and made her lesbian sexual orientation public. Subsequently she "came out" in an episode of her sitcom titled "The Puppy Episode." Her coming out prompted some critique from the religious right and particularly from Jerry Falwell, who named her Ellen DeGenerate. In an April 1997 edition of *Newsweek*, she responded, "Really, he called me that? Ellen DeGenerate? I've been getting that since the fourth grade. I guess I'm happy that I could give him work!" The coming-out episode proved to be the height of the show's popularity, and it was later cancelled due to declining ratings. A subsequent sitcom failed to garner a following, and it too was cancelled. DeGeneres returned to stand-up comedy for a time and also took some acting roles, including the voice of the forgetful fish Dory in *Finding Nemo*.

The talk show is light-hearted and fun with lots of audience reaction and participation. Forgoing the usual house-band led music of most talk shows, DeGeneres employs a DJ and opens the show every day with a dancing segment, with DeGeneres and members of the audience dancing together. It is exuberant, with few boundaries between the host and her audience. She has perfected the art of solidarity with both her audience and her guests—she might be a celebrity and famous, but she is also ordinary, enjoying many of the same things her audience does. Like them, she harbors fantasies about certain celebrities and shares mutual excitement with her audience when a huge star appears on the show.

DeGeneres makes no effort to hide her sexual orientation; in fact she quite aggressively markets herself as a lesbian entertainer. For one season she was a judge on America's most popular television show, *American Idol,* and made mostly humorous mention of her sexual orientation in virtually every episode. The *Dallas Voice* newspaper published an article about her titled, "Ellen: A Lovable Icon of 'Gay Normal?'" It pointed to her appeal with mainstream American women and attributed this to the effort she makes to have everyone see her as "normal." This has created some debate in African American circles, which highlight the similar way in which mainstream culture has embraced those who were deemed to be a "credit to their race."

Robert Putnam, author of the book *American Grace,* uses the analogy of the "Aunt Susan" principle to explain how America reconciles religiosity and tolerance. An "Aunt Susan" is someone who holds different views than we might but is someone who we know and love. Aunt Susan trumps theology, declares Putnam: "She doesn't win against the Bible for everyone but she's pretty powerful."

This same idea applies when it comes to human sexuality and personal relationships. When someone we know and love transforms an abstract notion or idea into a flesh-and-blood reality, we are far more likely to react with tolerance and embrace and shift our views. This occurs not because we have necessarily experienced a transformative intellectual conversion, but simply because we care about this person.

Ellen DeGeneres has become a fixture in many American living rooms because of her sexual orientation, not in spite of it. She invites us to embrace her and relate to her as a fellow human being, not simply reduce her to the particularities of sexual orientation.

BARRY TAYLOR

## *Doom*

"It's a Bloodbath in Hell!" "All Hell has run amok! Monstrous demons from another dimension use their gruesome talents to turn your space station into a blood-spattered slaughterhouse." These back-cover taglines aptly sum up the wild game play of id Software's *Doom* (1993). Throughout this seminal first-person shooter, the player assumes the role of a sole surviving, buzz-cut marine on a Martian outpost. The trans-dimensional gates of hell are open wide. Spiked imps; hoofed demons; flaming skulls; and shotgun wielding, demon-possessed humans now overrun the outpost. The player's mission is clear: terminate with extreme prejudice. Players experience *Doom* from a first-person perspective, through the eyes of the marine. The player's weapon protrudes into screen space. A portrait of the marine's face appears at the bottom of the screen—increasingly bruised and bloodied as the player's health levels decline. A generous assortment of chainsaws, shotguns, rocket launchers, and ammo boxes lay around the outpost's constricted hallways and flickering corridors, there for the taking.

*Doom* churns up a wide range of feelings in those who play it. On one hand, players report high levels of anxiety and paranoia, and even occasional vertigo or nausea at the game's dizzying pace. On the other hand, *Doom* also generates waves of adrenaline-soaked exhilaration and euphoria as evil is quite literally blasted into pieces. Following its launch, *Doom* quickly dominated the youth and adult video game markets, paving the way for other historic first-person shooter franchises such as *Quake*, *Half-Life*, *Halo*, and *Call of Duty*. By leveraging the power of shareware distribution channels, *Doom* also popularized the LAN deathmatch and user-generated content (or player mod) movements, each of which continues to enjoy a robust existence today. Interestingly, *Doom* was released during the same month as Joseph Lieberman's testimony before the Senate hearing on game violence. More ironically, however, *Doom* was released the same year as the nonviolent, first-person adventure *Myst*.

*Doom* is a dark game—literally and figuratively. Within the video game canon, *Doom* is the yang to *Myst's* yin. Fast-paced instead of contemplative. An immersive ambience of menacing growls instead of cooing birds. Destructive instead of constructive. Chaos instead of tranquility. Shadow instead of light. Each is a highly lucrative series in its own right, although it appears that *Doom* has gained the upper hand for today.

The moral backstory of *Doom* is quite thin, even superfluous. The Marine is stationed on the Martian outpost because he disobeyed a direct order to open fire on innocent civilians, choosing instead to assault his commanding officer. Seen from this light, the Marine is a noble figure. Nevertheless, the procedural rhetoric of *Doom* mounts a very different moral argument. Big gun or little gun, full speed ahead or sneak among the shadows . . . it really doesn't matter. Evil is inhuman. Violence is redemptive. "Vengeance is mine," sayeth the player, "because vigilantism is justice." Thus, the player becomes a pop culture variation on the Nietzschean *Übermensch*—a law unto himself in a godless world, carving out his own values in the face of nihilism and divine absence.

Thus, the world of *Doom* is not entirely dissimilar to the fallen world in which we live, but is it a world in which we *want* to live? In *Engaging the Powers,* biblical scholar Walter Wink argues that violence is the ethos, spirituality, myth, and religion that "undergirds American popular culture." He traces this myth to the primal story of Marduk and Tiamat—the Babylonian god of order and goddess of disorder. In that myth, Marduk defeats Tiamat, carving up her corpse and creating the cosmos from her broken body. Thus, human beings find that violence is literally in their very blood. Evil is indeed inhuman, because Tiamat is actually a dragon. To make war against evil is to carry out the will of the gods. Wink worries that mass media indoctrinates our young during their most vulnerable years. He makes a thoughtful point. On one hand, it seems implausible that video games like *Doom* could ever directly cause teenagers like Eric Harris and Dylan Klebold to gun down their classmates at Columbine High School. On the other hand, the doctrine of Christ's incarnation bears witness to our need for living, embodied examples of a new humanity that refuses to fight fire with fire. The authority of Christ derives not from might or power but from the Spirit. The way of Christ is the way of self-emptying love. The horizon of human history is not our *Doom*. It is hope.

MARK HAYSE

# Goth

You see them in almost every urban environment. People with heavily dyed, raven black hair; black clothing that is often ripped and layered; tattoos and piercings; slightly androgynous makeup (eye makeup in generous amounts is used by both sexes); heavy boots; and chains, belts, crosses and skull jewelry. They are Goths, a subculture that emerged in the UK in the early 1980s, a result of the splintering of the punk rock scene of the 1970s. Goth seems to have taken its name from a 1981 music magazine article titled "The Face of Punk Gothique." Goth is characterized and connected by specific associations in music, aesthetics, and fashion. It is one of the longest-lasting youth subcultures and shows no sign of abating.

Though the current incarnation is linked to developments in popular music and culture, the roots of the movement go much deeper and find their way back to eighteenth– and nineteenth-century England. The rise of the gothic novel during that period seems to have been a response to dramatic changes in cultural life. The rise of scientific rationalism erased confidence in religion, the industrial revolution shifted societal values, and long-held views of the world were challenged. The gothic novel addressed the shortcomings of the modern world by infusing it with tales of horror and the supernatural. The novels were filled with archetypes: virgin maidens, heroes, tyrants, fools, clowns, clergy, and monsters, all used as critiques of the way society was moving. The setting of these novels was equally important; they were usually situated in some gloomy castle or monastery, buildings filled with secrets. The gothic novel would not exist without the dark landscape as backdrop for the unfolding story, darkness being the key element in gothic literature and, as we can see, in contemporary goth culture as it manifests today.

Gazing at the ruins of European castles, the young romantic writers of the early nineteenth century added another layer to the gothic world. The movement's exponents included Lord Byron, Samuel Taylor Coleridge, and particularly Mary Shelley, whose novel *Frankenstein* is perhaps the most famous gothic novel of all. Note that Mary Shelley was a teenager when she wrote *Frankenstein*. Perhaps adolescent interest in the macabre transcends generations.

A strong anti-Catholic thread is woven into gothic novels, most of which are set outside of England, which had replaced Catholicism with Protestantism. The Catholic Church is always depicted as corrupt, as are its representatives—gothic novels are full of shady clergy and unchaste monastics who hide behind the authority of the church and prey on the innocents. Much like contemporary incarnations of the gothic, these first threads of gothic ideology were deeply distrustful of the status quo and the powers that be, suspicious of progress and modernity, and transgressive in their attitudes toward the mysterious, the sensual, and the sacred.

Goth culture as it emerged in late-twentieth-century Britain is but another iteration of the original gothic movement. Similar sentiments manifest: distrust of the status quo; a lack of desire for modernity; a deep fascination with the underbelly of modern life; and a mistrust of organized religion (contemporary gothic culture is suspicious of most organized forms of Christianity but remains surprisingly open to Christian faith itself, hence all the crosses and religious jewelry). The androgyny so often present in goth culture hints at the transgressive nature of its sexual attitudes. The black clothing, which tends to be gender-indifferent, is yet another signal. Goths inhabit the shadow world of modern life—in it, but not of it.

Other forms of the gothic emerge in popular horror films and apocalyptic disaster films. These movies confront us with our worst fears, whether it is the horror of modern city life rampant with murderers and serial killers or mass destruction via alien invasions, natural disasters, or evil criminal empires. The films are means by which we can confront our fears about modern life. Like the early gothic novels, horror movie plots often reappropriate elements of life that we claim to have left behind in our march into modernity—curses, the demonic, vampires, cannibals, haunted houses, and zombies. (The German term for Goths is *Grufties*—tomb creatures.)

Goth culture has always been about exploring not only the transgressive but also that which is not of the now—it is a rejection of the present state of society and culture and a search or desire for something beyond. Goths serve to remind us that we should not judge by externals and that clues about the true state of things lurk in the shadowy areas of popular culture.

BARRY TAYLOR

# Damien Hirst

Provocateur Damien Hirst placed sharks in formaldehyde, sawed rotting cows in half, and grew maggots under glass. He called it art, his critics called it stunts, and yet art buyers gobbled it up. No contemporary artist has focused more on death as a means of financing an extravagant life.

Damien Hirst was born in Bristol, England, in 1965, and grew up in Leeds with his mother and stepfather. In 1986 he was accepted onto the BA Fine Art course at Goldsmiths College, London, graduating in 1989. As a student he worked in a mortuary, which influenced his interest in the theme of death. In his second year, Hirst conceived, organized, and promoted "Freeze," an exhibition held in a disused Docklands warehouse. This event became the starting point for the "Young British Artists" movement.

Art collector Charles Saatchi attended this and future shows, where he was transfixed before the piece *A Thousand Years*, which depicts a rotting cow's head in a glass case along with maggots that feed off the cow, develop into flies, and are killed by an electric insect zapper. Saatchi bought the piece, becoming a patron who pumped money into Hirst's career, giving him a blank check to do whatever he could conceive of next. Hirst responded with a shark in formaldehyde, titled *The Physical Impossibility of Death in the Mind of Someone Living* (1991).

Throughout the following years, Saatchi continued to collect and commission Hirst's work. Some of the more notorious pieces include:

1. *Pharmacy* (1992), a life-size recreation of a British pharmacy
2. *Mother and Child (Divided)* (1993), a cow and a calf sliced in half in formaldehyde
3. *Away from the Flock* (1994), a dead sheep in formaldehyde
4. *Hymn* (1996), a gigantic head and upper body, based on an anatomical model of the human body

Between exhibits, Hirst made time to record a number one song for the 1998 FIFA World Cup with the band Fat Les. "Vindaloo" mocked the rallying cries of soccer hooligans but became an anthem nonetheless. Seemingly everything Hirst touched turned to gold.

Does Hirst use shocking, sensationalist materials in his works? No doubt. Is he very rich? No doubt. Is there intrinsic artistic worth in his most notable works? No doubt.

First, neither words nor pictures can do this artist justice. Being confronted with the works can be an overwhelmingly visceral experience. Whether working on a room full of butterfly wings fashioned into life-size Rose Windows or a reposing creature suspended in liquid, Hirst is the quintessential fin de siècle artist of the twentieth century. But where the last century had Edvard Munch and Gustav Klimpt expressing the public's psyche in paint with themes of anxiety, sex, and love, this generation has Hirst with themes of sex and death.

His work invites significant questions about religion. He labeled a cabinet full of pharmaceuticals *God*. He created a giant sculpture of *The Virgin Mother*, showing what was happening in utero as a cross section, in scientific detail. He reimagined *St. Sebastian* as a cow, tied to a rod and pierced by arrows. *The Sacred Heart of Jesus* was portrayed as a bull's heart, penetrated by needles and scalpels. He recast an eighteenth-century human skull in platinum, covered it in £15,000,000 worth of diamonds, and called it *For the Love of God*. Is he mocking our irreligious era, highlighting where our real treasure resides? Hirst's pieces are brutally stunning. His art reminds us that we are part of a system of life, death, and rebirth; that we are relational creatures, with only a short time to touch each other's lives. He salutes the history of religious art, while actively remaking it in his own direct terms.

As his fame has risen, Hirst has increasingly retreated from his earlier days as a wild child of British art. Since the birth of his children, he has spent most of his time at a farm in Devon. In 2003, Hirst had a public rift with his benefactor, Saatchi, and bought back a number of his pieces at market value. He took his art directly to the public, no galleries or benefactors needed. Damien Hirst will continue to create art that inspires, awes, or revolts, but it will never be anything less than engaging and frightening.

GABRIEL FERRER

# Michael Jordan

Michael Jordan, a leader of the Chicago Bulls in the 1980s and 1990s, redefined not only the sport of basketball but also the role of the superstar athlete in American popular culture. As Frank Deford wrote in *Sports Illustrated*, "what has made Michael Jordan the First Celebrity of the World is not merely his athletic talent, but also a unique confluence of artistry, dignity and history." Prior to Michael Jordan, athletes used to endorse shoes. After MJ, athletes wanted companies to build a new shoe (or even an entire clothing line) around them.

Jordan, born in 1963, grew up in a middle-class family in North Carolina. He pursued his love of basketball in high school and then at the University of North

Carolina at Chapel Hill, where he helped his team win the NCAA Championship and left after three years to join the NBA. Jordan arrived on the NBA stage in 1984, fresh out of North Carolina as the third overall pick for the Bulls in the association's deepest amateur draft. In 1986 he left his first major mark on the professional game, facing off against the Boston Celtics and their all-world forward Larry Bird. Having spent most of his sophomore campaign on the sidelines with a foot injury, Jordan scored forty-nine points in game 1 of the opening round playoff series and exploded for sixty-three points in game 2, losing both to a more experienced team. Regardless of the outcome, Bird could only shake his head at the press conference, victorious and still confused, as he said what everyone else was thinking: "I think it's just God disguised as Michael Jordan."

Jordan went from being a man to a brand, and from an icon to an empire. He defined the business of basketball as much as he defined the sport. His aerial assault changed how the game was played in the 1990s, as everyone hoped to live life above the rim. As impressive as his dunks were, his patented fade-away jumper was impossible to perfect and harder to defend. He had the stats, the titles, the awards, and the fanfare. By 1993, he had led the once-lowly Chicago Bulls to three consecutive NBA championships, becoming the first player to be thrice named Finals MVP. What could stop him?

Gambling allegations dogged him. His compulsive drive to win extended off the court, to the tables of Atlantic City. And one month after the 1993 championship, the father he loved, James Jordan Sr., was shot and killed during a car robbery. Michael Jordan announced his retirement. His number 23 jersey would be retired. A pall hung over the Bulls' new arena, the United Center. The house that Michael built felt empty.

Having conquered the NBA, Jordan sought a new challenge. He put on baseball cleats, playing for the Chicago White Sox—in the minor leagues. Evidently, his father, James Jordan Sr., envisioned Michael as a baseball player. Yet, Jordan's tall, lean frame seemed ill suited to the batting cage. He hit for a modest .202 average. When it came to baseball, Michael's athletic abilities proved limited.

His return to the NBA late in the 1995 season resurrected the Bulls' championship hopes, but they fell to the Orlando Magic in the playoffs. Jordan redoubled his efforts, and the Bulls once again claimed three consecutive NBA titles. Jordan burnished his legendary status in game 6 of the 1998 finals, securing the Bulls' victory over the Utah Jazz with a steal, sinking the come-from-behind, winning shot with only seconds remaining. Jordan had carried the Bulls to a "three-peat, repeat."

But Jordan was more than an athlete. His ability transcended basketball and sport, race and class, and eventually Nike, a company built on his image.

He had style, wearing a suit and tie to an office where most men wore shorts. When he shaved his head, others followed. He had a wide smile for his fans, an angry stare for his opponents, and an aura that was all business. He defined manhood in the 1990s.

Jordan empowered the next generation of NBA stars to be more than they hoped they could be, to work hard and be perfect. When Carmelo Anthony joined Nike, he declared himself Jordan's "student." Dwyane Wade, Kobe Bryant, and LeBron James, like many others, wanted to believe in his deity. A generation of people strived to emulate Jordan, believing they could "be like Mike" if they drank enough Gatorade and ate enough Wheaties. Nike's famous ad spots claimed that "it's gotta be the shoes," so people bought the shoes, millions of pairs. But with all the effort there still hasn't been another Michael Jordan. There may never be. We all fall short.

MATTHEW KITCHEN

# Left Behind

In 1995, Tyndale House, an evangelical Christian publishing company, took a chance on an apocalyptic novel called *Left Behind*, the first in a proposed series. One of the coauthors, Tim LaHaye, was well known as a conservative evangelical theologian and author of several dozen books. The other was Jerry Jenkins, who had described himself as "the most famous writer no one's ever heard of"; he had ghostwritten highly successful sports biographies but did not achieve similar sales with the fiction he had published under his own name.

Tyndale hoped to sell around 75,000 copies of the first novel. Yet the story—which centered around a group of recognizably human characters who were forced to confront life after a sudden rapture that removed all true Christians from the earth and ushered in a painful period of tribulation—unexpectedly caught on. In part, this early commercial success was due to the negative publicity generated by fellow evangelical Christians who strongly disagreed with the time line of Jenkins and LaHaye's premillennial vision. By denouncing *Left Behind* to one another and the media, its detractors inadvertently created buzz about the book, publicity that was compounded by other readers who loved the novel's combination of theology and potboiler suspense.

By mid-2008, the Left Behind series had sold a combined 63 million products, including sixteen adult novels, dramatized audio versions, a children's series, and spin-off devotionals. At the peak of excitement about the series, four Left Behind novels sat on the *New York Times* bestseller list, an astonishing feat since the *Times* did not canvas sales from Christian bookstores.

Several theological themes emerge from a close study of the series. First, the novels express confidence about the exact time line of apocalyptic events that are ambiguous in the Bible. Characters who become Christians after the rapture are ever after one step ahead of events; using the Bible as a calendar, a map, and a how-to guide, they are able to recognize the rising antichrist and anticipate further disruptions, such as the Four Horsemen of the Apocalypse. In contrast, the followers of the outwardly charming Nicolae Carpathia, the antichrist, hail him as a hero who will rebuild and unite the world in the wake of the traumatic rapture. Even by the eighth novel, *The Mark,* they remain tragically deceived, despite the fact that Carpathia, who has been resurrected from the dead, is now indwelt by Satan. The novels are thus a form of Christian Gnosticism, in which a select few are privy to the most important sacred teachings, while the masses stubbornly fail to understand.

A second theme of the series is its intense evangelism. Within the story, characters discuss conversion to Christ as "making the transaction"; conversion is presented almost as a business deal in which believers promise to align themselves with God's will and oppose the machinations of the antichrist. In return, although God cannot grant them protection against the apocalyptic storms unleashed on the world in accordance with prophecy, his followers get the promise of eternal salvation and peace—a heavenly reward glimpsed at the close of the twelfth novel, *Glorious Appearing.* Of course, the point of the series' many sermons, conversations, and prophecy discussions is to convert the real-life readers for whom the fictional characters act as stand-ins. The series' evangelistic purpose is didactically entrenched in every plot line to urge readers to embrace the Christian message before it is too late.

A final theme is the interplay of hope and hopelessness throughout the series. In one sense, *Left Behind* and its successors express a dystopian cynicism about the world and its future prospects: humanity stands condemned and no amount of good works can change the apocalyptic future God has foretold, complete with plagues, earthquakes, and death on a massive scale. At several points, the novels debunk the notion that merely being a good person or doing good deeds can effect salvation. Good works count for little or nothing, while "making the transaction" of an individual evangelical Christian conversion represents the difference between heaven and hell. On the other hand, many readers find the novels hopeful in the simple (perhaps simplistic) way they restore the power to make that transaction to any individual believer. No priest, no political leader, no intermediary stands between any Left Behind character and his Bible. However, what might seem to be a commitment to *sola scriptura* is more a supra-scriptural reading—something that goes beyond the text and in the end stands outside it.

JANA RIESS

# Nelson Mandela

The Chilean writer Ariel Dorfman once made the point that for all his immersion in the question of memory, he could not remember when he first heard Nelson Mandela's name. This is likely true of many of us; the iconic struggle and achievements of the dominant political figure of the late twentieth century are so embedded in the culture of a generation of people that we may think of Mandela as a kind of global grandfather (just as the rainbow nation of South Africans is apt to refer to him affectionately by the tribal honorific "Madiba"), without ever really facing the monumental nature of his suffering and impact on humanity. Freedom concerts, truth and reconciliation commissions, and impersonations by Morgan Freeman aside, Mandela's fight and his victories are indeed monumental.

Born in 1918 during the last months of the First World War as the son of a tribal elder who died when Mandela was nine years old, the man who would free a nation showed early promise by completing school work a year ahead of time; and he revealed a revolutionary streak by responding to an upcoming arranged marriage by fleeing to the big city. The enshrinement of apartheid policy by the ruling white Afrikaner National Party in 1948 coincided with Mandela's immersion in politics. He joined the African National Congress (ANC) campaign, rejecting laws that segregated black and "coloured" people and serving poor defendants as a lawyer.

While influenced by Gandhian nonviolence, not least the need to avoid shredding the dignity of your opponent in pursuing your own cause, Mandela eventually became the leader of the ANC's armed wing Umkhonto we Sizwe (MK). Against the threat of sporadic, unorganized violence and the assertion that the transformative potential of nonviolent struggle had been exhausted by a culture of reactive legislation, the transition to organized violent means appeared inevitable, for its supporters at least. Restraining violence in the aftermath of such horrific state repression as the 1960 Sharpeville

Massacre, in which sixty-nine black people were shot dead by the police, seemed impossible. MK's strategy, at first limited to infrastructural sabotage, eventually, after Mandela was imprisoned, gave way to MK targeting and killing people; it is characteristic of Mandela that he criticized his own party when it attempted to sanitize the historical record of the struggle by deleting its own human rights violations in the report of the Truth and Reconciliation Commission.

In 1964, after a long trial on charges that would not exist if apartheid had not been state policy, Mandela was sentenced to twenty-seven years in prison and removed to Robben Island, a boat ride from Cape Town. Conditions were barbaric. His work in a shadeless lime quarry permanently damaged his eyes; he was permitted to receive only two letters and visitors every *year*; his cell was smaller than the average American half bathroom. A neighboring cell mate wrote despairingly to his own wife that he could no longer remember her face. It is a common error to downplay Mandela's involvement in violence so as to uphold his peacemaking; this is as unhelpful as romanticizing his prison experience. It was not revolutionary romance. It was hell on earth.

And then—the miracle. Having been arrested before President Kennedy's assassination, he was released in 1990, with George H. W. Bush in office. Twenty-seven years—a few eras, really—had passed, and he was now an old man. His long walk to freedom, which seemed at the time to be the final insult of a government dragged kicking and screaming to the negotiating table, became a symbol of ultimate dignity—the freedom fighter victorious, making his own way to his own destiny.

What was astonishing is that spending nearly half his life behind bars had not left him bitter. In fact, his refusal to endorse deadly violence and his disavowal of revenge helped South Africa avoid a full-blown civil war. He spent the next twenty years shaping a new, fragile nation, and ended up as the personification of political grace. Mandela had become a man who knew how to turn insecurity into the impetus for inner liberation, a man who knew that the only way to transform poisoned relationships is for one party to start nurturing the other and who embodied Pascal's notion of the healing man: one who is able to sit still and think for ten minutes before speaking. He was a man out of his time, but whose time needed him like oxygen. We may not remember when we first heard his name, but we should remember who he is.

GARETH HIGGINS

## *The Matrix*

Culture critic and philosopher Slavoj Žižek says that *The Matrix* functions as a Rorschach test in which all perspectives and beliefs can be found. He goes on to compare watching *The Matrix* to looking at "the proverbial painting of God, which seems always to stare directly at you, from wherever you look at it—practically every orientation seems to recognize itself in it." With all of the theological, technological, and philosophical issues being tossed around in *The Matrix,* it is easy to see why the film has been such a common topic of study and debate and why people are still interested in its content since its release in 1999.

*The Matrix*, a sci-fi action movie written and directed by Andy and Larry (later called Lana) Wachowski, is the first of a trilogy that includes *The Matrix Reloaded* (2003) and *The Matrix Revolutions* (2003). Keanu Reeves stars as a computer hacker, Thomas A. Anderson, who is known by the alias "Neo." After receiving a cryptic message on his computer about "the Matrix," he is introduced to famous female hacker named Trinity who claims that a man named Morpheus has all the answers Neo is looking for. When Neo finally does meet Morpheus he is given a choice between two colored pills: a blue pill that will return him to the old life that he has known or a red pill that will allow him to fully learn the truth about the Matrix. After taking the red pill, Neo wakes up in a pod filled with slime and connected by cables to a column that supports hundreds of similar pods. Morpheus and his crew take Neo on to their ship, the Nebuchadnezzar, and begin to explain to him the new reality he has just awoken to.

Neo finds himself in a time close to the year 2199, in which machines have won a war against humans and are harvesting people to use as their energy source. The world that Neo previously knew is actually a simulation created by the machines called "the Matrix," which is intended to keep the humans they are harvesting docile. Morpheus leads a resistance team that unplugs humans from the Matrix. He believes that Neo is "the One" prophesized to end the war and free all of the captive humans. Neo is trained to understand and manipulate the Matrix through simulations so that once he reenters the virtual world of the machines he is able to have abilities that defy normal physical limitations. He is taught that there are agents inside the Matrix whose purpose is to protect the simulation and are able to possess any "plugged in" body in order to eliminate the threat. Much of the trilogy is taken up with Neo's struggle to defeat these agents.

The complex plot was wrapped in a remarkably stylish package. Neo's long, black, leather coat shimmered under city lights. The bullet-time effects employed for a rooftop shootout thrilled moviegoers. The gravity defying fight scenes set a new standard for action films. The Wachowskis borrowed from the best of cyber-punk, Japanese anime, and Hong Kong martial movies to create a startling, cinematic game changer.

*The Matrix* was at first embraced as a messianic allegory with Neo being the Christ figure amid traditional Christian illustrations such as Trinity, Nebuchadnezzar, and Zion. However, as the trilogy unfolded there were many references to Hinduism, existentialism, and Buddhism that made the original Christian claim of the film seem too narrow a scope. What *The Matrix* does provide us is an example of the bricolage of how thought and belief systems interact and function in a postmodern age. The film can be seen as another interpretation of Plato's allegory of the cave or Calderón de la Barca's *Life Is a Dream*. Even though some language is taken from the Christian world, it is intermingled with the Greek mythology of Orpheus and Buddhist thoughts on enlightenment. All these streams of thought and faith systems are intermingled into one story, displaying how popular culture now processes and engages contemporary religious pluralism.

STEVE SUDUTH

---

## Mitford Series and Jan Karon

When Chariot Victor, a small Christian publishing house, brought out Jan Karon's first novel in 1994, no one predicted that the Mitford novels would be a phenomenon: by the time Karon (1937- ) decided that she had "said everything I had to say, done everything I had to do with Mitford," she'd written a nine-installment series (picked up by Penguin in 1996) of *New York Times* bestsellers, not to mention numerous spin-offs: Christmas gift books; a cookbook; a Mitford bedside companion, which includes crossword puzzles; and a commonplace book (in two volumes). The final Mitford novel was *Light from Heaven*, published in 2005.

The novels follow an Episcopal priest, Father Tim Kavanaugh, as he ministers to his friends and neighbors in Mitford, North Carolina (a thinly disguised Blowing Rock). Over the course of the novels, Father Tim gets married, takes in some stray children, wrestles with his own childhood demons, carries on a correspondence with his cousin, gardens, tends to the dying, makes meatloaf, becomes something of a father figure to his maid, prays, preaches, and reads a lot of poetry.

The novels are not heavy on plot; they are heavy on faith. "In my books," Karon has said, "I try to depict not a glorious faith with celestial fireworks, but a daily faith, a routine faith, a seven-days-a-week faith. Father Tim's faith is part of his everyday life. . . . I try to depict how our faith may be woven into our daily life, like brandy poured into coffee. I believe that spirituality needs to be basic, common, everyday." Several bedrock evangelical themes pervade the novels. Among other things, Karon stresses the authority of Scripture—a theme made clear in the first chapter of the debut novel *At Home in Mitford*, when Father Tim is adopted by a large stray dog. Said dog doesn't respond to normal canine commands; rather, he sighs with contentment and docilely sits down every time he hears a verse from the Bible. Evangelism and conversion also figure prominently. In *At Home in Mitford*, for example, Father Tim counsels a stressed-out businessman, who eventually prays "the sinner's prayer." It turns out that a jewel thief on the lam was hiding in the church attic; he overheard Father Tim's ministrations to the businessman, and he too prayed the prayer, turning his life over to Jesus, and, eventually, to the police.

On the surface, Father Tim is the main character of Karon's novels, but the real protagonist of the series is Mitford itself. As literary critic Scott Romine has noted, readers meet Mitford even before they meet Father Tim. Mitford is unspoiled, a place set apart. Neighbors are friendly; eccentricities are lovable and loved. It is a town that, in the words of its mayor, "takes care of its own." Karon herself understands that the small-town feel, the sense of community, is what energizes the novels: she says she wrote to "give readers an extended family."

But the community so powerfully depicted in Mitford has come in for criticism. Reviewers and critics, including a reviewer for *Christianity Today*, have chided Karon for creating a small-town community that is virtually all white.

Emily Satterwhite has connected the Mitford series to other middle-brow, late-twentieth-century novels set in Appalachia, such as Adriana Trigiani's Big Stone Gap trilogy. This subgenre of feel-good Appalachian fiction, argues Satterwhite, "reassured white high-middlebrow readers of the presence of Appalachia as a refuge for 'real' American values, folkways, and racial homogeneity."

This is not just a sociological but also a theological point: the novels, in the words of Caryn D. Riswold, fail to portray "the idea of Christian engagement with the world—the church as prophetic presence in the world."

In other words, the Mitford books will never be mistaken for social gospel novels. Karon's characters are primarily focused on the pursuit of personal holiness and good relationships with one another (and sometimes the pursuit of a therapeutic healing of wounds inflicted by difficult family situations). Redemption involves, among other things, stitching together children who have been cast to the four winds by parents who couldn't care for them, or getting sober after many years on the bottle. That redemption is found, implicitly or explicitly, through Jesus Christ. To wit, a pointed scene in *Shepherds Abiding*, in which Father Tim sets out to restore a badly damaged nineteenth-century crèche: an angel was missing a wing, a camel was short an ear, and the three kings needed noses and crowns. "One needn't be a Leonardo da Vinci to see that the whole parcel needed redemption, save for the Babe, whose figure in the attached manger was amazingly unharmed." In Mitford, Jesus redeems, and he uses ordinary people like Father Tim and his fellow Mitfordians in the process.

LAUREN F. WINNER

## Philip Pullman and His Dark Materials

G. K. Chesterton, the eminent nineteenth-century Christian apologist, likened his quest to find out what he believed to that of searching for a heresy and discovering Christian orthodoxy. Philip Pullman, born in 1946, follows an analogous course in his fiction. In the midst of his criticisms of Christianity and its institutions, he ends up affirming self-sacrificing love and the message of Jesus.

Pullman spent most of his childhood in North Wales. In his early career he served as a teacher, including eight years at Westminster College, and now writes full-time. While he has authored over twenty books, including the Sally Lockhart Quartet, the His Dark Materials trilogy is the most famous, honored, and controversial of them all.

*The Golden Compass* (originally published as *Northern Lights* in 1995), *The Subtle Knife*, and *The Amber Spyglass* set out to rewrite the story of Milton's *Paradise Lost*. Instead of Satan being the diabolical power in rebellion against the benevolent God, His Dark Materials assumes that God is actually an imposter, merely the first and most powerful angel that assumed such titles as God; the Almighty; and, the most prominent, the Authority. This Authority built churches and Magisteriums throughout all parallel worlds to impose his will on everything and everyone.

This background sets the stage for the story in His Dark Materials, where the girl, Lyra Belacqua, becomes critical in overcoming the Authority. While the great powers of the worlds gather to wage war against the Authority, Lyra focuses on saving her playmate Roger Parslow, who has been kidnapped. This task leads her to help others, including the armored bear Iorek Byrnison; the Gypsies; the people of Cittàgazze; the shadows imprisoned in the Land of the Dead; and, ironically, the Authority himself. She is aided on her quest of compassion by her daemon Pantalaimon, an animal distinct but indivisible from Lyra; her unique ability to read an alethiometer, literally a truth meter that resembles a golden compass; and two friends from a different world—Will Parry, who becomes the wielder of the subtle knife, and the ex-nun Mary Malone, who creates the amber spyglass.

Lyra discovers that the only way to help her friends is also the way to save all the parallel worlds from the Authority's tyranny. She must help restore Dust, the source and substance of everything. The Authority and his cruel institutions have strangled the creation of Dust, and his attempt to rule all possible worlds has opened holes between worlds that suck out Dust. His Dark Materials reaches its climax when Lyra decides to have all the holes between the worlds sealed up, even though it means that she will be forever separated from Will, her true love. She sacrifices her own desires in order to bring peace and freedom to everyone else.

Pullman's trilogy thus concludes that the way to overcome evil in the world is through self-sacrificing love, a surprisingly Christian response for someone the *New Yorker* said was "one of England's most outspoken atheists." Although the Catholic League—an advocacy group that fights anti-Catholicism in U.S. culture—was publicly critical of Pullman's work, the Archbishop of Canterbury, Rowan Williams, said the trilogy should be included in religious education classes, while the editors of the neoconservative journal of religion and politics, *First Things*, called the story "an Almost Christian Fantasy."

Following the His Dark Materials trilogy, Pullman has continued to engage Christianity. In *The Good Man Jesus and the Scoundrel Christ*, his subsequent literary foray into religion, Pullman tells the tale of twin brothers—one Jesus who preached compassion and the other Christ who distorted this message in order to establish churches and religious hierarchies. The book continues Pullman's exploration of the themes in His Dark Materials: the primacy of loving one another and institutions that distort this message. One can imagine that *The Book of Dust*, Pullman's promised companion to His Dark Materials, will continue to develop these subjects.

Although Pullman's His Dark Materials series is intentionally set in opposition to C. S. Lewis's The Chronicles of Narnia—both stories begin with a girl entering a wardrobe, but Pullman has the girl returning to her world rather than entering another one—perhaps their legacy is very similar. Both explore the drama of faith and love; of good and evil; and, in doing so, both offer engaging stories.

JASON KING

## *Rent*

"*Rent* was born of loss," producer Jeffrey Seller said. Initially famed for the death of its young creator, Jonathan Larson, the night before it opened in 1996, *Rent* ran for thirteen years, becoming the fifth-longest-running show in Broadway history when it closed September 7, 2008. It grossed close to $300 million and won every major best musical award, including the Tony Award, New York Drama Critics Circle Award, Drama Desk Award, and the Outer Critics Circle Award. It also won the Pulitzer Prize for drama, one of only seven musicals to ever do so.

But its impact ran wider than awards and profit. It introduced live musical theater to a new generation, and for these "Rentheads" it was a life-changing communal experience. Benjamin Hicks, an original cast member, said as much when he returned to the final cast. "It's not just a show. It changed my life." Audience members used words like sacred, ritual, and community to describe what they had seen. Sobbing was common during performances.

It sounds oddly familiar. A group of people on the fringe of society creating new community around a legacy, having their lives changed, and going on to tell others. Is *Rent* really a musical about starving artists with raging social consciences trying to find meaning on the brink of death? Or is it about something more universal?

This musical transcends its story and medium, becoming communal ritual and a near-religious experience for its audience. In lyrics, cultural references, character arcs—even in staging the party song "La Vie Boheme" like da Vinci's *The Last Supper*—it seems haunted by the true-myth of Christ's presence, his life-crushing death, and impossible resurrection.

Not everyone agrees. Many within church circles have dismissed *Rent* as a celebration of carnality and promotion of homosexuality. Looking mostly at the behavior, addictions, and lifestyles of the characters, they miss the heart of this musical. They also miss a bounty of parallels and references to Jesus and his teachings. They miss the Christlike Angel, the transvestite who does nothing but love, encourage, and make peace. They miss the Christmas choruses that humorously critique how we treat the homeless. They miss the dozens of lyrics cut and pasted from Scripture. In the musical, Mimi begs, "Light my candle." In the Bible, Jesus celebrates, "He who lights a candle." They sing Jesus' words, "Let he among us without sin be the first to condemn." Both Jesus and the *Rent* cast cry out, "Don't forsake me." And finally, "How do you measure a life?" they ask. Their answer and Jesus' whole message is the same: "How about love?"

Jesus isn't preached in *Rent*, but the essence of the gospel is incarnated in these characters who, like the disciples, represent the least of the least. Can the grace of God be found on a stage of transvestites and drug addicts? Is it blasphemy to suggest a transvestite dying of AIDS as the figure most like Jesus? Not if Jesus indeed came to love sinners and dine with tax collectors. This Jesus does not speak exclusively to the rich, religious, and righteous.

"*Rent* is one of the most beautiful celebrations of life that exists," final cast member Renee Elise Goldsberry said. With its songs rooted in questions like "how we gonna pay," "how do you measure," "how about love," "why am I the witness," "will I be alone," and "will I lose my dignity," *Rent* proclaims the yearning of a generation to find community among those who will take them for who they are, love them, and help them discover a worthy measure of their days. On the brink of death, with nothing more important to question than the very purpose of their life, they find the answer Jesus gave—love—and sing it loudly, asking us to count the minutes of our lives. *Rent* is a haunting cry for glory and significance, for community and worth, and an echo of the very questions that drove Jesus to the cross and the disciples to their knees.

R. W. BONN

## *SimCity*

*SimCity* popularized the so-called "god game"—a real-time strategy simulation in which the player guided and directed the emergent growth of a digital ecology. First released in 1989, *SimCity* set up the rules and tools. The player then put them to work as a virtual city planner. One-half education and one-half entertainment, *SimCity* captured the imagination of young and old alike. Zoning and budgeting. Building up and tearing down. Police stations. Public utilities. Rivers, roads, and rails. As the game evolved minute by minute, little "Sims" gradually moved into the neighborhood to take on a life of their own. Some cities sprang up from farmland, while others grew from preloaded scenarios such as San Francisco, Boston, and Rio de Janeiro. In these preloaded scenarios, the player had limited time to prepare for eventual crises such as earthquakes, nuclear power plant meltdowns, and widespread flooding. From a bird's eye view, players constantly scanned north, south, east, and west for critical environmental needs to address before chaos broke loose. A series of graphs, charts, and Sim opinion polls communicated the health and well-being of *SimCity*, while a complex arrangement of buttons, cursors, drop-down menus, and on-screen icons allowed the player to plan the next stages of development.

In contrast to the immediacy of a first-person shooter like *Doom*, *SimCity* felt like a very abstract—even impersonal—game. Seen only from a distance, no single Sim had a real life of her own. Statistical trends directed game play, not life stories. *SimCity* was a virtual ant farm, a digital hive, a collective swarm lacking individual personalities. Some players let their games run all night long, just to see how *SimCity* would develop by daybreak. *SimCity* is not the first commercial god game in the video game canon. That honor belongs to Mattel's relatively simple *Utopia* (1982) for the Intellivision. However, *SimCity* eventually led to *The Sims* (2000)—undoubtedly one of the best-selling PC video games of all time. To date, *The Sims* has sold sixteen million shipped copies. All games in *The Sims* franchise have sold over eight times that number.

Apparently, *Wired* editor Kevin Kelly is right: "Godhood is irresistible." Designer Will Wright created *SimCity* after a now-legendary experiment with his first game, *Raid on Bungeling Bay* (1985). *Bungeling Bay* was a very ordinary shoot-'em-up, a top-down scroller in which would-be helicopter pilots pummeled military islands with heavy ordinance. Bored with his own work, however, Wright decided to write a utility program that would design the islands all by itself. Surprising even himself, Wright kept tweaking the island-building utility even after finishing the game. He explains, "I had a lot more fun building the islands than I had destroying them. Pretty soon I realized that I was fascinated by bringing a city to life." Without intending to, Wright stumbled across the intoxication of *creatio ex nihilo* (creation out of nothing)—or at least the next best thing to it. Through a complex code of algorithms and equations, video game life emerges in the playful image of its creator. Of course, as all who play with toy soldiers and building blocks come to know, wreaking havoc on creation brings deep satisfaction too. After all, the Lord gives, and the Lord takes away. In *SimCity*, gods who grow weary of creating can unleash their own natural (and unnatural) disasters, just to see what happens.

Is this what being God is like? Switching back and forth between divine persuasion and divine coercion like an impetuous child? Conceiving of the universe as a binary system ultimately reducible to ones and zeros? Hopefully, video game metaphysics do not accurately mirror the nature of divine-human relations. In video game worlds, the exhilaration of creation inevitably gives way to the tedium of management. Tedium produces disinterest, and disinterest fosters loathing. And once *that* incurable disease sets in, the only cure is the off-switch, perhaps preceded by a bit of gleeful sadism. Why not start over again? After all, they're just Sims.

Thankfully, Hebrew Scripture foresees a day when divine *shalom*—not divine wrath—will fill all Creation. Christian Scripture tells of a divine, suffering love that acts sacrificially to reconcile all things. Turns out we human beings are more than just Sims after all. We bear the *imago Dei*—a sacred mixture of one-part relationship and one-part creativity, bound together by love. Would it be too much to suggest that our fascination with video games may reflect that image somehow? Nonetheless, our best works are ever outdone by a divine covenant love that will not let us go. This is the gospel. Good news indeed.

MARK HAYSE

# Quentin Tarantino

When Quentin Tarantino was twenty-eight years old, he made a film about seven men who rob a diamond store and get killed or kill each other. While planning the robbery, they eat breakfast together and discuss the morality of tipping waitresses. At one point in that film, *Reservoir Dogs,* it's revealed that one of their members is an undercover cop. Popular tunes of the 1970s flutter in and out of the background, one of the men gruesomely tortures another, and they all look great in black suits, white shirts, and black ties. A new force in filmmaking was born, Puritanical moralizing was inspired, and a generation of film students knew whose work they now had to live up to. *Reservoir Dogs* (1992) had opened the floodgates of Hollywood financing to Tarantino, and a couple of years later he produced *Pulp Fiction*, a dizzying narrative labyrinth of crime in Los Angeles. The ultraviolence, cheesy music, and self-referential dialogue about pop stars and burgers were wheeled out again, but this time with extra aplomb and a bigger budget. But more than that, Tarantino conjured a fully realized, imagined world in which women are archetypally beautiful or duplicitous, and men are either warriors or weak.

It was as if a bomb had exploded in the lobby of every theater in America—cinema was changing forever. Audiences had never seen a mainstream film so in tune with their own pop culture sensibilities that was also so literate, dependent even, on a continuum that could include both the highbrow films of Jean-Luc Godard and the kung-fu silliness of the Hong Kong-based Shaw brothers. And more important, the narrative structure of *Pulp Fiction* risked alienating the public by jumping around as if time didn't matter at all. The last scene of the movie includes a character walking away intact and happy from a crime scene, but twenty minutes earlier we had seen the same character die at the hands of one of the film's several antiheroes. Tarantino was making a film whose structure felt like the way we experience life. It's incomplete, and it's not always clear who the protagonist is. We rarely realize the moments of greatest significance while they are happening to us, driven by the desire to stay afloat in an uncertain world.

Even the violence of *Pulp Fiction* found an antidote to its detractors. Sure, we see horrific things happen to bad people, and we are even invited to revel in it, but this is a film that climaxes with its central character repenting of his own murderous instincts, using a (paraphrased) speech from the book of Ezekiel, of all things. Los Angeles in *Pulp Fiction* looks like the kind of place where anything can happen, to anyone, at any time; which, of course, it is—whether you're an aspiring starlet just arrived on the bus from Indiana or a murdered partygoer victimized by the selfish, idiotic cruelty of the Manson family. It's the kind of place that cries out for redemption and justice.

It's too easy to write off Tarantino's films as the attention-grabbing cries of an adolescent sensibility or the violent fantasy projections of an underdeveloped mind: *Pulp Fiction* is a film that makes fun of people doing stupid things and presents a man walking away from killing as its most heroic act. Tarantino's later films are variations on the theme of how to survive ordinariness without losing your soul; in *Kill Bill* (2003), maternal instinct transcends all others; in *Inglourious Basterds* (2009) the very representation of war on screen is satirized as a poor substitute for actually doing something about conflict between people.

Tarantino is not necessarily wise, but he is smart—very smart. His films, more than those of any other single director, are the most obvious standard-bearers for what happened to cinema after the 1980s blockbuster gave way to the rise of indie films in the 1990s. They gave audiences an appetite for something meatier; they made us laugh at ourselves; and they injected even the most depraved scenario with nothing less than an adrenaline shot of the holy. Tarantino's films were in the world, but not of them; but once they were unleashed, they created a new world of their own.

GARETH HIGGINS

## Tupac Amaru Shakur

Tupac Amaru Shakur (1971–1996) is one of the most renowned rap artists of all time. His reputation has grown even with a generation that might not have been alive during his rise to fame. *Rolling Stone* magazine identified him among the top one hundred musical artists of all time, and his albums have sold more than seventy-five million copies around the world. What is his appeal?

Tupac lived what he spoke and sang. He communicated with all who were downtrodden and set apart from society, and he was a mouthpiece for those who had no voice. His music, poetry, and presence created a sense of hope, vision, and a realistic approach to life that connected with his devoted fans. Perhaps most profoundly, Tupac created a link between God and humankind. He was an irreverent, profane, natural theologian. In an interview he stated:

> God has cursed me to see what life should be like. If God wanted me to be this person and be happy here, he wouldn't let me feel so oppressed . . . he wouldn't let me feel the things I feel, he wouldn't let me think the things I think. So, I feel like I'm doing God's work, you know what I'm sayin'. Just because I don't have nothing to pass around for people to put money in the bucket don't mean I ain't doin' God's work . . . because ain't these ghetto kids God's children?

Tupac was a prophetic voice for his generation. He expressed a quest for meaning and hope in the midst of suffering—issues that are universal and timeless. He was the visual articulation of an ongoing generational divide. However, he also represented the nihilism, despair, and dystopian worldview that so many experience every day. Tupac was both sides of the coin: a hopeful visionary riddled with despair and pain. He asked, "If you're in hell, how can you live like an angel?"

Tupac spoke to "thugs," which for him meant those who were downtrodden, those who did not have anything, those who were without hope. The acronym THUG LIFE meant "The Hate U Give Little Infants F**ks

Everyone." NIGGA for him meant, "Never Ignorant Getting Goals Accomplished." To these acronyms that he derived from thug culture, Black street culture, and ghetto-centric reality, he endowed a kind of religious passion that edified those who lived the THUG LIFE or who identified as a NIGGA, and gave them a transcendental force (a connection to God). They were cooperating with the best forces of the universe. Blacks were not the only ones who connected with this message. Asians, poor Whites, Latinos, and Africans also saw in Tupac's music a contextualized pathway to both their problems and to God.

Tupac's iconic image did not die on September 7, 1996, when he was fatally shot by three men in Las Vegas. His death nearly a week later made him into an even bigger presence on the American pop culture landscape. Walk by almost any open-air market and you will see Tupac's face on a pillow, shirt, cake, or even a tattoo. When Tupac died, Tony Danza, Mickey Rourke, James Belushi, and Madonna were just some of the celebrities in mourning. They recognized his powerful impact. Many were astounded knowing how much Tupac had accomplished in only twenty-five years.

Tupac's life was marked by well-publicized arrests, including a controversial and contested prison sentence for sexual assault, and he was often in the news for lyrics that appeared, on first glance, to promote violence. Even so, Tupac shared common ground with Jesus. Both were hated and despised by church officials. Both had issues with untrustworthy friends. Both had prophetic messages that were not received well by the cultures of their times. Both spoke truth and light into people and systems. And both died violent deaths, which left a remarkable imprint on society. Although Tupac was in no way a Christ figure, there was a socio-theological connection between Tupac and Jesus. Tupac felt that Jesus related to and understood the poor. Jesus comprehended the nitty-gritty elements of life as he lived them. Religious dogma made Jesus inaccessible or out of reach. Through his music and poetry, Tupac created new pathways to Jesus.

It is easy to ignore someone like Tupac because of his obvious derisive posture and media-enhanced disrespectful attitude. But when we go a little deeper, we are able to see much more than "F bombs" and illicit sexuality. We see a person admitting his sins openly, embracing his humanity, and attempting to make the connection to God.

DANIEL WHITE HODGE

# Joss Whedon

"Note to self: religion freaky." This statement from *Buffy the Vampire Slayer* (1997–2003) could in fact sum up the religious approach of series creator Joss Whedon in all of his television programs to date: *Buffy, Angel* (1999–2004), *Firefly* (2002–2003), and *Dollhouse* (2009–2010). Whedon, a third-generation television writer and professed atheist, continues to cycle back to questions of self-sacrifice, redemption, the nature of evil, and the perils of "group think." His groundbreaking television series have appeared to be of two minds about religion. Without exception, they expressed grave suspicion of religious institutions (and indeed, almost all institutions, including government), but also without exception, they celebrated what *Buffy* coproducer Marti Noxon has called "a yearning for belief."

On *Buffy*, cosmic possibilities seem limitless on the one hand—there are untold demigods, demons, and alternate dimensions (including a land of perpetual Wednesday)—but the show is decidedly close-mouthed about a capital-G God. In the fourth season, for example, vampires take over a church, a building they have always feared as powerful, even lethal. But the place turns out to be "nothing," one sniffs. "Where's the thing I was so afraid of . . . you know, the Lord?" God in the traditional sense is absent from the church; there isn't even a priest or minister to be found. There is, however, a vampire slayer who strides in as a savior to the hostages in the pews. In the Whedonverse, "God" is to be found in human acts of moral courage, as people risk everything for others.

This humanism extends to the show's treatments of religious leaders. Whereas other television series have often depicted clergy in a positive light (e.g., *7th Heaven*), the Whedonverse typically regards religious leaders with suspicion. *Buffy*'s third season opened with an episode about a street preacher who literally sucked the life out of the teenagers in his ministry, and the final season's supervillain was a defrocked killer priest (deliciously portrayed by Nathan Fillion), powered by regular infusions from a pure, primordial First Evil. *Angel*, *Buffy*'s darker spin-off series, took an even more skeptical turn in its fourth season, when a goddess named Jasmine (Gina Torres) engineered various machinations to obtain a human birth and take over the world. Under her spell, Earth's inhabitants committed all manner of evil in the name of establishing world peace. The episode "Shiny Happy People" exposed the dangers of religion as a form of mind control, as Jasmine subtly hypnotized everyone around her and caused them to believe that the evil they were perpetrating was actually for the greater good. In that story arc, people believed that the world had become a happier, better place, but the cost was the loss of all free will—to a deity who was more likely to eat humans than protect them.

In all of Whedon's television series, the theme of redemption is paramount. On the futuristic *Firefly*, a smuggler's spaceship is populated by a motley crew of individuals trying to flee old lives and build new ones, from former soldier Captain Mal (Nathan Fillion again) to wunderkind River Tam (Summer Glau), whose formidable intellect has already unleashed dangerous powers in the imperial Alliance and within River herself. Notably, one of the characters on *Firefly* is Shepherd Book (Ron Glass), the closest Whedon ever gets to a positive portrayal of clergy. But Shepherd is fleeing a past himself, finding in a simple monastic spirituality the moral courage he perhaps did not demonstrate when he was in the upper echelons of the Alliance. All these characters are seeking redemption, which in Whedon's world is sometimes forthcoming but just as often slightly out of reach.

Whedon has stated that all of his series wind up focusing on what it means to create a family. In *Buffy, Angel, Firefly*, and *Dollhouse*, disparate people (as well as vampires, witches, aliens, and demons) often discover that the most powerful family is the one you choose for yourself. Family for Whedon is the incomparable connection that can exist only among those on the margins, fighting impossibly powerful establishments. They have only each other for understanding and much-needed gallows humor. In all four shows, the series finales depict what becomes possible when such an unstoppable "family" chooses to fight against evil and for one another, often at the cost of their lives. If this can be called religion (and why can't it?), then all four series are infused with deep spiritual power.

JANA RIESS

## *The X-Files*

The *X-Files* premiered on FOX in 1993 with FBI agent Fox Mulder (David Duchovny) working on a series of unexplained and unsolved cases known as the x-files. Believing wild, "crack-pot" theories of aliens, ghosts, and the supernatural, Mulder starts down a long road of uncovering government conspiracies and discovering proof of the supernatural.

But Mulder isn't alone. The bureau has assigned the scientist, medical doctor, and FBI agent Dana Scully (Gillian Anderson) as Mulder's partner. They hope Scully will discredit Mulder's unorthodox investigations and reports by offering a more scientific perspective of these x-file cases. Within the first five minutes of the series, we are introduced to what will become a love affair between science (reason) and faith.

Throughout nine seasons of banter between the modernist Scully and postmodernist Mulder, the unlikely duo forms a bond, trusting only each other. This bond grows stronger as they fall deeper into an intricate web of deceit that reaches not only into the FBI but into a global shadow government known as the Syndicate. This Syndicate is bent on hiding the truth about the existence of Extraterrestrial Biological Entities (E.B.E.s), and their plans for the human race, by dealing in misinformation and fabricated "truths."

*The X-Files*, created by Chris Carter, became a huge cultural phenomenon, earning the record of longest-running sci-fi series in U.S. television history, at nine seasons. (It was later surpassed by *Stargate SG-1* with a ten-season run.) Out of 102 award nominations, the show won twenty-six awards across a wide range of categories, including editing, acting, music, and even makeup design.

The *X-Files* has influenced countless other TV writers hoping to expand the complexity of plot lines within the television medium. These include J. J. Abrams's series *Alias* and *Lost*, with their intricate mythologies; Joss Whedon's *Buffy the Vampire Slayer;* and Russel T. Davies's *Torchwood* (a BBC series spin-off of *Doctor Who*). All three men have claimed inspiration from Chris Carter's world of paranormal investigation and comprehensive plot lines. Mulder and Scully even made character appearances on an eighth-season episode of *The Simpsons*, titled "The Springfield Files." Ranked as the second-best cult TV show by *TV Guide*, and as the fourth-best piece of science fiction by *Entertainment Weekly*, the *X-Files* has truly made its mark in cultural history.

Many "X-philes" (a term describing fans of the show, from the Greek root *philos*, meaning love) were intrigued by the premise that faith and science could coexist. With slogans like "I Want to Believe" and "The Truth Is Out There," this show was a perfect setup for exploring the epistemological process of finding truth; defining truth; and asking, ultimately, if we'd be happy knowing the truth.

There is a pivotal moment in the second *X-Files* feature film, *I Want to Believe*, where Dana Scully has a frank discussion with ex-Catholic Priest Joseph Crissman debating a theology of forgiveness and the validity of his priesthood. Scully believes this man is lost, with no chance for redemption. Father Crissman believes his psychic abilities were granted by God, to help solve murders and gain redemption (as penance) for having molested altar boys many years ago. While Crissman is repentant, regardless of his sin's absolution, consequences still linger. The sins of the past do affect the present and the future, and it may be possible that Crissman's actions led to the very case our agent-duo is investigating.

Like all good, classic *X-Files* endings, we are given the questions and then left to discover the answers for ourselves. Instead of giving away his answers, Chris Carter seems to understand Jesus' words to "seek and ye shall find." When we read the slogan "The Truth Is Out There," it is not to boldly claim that we have all truth right here. No, truth is something we must work to find; it will not be simply dropped in to our laps.

"I Want to Believe" also bolsters the seeker's journey. This is not a journey with a mind so open that one would accept anything without reason. This is a journey where faith meets skepticism and the facts lead the believer just as the believer encourages the skeptic to question and discover. The *X-Files* therefore asks us to embrace mystery *and* absolute truth. So be willing to seek, for the truth is out there.

ERIC BUMPUS

# The Oughties

$A$s the third millennium dawned, our faith rested in technology. Broadband made it possible for us to interact with each other anywhere at any time, to explore and express ideas, to buy and sell online, and to research anything via the Internet. We experienced the world from the comfort of our chairs. Services provided by Google, Facebook, and Twitter became so ubiquitous that they became verbs. YouTube allowed users to broadcast themselves, no matter how mundane or arcane the subject. Apple's sleek designs made iPods indispensible friends. Cellular technology transformed our phones into multimedia devices—we listened to music, played games, watched movies, and accessed the Internet with complete, wireless mobility.

Globalization benefited many countries, especially China, India, and Brazil. These new economic powerhouses reconfigured the socioeconomic shape of the world. The Human Genome Project confirmed our connections on a micro level. America elected its first African American president on a campaign that utilized social media and graffiti art.

A new generation embraced the throwback innocence of *High School Musical*. *Glee* blended sexual experimentation and eclectic spirituality into a musical mashup. (Only in *Glee*'s rarefied air could an episode like "Grilled Cheesus" make utter sense.) File sharing devastated the music industry, allowing fans to download entire music collections via BitTorrent. DVR technology undercut the TV business with viewers zipping past formerly pervasive commercials. Audiences flocked to computer-generated fantasy films like *Shrek*, *Finding Nemo*, and *Avatar*. Hollywood turned to comic books (*Spider-Man*), toys (*Transformers*), and theme park rides (*Pirates of the Caribbean*) for "new" ideas. The affordability of digital cameras and editing allowed documentaries like *Bowling for Columbine*, *Super Size Me*, and *An Inconvenient Truth* to achieve unprecedented social impact. With Catholic priests in the news for cases of sexual abuse, author Dan Brown tapped into suspicions regarding church authority to elevate the sacred feminine in *The Da Vinci Code*.

It was a time of environmental upheaval, even as eco-consciousness became part of our daily lives. Nature reminded us of its fury—tsunamis in the Pacific Rim devastated Thailand and Indonesia, Hurricane Katrina wiped out New Orleans, and huge earthquakes rocked China, El Salvador, and India, to name only three.

But the Oughties will be remembered for the rise of global terrorism. The 9/11 attack on the World Trade Center—followed by additional bombings in Bali, Madrid, London, and Mumbai—brought religion back to the forefront of public life. The twentieth century had consigned religion to the private sphere, but these terrorist attacks, rooted in the rise of global fundamentalism, thrust religion back onto the world stage. The "new" atheists like Sam Harris, Richard Dawkins, and Christopher Hitchens decried religion as the root of what ails us. Nations responded to terrorist threats with lengthy and protracted wars in Iraq and Afghanistan and an obsession with security. A global financial crisis followed in the wake of overspending and fear. Religious literacy became an unlikely currency in a highly mediated era.

# Banksy

Banksy is an anonymous British street artist, activist, filmmaker, and leading figure in the contemporary street art movement. He works with various mediums, including stencils, paint, print, mixed media, and site-specific installations. His art is politically charged and socially minded, often combining his signature stencil technique with sardonic aphorisms, irony, and satire in order to critique prevailing power structures and socioeconomic inequalities. Common targets include capitalism, imperialism, authoritarianism, war, and pollution.

Banksy was born and raised in Bristol, England, sometime in the early 1970s. He became an active graffiti artist amid the Bristol underground, an ethnically diverse subculture known for its awareness of racial tensions and hybridity, in the early 1990s. The movement fostered the development of hybrid musical genres such as Drum 'n' Bass and Trip Hop. Some observers contend that the sparseness of Banksy's stencil style and his sensitivity to social issues typify the ethos of the Bristol underground scene.

Banksy also cites the Situationist International, a Marxist avant-garde artists' collective that used a subversive technique called détournement in the 1950s, as a significant influence. Détournement endeavors to turn expressions of capitalist systems, such as advertisements, against themselves by altering their meanings through subversive pranks and juxtapositions. In his book *Wall and Piece,* Banksy writes, "Any advertisement in public space that gives you no choice whether you see it or not" is "yours to take, re-arrange and re-use." He has proclaimed that the true vandals are the corporate institutions that endeavor to make us feel like we are defective unless we purchase their products.

Banksy's art is not limited to critiques of consumerism. His work consistently assumes an antithetical posture of resistance toward authoritarian systems and institutions that he views as propagators of social injustice, inequality, and oppression. In *Wall and Piece*, Banksy claims that, "The greatest crimes in the world are not committed by people breaking the rules but by people following the rules. It's people who follow orders that drop bombs and massacre villages. As a precaution to never committing major acts of evil it is our solemn duty never to do what we're told, this is the only way we can be sure."

Banksy has employed this spirit of anarchism in attacks on the institutionalized art world, which he views as an elitist enterprise comprised of the "trophy cabinets of a few millionaires." In the early 2000s he mocked the system by performing a series of subversive acts that involved sneaking his own works of art into museums such as the Louvre, Tate Gallery, and Museum of Modern Art. More recently, Banksy has turned his gaze to the street art scene itself, directing the Academy Award nominated film *Exit through the Gift Shop,* which met with some controversy concerning its legitimacy as a candidate for the Academy Award for Best Documentary Feature. Banksy's subversive proclivities led many to question the viability of the film, and some maintain that the film is indeed a hoax.

The artist's allegiance to anticapitalist principles has also been questioned by critics who observe that prices for his works at auction have commanded upwards of half a million dollars. In a 2007 interview with *The New Yorker,* Banksy said that he was uncomfortable with the money his work commanded, stating, "I don't think it's possible to make art about world poverty and then trouser all the cash, that's an irony too far, even for me." In the same interview he made the incredible and unverifiable claim that his solution was to give all the money away.

Whatever the case, it is clear that Banksy's sympathies lie with the oppressed and disenfranchised. The anonymity the artist maintains allows his work to function as a sort of urban lament, providing a voice of protest against a myriad of social injustices. In 2005, he produced a series of paintings on the Israeli West Bank barrier depicting the efforts of Palestinian children attempting to circumvent the wall of concrete that stands between them and the Holy Land. In the scene, one little girl tries to use helium balloons to carry her over the wall, while a boy endeavors to traverse the boundary by means of a painted-on ladder. That same year, the artist produced a series of stencils depicting tortured Guantanamo Bay detainees in Cuba, London, and New York, indicting the powers that be by writing their sins, quite literally, on the wall.

CHRISTOPHER MIN

# David Beckham

Football (soccer) star David Robert Joseph Beckham OBE (Officer of the Order of the British Empire) was born in Leytonstone, England, in 1975 and has become one of the most recognizable sports figures on the planet. Since debuting at age nineteen for Manchester United in the English Premier League in 1995, Beckham has enjoyed major success with a number of football clubs and at one point was captain of the English national team. He became one of the highest paid footballers in the game when he signed a three-year deal with Manchester in the late 1990s and has continued to generate a huge income through contracts and endorsement deals throughout his career. His earnings culminated with a contract worth an estimated $6.5 million a year when he signed with LA Galaxy to become the figurehead for American soccer in 2007.

Having emerged through the ranks of youth soccer, he honed what were to become his signature abilities—dazzling passing skills, precisely placed long-range free kicks, and a spot-on crossing ability—through a lifelong commitment to training. Rumor has it that he used to practice barefoot in order to gain a sense or feel for the ball. So legendary is his ability that a 2002 movie, *Bend It like Beckham*, showcases his influence. The movie tells the story of Jess, the young daughter of Punjabi parents, who is infatuated with soccer and overcomes parental resistance and gender biases to achieve success. The film hints at the larger import of Beckham, for it is not only his ability on the field that makes Beckham a phenomenon but the fusion of a number of things (sport culture, celebrity power, and commodity culture) that make Beckham a global celebrity whose fame transcends the sport that gave rise to him. In November of 2003, he was declared the Greatest Pop Culture Icon in the world on the VH1 cable network's show of the same name, above Elvis Presley, The Beatles, Madonna, Martin Luther King, and a host of other figures.

When the LA Galaxy signed David Beckham in 2007, his celebrity was evident in the welcome he received. Los Angeles heralded his arrival not only by the usual round of press conferences and sports-based interviews but also by celebrity-hosted parties and a frenzied, paparazzi-driven outpouring of almost cult-like fascination with his every move. His debut game for the Galaxy was a celeb-fest, with everyone from Tom Cruise and Katie Holmes to then-Governor Arnold Schwarzenegger in attendance. His celebrity wife, Victoria Beckham of Spice Girls' fame, only added to his star power and cultural fascination.

But perhaps the most interesting aspect of Beckham's influence lies off the soccer pitch where he honed his gifts and made his career. He has contributed to the redefinition of masculinity in the late twentieth century. Beckham is perhaps the first footballer to attract large numbers of female fans in what has traditionally been a male-dominated sport. It has been said that men want to be him, and women want to be with him. Men admire him for his athletic gifts, which he has always linked to hard work and relentless commitment to excellence, but he has also been very forthright about his love of style and fashion. He appeared publicly in a sarong and is famous for continuing experimentation with his own hairstyle. He has also championed male grooming such as eyebrow waxing and facials. "I'm not scared of my feminine side, and I think a lot of the things I do come from that side of my character," declared Beckham in his 2000 biography, *My World*.

Beckham is also a renowned family man, frequently photographed in the role of husband and devoted father, ferrying his children to school and accompanying them on after-school outings. None of this is particularly radical or out of the ordinary, but his celebrity power has been instrumental in countering typical gender stereotypes and collapsing old perceptions about what it means to be male. Personal grooming and beauty products have long been seen as more feminine, but Beckham has succeeded in breaking that view and creating a new man—commonly termed "metrosexual"—who values attention to appearance, personal grooming, and the discovery of manhood in actions and attitudes that have long been dismissed as not part of what it means to be truly male. This element, even more than his sporting ability, is Beckham's greatest contribution to popular culture.

BARRY TAYLOR

## *The Daily Show*

Few would have predicted that Comedy Central's blockbuster series *The Daily Show* would rise from a spoof of network newscasts to become the primary news source for a generation alienated by politicians and the reporters who enabled them. It began modestly in 1996 with host Craig Kilborn, who seemed content to upgrade his mockery of pop culture from *Talk Soup*. But Kilborn clashed with the creator of *The Daily Show*, Lizz Winstead, and her growing interest in political news. Kilborn's exit made room for Jon Stewart to slip behind the desk in 1999. Stewart emerged as "satirist-in-chief" during a remarkably contentious decade in American politics.

*The Daily Show* has been an anchor for Comedy Central, generating more than 2,000 topical episodes. It earned numerous Emmy Awards for the sharp writing team led by executive producer Ben Karlin. It also spawned the best-selling *America (the Book): A Citizen's Guide to Democracy Inaction,* whose audio version won a Grammy for Best Comedy Album. *The Daily Show* launched correspondents Stephen Colbert, Steve Carell, and Ed Helms into major comedy careers. In 2005, *The Colbert Report* was spun off as a pointed satire of partisan news programs like *The O'Reilly Factor*. The unwavering braggadocio of the Colbert character grew into its own cultural phenomenon, with fans forming "The Colbert Nation."

While some may reduce *The Daily Show* to a mockery of newscasts and the political process, Stewart and his creative team became motivated by more than laughter. In an era of post-Monica-gate cynicism, Democratic and Republican party conventions provided ample material for satire. *The Daily Show*'s election coverage, "Indecision 2000" (and 2004, 2008, and 2012) offered authentic bite, with correspondents securing genuine scoops. Stewart has interviewed countless senators, cabinet members, and heads of State. What inordinate influence for a self-proclaimed "faux news" program.

After the traumatic events of 9/11, *The Daily Show* took a hiatus during a time of national mourning. Stewart returned as the voice of New Yorkers and Americans changed by a daunting day. Once the United States went to war in Afghanistan (2001) and Iraq (2003), *The Daily Show* offered a sober dose of sanity. A prophetic purpose emerged in the wake of the Defense Department's near media blackout with *The Daily Show*'s coverage of a "Mess O' Potamia."

Stewart's most galvanizing television moment may have occurred on somebody else's show. In 2004, he took the hosts of CNN's *Crossfire*, Tucker Carlson and Paul Begala, to task for not reporting the news in a conscientious and insightful manner. He insisted, "You're doing theater when you should be doing debate." Stewart pleaded, "Stop, stop, stop, stop hurting America." *Crossfire* was canceled shortly after Stewart's appearance. Yet some questioned whether *The Daily Show* could hide behind claims to be a fake news program when guests like John Kerry were campaigning for elected office.

Stewart and Colbert eventually dropped nonpartisan pretense with their "Rally to Restore Sanity/March to Keep Fear Alive." Held on the Washington Mall one week prior to the November 2010 election, the rally lampooned Glenn Beck's earlier "Restoring Honor" event. Stewart's stated goal was to convince a polarized America to "take it down a notch." While the rally included plenty of humor, Stewart concluded with an unvarnished "moment of sincerity." The satirist had crossed over into statesman.

While Stewart acknowledges his Jewish roots on a regular basis, he has not made overt connections to the biblical prophetic tradition. He speaks truth to power, or at least exposes hypocrisy wherever it may appear. Stephen Colbert draws on his Catholic social teaching to maintain his satirical edge. In his testimony before Congress on behalf of farm workers, Colbert referenced

Jesus' advocacy for the least of these in Matthew 25:40. He has also named Jesuit priest Rev. James Martin the "official chaplain" of the Colbert Nation.

What other network news program retained a "senior theology correspondent" to report on "This Week in God"? While televangelists provided countless clips in the early days of *The Daily Show*, all faith traditions eventually filled the five-minute segments. After pressing the seemingly random generating "God Machine," correspondents chided Jews, Catholics, Protestants, Mormons, Buddhists, Hindus, Muslims, Scientologists, and even atheists. *The Daily Show* is an equal opportunity offender.

Viewers tempted to lose faith may find some comfort in the concluding "Moment of Zen." While such moments sometimes veered toward the absurd, they also left space for life's unexpected surprises and joys. While corrupt politicians or preachers may cause us to question life's purpose, glimpses of the silly, the significant, or the sublime could give us a reason to tune in tomorrow.

CRAIG DETWEILER

## *Extreme Makeover*

Promising to be the ultimate ugly duckling transformation, *Extreme Makeover* was a plastic surgery reality TV show that aired on ABC from 2002 to 2006. Participants volunteered to undertake a physical renovation that took place over several weeks. The show developed an "Extreme Team," made up of the best and brightest in their respective fields, including plastic surgery, cosmetic dentistry, eye surgery, personal training, and hair and makeup artistry. Participants were average Americans who wanted to improve their physical appearance, because as the show pointed out, who hasn't wanted to change something about themselves?

*Extreme Makeover* brought a somewhat forbidden topic into mainstream culture, celebrating the changed participants' new look with a big "reveal" to friends and family. This public visibility was a dramatically different response to plastic surgery, especially compared to the hush-hush nature of clients using back doors and denying that they had "work done." *Extreme Makeover* invoked strong responses, from those who found the normalcy of plastic surgery to be an outrage to those who were relieved to acknowledge that appearances matter. *Extreme Makeover* was the precursor to the many shows featuring plastic surgery that emerged around the same time, including

*The Swan*, *Nip/Tuck*, and *Dr. 90210*. It also spun off into the stories of familial hardship that featured in *Extreme Makeover: Home Edition*, which has been far more successful than its original predecessor.

The *Extreme Makeover* phenomenon prompts intriguing reflection on the issue of beauty. Swiss theologian Hans Urs von Balthasar offers an interesting perspective in his seven-volume series, *The Glory of the Lord*. He introduces the term "theological aesthetics" to describe the concept of divine love. His assertion is that just as Christian revelation is absolute truth and goodness, so also is absolute beauty. This vaguely echoes Plato, who asserted that every experience of beauty points to infinity.

This approach to a theology of beauty showcases the beautiful as a reflection of God's creative handiwork and as such will point the viewer toward transcendence. Beauty is not seen as a superfluous notion, but as a revelation of God's redeeming work in the world. It seems that this idea may interact with the theological concept of common grace and that beauty points to God's grace.

If, in fact, God is in favor of beauty, how does this shape a theological understanding of the beauty industry? For example, how does liposuction point to God? Theoretically it seems that the human form itself would qualify as a beautiful work of God's creation, yet there are divergent perspectives on beauty as it applies to the human body within the scope of religious faith. Some think that making major changes to one's appearance encourages conformity to cultural ideals of beauty. Others contend that because earthly bodies are temporary, it is of little importance whether major changes are made or not. However, this issue is much more complicated, especially when considering instances of reconstructive surgery, which, in some cases, are permitted within certain religious perspectives while purely cosmetic improvements are frowned upon.

The human quest for identity, autonomy, and belonging in some ways is tied to appearances. Presentation of oneself is a rich source of signification. It serves as a first impression and a visual, nonverbal communication of personhood. It also signifies status as well as belonging. Appearance and presentation are avenues to convey or discover who one is by means of self-expression and provide an opportunity to participate in a broader cultural experience.

Ironically, the process of identity formation involves a long period of blending in to fulfill the need of belonging, which is most visually expressed through personal presentation of fashion and adornment. At times these visual presentations are not very personal, as the choices made can be dictated by advertising and peer influences, yet simultaneously are very intimate because of the close ties to the very core of identity. To dismiss appearances as extracurricular to the human experience is to irresponsibly and inappropriately bypass a crucial piece of developmental formation. At the same time, finding the significance of one's personhood solely in appearances and cultural ideals of beauty can be equally damaging. As with most complex issues, theological discernment is of indispensable importance.

MINDY COATES SMITH

# Facebook

In February 2004, Harvard sophomore Mark Zuckerberg launched an online social network called "The Facebook," the name inspired by the yearbook-style guides given to incoming students at many colleges to acquaint them with their new classmates. Over the next seven years, Facebook morphed from a small Harvard staple to a worldwide revolution. It spread first to other universities and high schools before opening to the public in 2006. Spanish and French versions were launched in 2008; within two years, it was available in more than 70 languages. By July 2010, the site boasted 500 million active users, half of whom had joined within the previous year. Seventy percent of its users lived outside of the United States, and it had become the second most visited site in the world, trailing only Google. Months later, Facebook's founding was the topic of a critically acclaimed film, *The Social Network*, and Zuckerberg was named *Time*'s Person of the Year. In 2011, more than thirty billion items (such as links, photo albums, and blog posts) were "shared" by users each month, and the site was widely credited with inciting the Egyptian revolution.

   Given all these facts, it would not be an exaggeration to say that Facebook has revolutionized the way the world interacts. Facebook makes it possible to spread personal information at a viral rate, all without any form of direct human contact. A simple change of relationship status is sufficient to inform all of one's friends about an engagement. A user can view pictures from a friend's birthday party that took place the night before on the other side of the country or the world. A status update can notify friends of a bad day, an illness, a terrible breakup. Users don't even need to be proactive in order to find this information—it is all available for their consumption as soon as they log in, when their News Feed displays recent and discussion-generating posts. Thus, thanks to Facebook, the spread of personal information has significantly increased while the need for personal contact to obtain this information has drastically decreased, which raises interesting questions about the nature of intimacy and relationships in the present day.

Facebook also has implications for public discourse, as news information via links and status updates can also be disseminated at warp speeds. In addition, the "comment" feature on status updates, notes, and shared items allows for discussion among friends of friends from all over the country and the world. Thus, Facebook provides unprecedented opportunities for the dispersion of ideas and information and for dialogue about these things, both locally and globally.

Facebook's widespread popularity is a testimony to human desires for identity and relationships. Users' profiles provide them with an opportunity to create an identity for themselves, shaped by the interests and activities they choose to share, the books and movies and music they like, and the pictures they choose to post. The amount of time and energy that is invested into fashioning these profiles attests to the desire of individuals to be known, and to be known as accurately as possible. It is important to note, however, that the personas created are not as much reflections of who the users are—though there are certainly elements of that on every page—as who they would like to be. Rarely has large-scale impression management played such a prominent role in society. With regard to forming relationships, Facebook provides an incredibly easy way to stay connected with others. One click of a button joins a user with another person indefinitely. Staying in contact is just as simple; all it takes is a quick note on a friend's wall; a message; or even a "poke," for which no words are needed. The opportunities for connection that Facebook provides, and the zeal with which its users utilize these functions, illustrate humans' inherent desire for relationship. Individuals in every generation have their own ways of making themselves known and connecting with other people, and Facebook is a prominent way in which these desires are manifested today.

Not all is rosy, however. The amount of information people can disclose on Facebook, and the amount that they can find about their friends without any personal contact, raises questions about voyeurism and exhibitionism in the present day. The rise of Facebook parallels that of reality television, in which subjects reveal their lives with surprising candor and viewers watch with morbid curiosity. Similarly, the inordinate amount of time spent on Facebook reflect the degree to which individuals today are willing to publicly disclose details of their own lives and the curiosity that they have about the lives of others. Facebook's seemingly impenetrable armor took a huge hit after it went public on the U.S. stock exchange in May 2012. Less than positive future earnings potential dampened Wall Street's fervor, and growing user concerns about the ownership of personal information are challenging Facebook's hegemony. But those darker threads have not diminished our fascination with self-disclosure and our desire for social capital. Regardless of Facebook's long-term outlook, we will never be the same again because of it, and privacy in some sense seems to be the remnant of a bygone era.

ELIZABETH LIN

# Got Milk? Ads

A simple question, "Got Milk?" became one of the most recognizable advertising campaigns in recent history. With more than 90 percent consumer recall, the involvement of over 250 celebrities, and a tagline that resulted in countless parodies, "Got Milk?" grew into a surprising pop culture phenomenon.

In 1993, the California Milk Processing Board hired a San Francisco-based ad agency, Goodby, Silverstein & Partners, to help revive flagging milk consumption. A television commercial focused on a lonely worker inside the Aaron Burr museum. As he listens to the radio and eats a peanut butter sandwich, he is surrounded by the answer to a radio contest about the famous duel between Burr and Alexander Hamilton. But when the radio station calls him for the answer, he runs out of milk to wash down his mouthful of sandwich and cannot be understood. He mumbles and shouts, "Awan Brur," to no avail. The haunting and comical question follows, "Got Milk?"

TV commercials featuring a range of everyday people who missed out on great opportunities because they didn't have milk to wash down sticky peanut butter or chocolate cake put the campaign on the cultural radar. But it was the creation of a series of print ads for national magazines that lifted the campaign into the success stratosphere. The National Milk Processor Board licensed the "Got Milk?" tagline in 1998 and launched a national print campaign, featuring celebrities, each with the now-familiar milk-moustache, expounding the benefits of drinking milk.

Unlike other campaigns that might be directed at a single demographic, such as teenagers or the elderly, "Got Milk?" aims at everyone, in all walks of life. The *Today* show's Meredith Viera tells busy, working women and moms that she stays strong by always making time to drink milk, because it is good for "your health . . . and your waistline." Teenagers get Miley Cyrus or ice-skater Michelle Kwan, extolling the virtues of milk as both a "cool" drink and a part of a healthy, strength-building diet. Men of all ages get rock stars, sporting heroes, and even Batman, telling them about the strength and body-building capacities of milk.

While the ads seek to reach every social demographic, they also employ a technique called buttonholing, in which it directly addresses the potential consumer as "you." "What can milk do for you?" the celebrity asks. It seems as though this well-known personage is addressing the single reader of the ad, and not the millions of others who are looking at the same thing. That personal connection adds more weight to the advice and encouragement that the celebrities offer us. And what are they offering?

The ads sell milk, but they also sell us views on health, well-being, and particularly body image. Many of the "Got Milk?" ads found in women's magazines focus on the potential of milk consumption to contribute to a sexy and desirable physique. The Meredith Viera milk ad portrays her holding an hourglass-shaped glass of milk—a popular way to capture female desirability. Though she is dressed conservatively, there is a hint of sexual provocation in her knee-revealing skirt, furthering the idea that drinking milk can make one svelte, sexy, and perhaps even famous. Men are subject to other messages. Singer Steven Tyler of Aerosmith tells us that milk can make "our bones rock hard," even beyond our youth.

Beyond the given of human physicality, our bodies are molded and shaped by our interactions with ideas and perspectives on the body. "Got Milk?" speaks directly to our culturally mediated sense of body. The celebrity presence in the ads functions as a voice of authority, directing us to what is cool and important, telling us how we should look and feel about ourselves. Milk is held forth not simply as something to drink but as a means to a culturally desirable end—a perfectly embodied self.

"Got Milk?" offers a model of physical perfection and a means to its achievement. The space between the ad's ideal and our own perceived shortcomings creates tension, providing the occasion for thinking theologically about the body. Our very sense of ourselves is subject to multiple layers of socioculturally constructed meanings. These must be acknowledged when we discuss embodiment. But our bodies are more than the product of media conditioning or influence. Our body is something we receive, not just something we construct. We must understand the meanings we ascribe to our bodies, but we must also interpret them in ways that nurture what we are given—both in relationship to God and one another.

BARRY TAYLOR

# Harry Potter and J. K. Rowling

In 1990, author J. K. Rowling was on a train from Manchester to London when she conceived the idea for the Harry Potter series. The story begins with the newly orphaned baby Harry being left on the doorstep of his Uncle Vernon and Aunt Petunia Dursley's home after his parents' deaths. Then the narrative skips ahead to Harry's eleventh birthday, when he receives an invitation to attend Hogwarts School of Witchcraft and Wizardry.

Harry soon learns not only that he had inherited magical abilities from his parents but that his parents had been murdered by the evil wizard Lord Voldemort and not involved in a car crash as his uncle and aunt had led him to believe. At this moment, Harry begins his journey to becoming a wizard. As he seeks the truth behind his parents' deaths, he discovers that he may be the "Chosen One," foretold in a prophecy, who would come to destroy Voldemort once and for all.

This fantasy series of seven books took the literary world by storm in 1997 with the UK publication of *Harry Potter and the Philosopher's Stone* and in 1998, with the U.S. version titled *Harry Potter and the Sorcerer's Stone*. Overall, the series has sold over 400 million copies, been translated into sixty-seven languages, and earned Rowling the title of first (and so far, only) billionaire author. With the main series, supplemental books, eight films, and a theme park at Universal Studios, the Harry Potter universe has been inextricably and permanently embedded into global culture.

But not everyone has been pleased by the success of Harry Potter. Many evangelical Christian groups condemned the story for its depiction of witchcraft. But where boycotts and book burnings have failed, a discussion of the series from a theological standpoint may prove beneficial to cultural interaction.

And perhaps, waiting to voice concerns until the end of any series would be better than jumping right in to voice complaints that may be inaccurate later. J. K. Rowling stated in a 2007 interview that the reason she did not respond to the religious criticism early on was because it would spoil the end of the story for her readers. So what is the story about?

On the surface, it is the age-old tale of good versus evil, but under the surface, Rowling has painted a picture of racial and ethnic discrimination within World War II. With Lord Voldemort's desire to rid the world of all but the "pure-blood" wizarding line, he gathers his Death Eaters to help him eradicate anyone who is half-blood or nonmagical (referred to as Muggles). There are clear undercurrents here of Adolf Hitler's genocide against the Jews in Europe in the 1930s and '40s.

This analogy is epitomized by the casting of the Malfoy family in the film series. Their blond hair and blue eyes could not be a better representation of Hitler's Aryan race. But, beyond the racial discrimination, Rowling also depicts the inequality between economic classes (the affluent Malfoys vs. the poor Weasleys). She continued her theme of inclusion post-series, attacking sexual discrimination by announcing that Albus Dumbledore, headmaster of Hogwarts and a hero of the series, was a homosexual. Rowling effectively demonstrates that all people have equal worth, value, and dignity.

Another theme of the series is power over death, which characters seek to achieve in radically different ways. Voldemort craves to conquer death in order to achieve immortality. In the first book, he hopes to attain the Sorcerer's Stone, which is said to grant immortality to the one who possesses it. By the end of the series, we learn that Voldemort had long ago split his soul into seven pieces, hiding them in various objects so that they could help him return to life should he ever die. He fears death above all else.

Harry and Dumbledore also exchange words about death and the afterlife in the final installment of the series. Harry reads two Scripture passages on the tombstone of his parents and of Dumbledore's mother and sister, verses which Rowling has stated sum up the entire series. The first is from Matthew 6:21 ("Where your treasure is, there will your heart be also") and the second from 1 Corinthians 15:26 ("The last enemy to be destroyed is death"). This latter passage alludes to a life after death, not a life without death, which is what Voldemort sought. At the end of the series, Harry emulates Jesus' self-sacrifice by giving himself willingly in order to save others, but he returns triumphant to vanquish evil once and for all. Here Rowling reveals her strong Anglican roots and convictions, as the series works through the mystery of death that affects all living beings.

ERIC BUMPUS

---

# iPod

*"The iPod is to music what penicillin was to medicine."*
*Paul McGuinness, manager of U2*

October 23, 2001, may have been a date lost in the infamy of the events of September 11 of that same year, but it is imbued with cultural significance for entirely different reasons. On this day, Apple, the Palo Alto-based software and computer company, released its new portable media player, the iPod. This product proceeded to change the way we listen to music and perhaps even our way of life. There were other media players before the iPod, but they tended to be big and clunky or small but with difficult or dysfunctional user interfaces. Apple saw a gap in the market and released its iconic player. It was designed to interface with the recently launched online music store iTunes, a computer application that allowed the user to purchase and manage audio and video on a personal computer.

Initial reactions to the device were mixed, with many critics complaining about the high price tag of $400, the lack of compatibility with Windows software, and the somewhat-unconventional scroll wheel—a novel means of accessing the information contained on the device. But regardless of the critics, the price and the incompatibility, the iPod was a success with consumers. Soon the white headphones signaling ownership of the device had become ubiquitous. By April 2007 Apple claimed sales of a hundred million of these devices, and it has become the dominant digital music player in the United States.

As Melville wrote in *Moby Dick*, there is a certain significance that lurks in all things, and the iPod has come to signify a number of key things. The iPod was distinct from the beginning. Like all Apple products, the design element was as important as the function. It was a vision of economic design and structural beauty combined with technical capability. It was small in size, using a 1.8" hard drive (while competitors were using 2.5" drives at the time), and initially available only in white, amplifying the clean, but not sterile, look of the product. It was simple: a small information screen, revolutionary central wheel giving easy-to-use navigation, a center select button and four additional buttons around the wheel, and nothing else.

Its form was so distinctive that it created a sense that users were holding a new category of object, which is exactly what they were doing. There had been nothing like this before. Religious attachment and devotion to Apple only grew.

In *The Language of Things*, Deyan Sudjic writes that an object becomes an archetype when it has a "form that can communicate what it does and what the user needs to do to make it work." The iPod didn't come with a huge instruction manual; the packaging and instructions were as concise and economical as the device itself. It was to be experienced, played with. One was supposed to interact with the device and feel one's way into using it.

While Steve Jobs made the headlines, German designer Dieter Rams influenced the design of the iPod and other Apple products. Rams's design philosophy was to eliminate the superfluous in whatever he was creating. A key part of his design process involved breaking down a design to its most functional while retaining a sense of beauty in form as well as use. In this aesthetic, Apple seems to have found a mentor, but its products have moved beyond that idea. The iPod feels good to touch and use, but it is also the herald of a whole new world of user interaction. The significance of a device like the iPod is that it brings together multiple technologies. It began life as a digital media player, but with the introduction of iPod Touch it has become so much more: a camera, a gaming platform, and an e-mail and text-messaging device. It is now a means by which we can access the world in ways inconceivable a few short years ago.

iPods tell us a story about ourselves and about the brave new world of digital culture in which we find ourselves. The company's brief to Chiat-Day, its advertising agency, was simply empower the individual. By beginning with *i*, the iPod put our tastes, our likes, our passions front and center. It helps us navigate the complexity and bewilderment of the information age. The iPod is a visual prop and a prophetic tool for managing the complexities of the present. The last-minute addition of a "shuffle" function, which allowed the device to play music randomly, became a metaphor for how we can manage chaos: one piece of information at a time, creating a personalized collage of all our various interests. Music buying went from a personal experience at record stores to an online transaction at the iTunes store. Singles made a comeback. We now held our personal soundtrack and playlists in the palms of our hands. Will music grow less communal and more individual? Only Apple knows for sure.

BARRY TAYLOR

## Lost

The complex six-year story arc of *Lost*, J.J. Abrams's acclaimed television drama, follows the all-too-human survivors of Oceanic Flight 815 from their crash in the Pacific on a mysterious island, through various dimensions. Dozens of books, novels, and blogs were spawned to deconstruct clues and theorize about story lines. Showrunners Carlton Cuse and Damon Lindelof created a Web site, the Fuseluge, to interact with die-hard fans and include them in the storytelling process. *Lost* delighted thoughtful viewers and demanded intellectual involvement. Devout fans formed a fervent cult following.

*Lost* is infused with religious and biblical references, names, symbols, and archetypal stories, from Mr. Eko's Scripture-etched Jesus stick to Charlie's

Marian and angelic visions to the Jacob and Esau (Man in Black) storyline. Statues of Egyptian deities such as Set are at home on the island. Eastern religious traditions are also explored, including Hindusim's ideas of karma, incarnation, and communal cosmic dreaming; and Buddhist teaching (Dharma), Sangha (community), reincarnation, and release from Samsara. Taoist symbols of yin and yang are especially prevalent in the Dharma Initiative propaganda and in the balance of negative and positive energy on the island. The character John Locke, one of the leaders of the Losties (the original group of survivors), embraces a nature mysticism that echoes Emerson's transcendentalism. Despite the proliferation of religious imagery (which continues to the very end of the show, where Jack and his father are conversing in front of a stained-glass window that depicts the symbols of multiple religions), the show eschews organized religion and is ultimately atheistic—there is no higher power in charge. "God's got nothing to do with it," according to Sawyer, the show's antihero. *Lost* replaces religion—or at least "Religion"—with individual freedom and determinism girded by human community.

What distinguished *Lost* from other finely crafted TV series was the depth of its theological and ontological questions. What is the purpose of human life? What happens when I die? Do we live in a moral universe? Is a higher power orchestrating my life, or am I radically free? Am I my brother's keeper? And most importantly, what is *really* "Real"? Survivor Dr. Jack Shephard's poignant question to his father in the penultimate scene is simply: "Are you real?" Closure comes, in a very Buddhist and Hindu fashion, when the main protagonist awakens to what is really real: his own mortality and his spiritual journey.

Among the many religious or philosophical themes interwoven into *Lost*'s plot, three emerge most prominently: redemption, free will versus fate, and the show's core value of human community. Damon Lindelof described the show as a tale of individuals "searching for redemption in the face of their flaws and struggles."

Jacob (a mortal infused with special powers and guardian of the island) had one cardinal rule: do not interfere with human free will. As he explains to Richard Alpert (Ricardis), he brings people to the island to prove to his brother (the nameless Man in Black, aka the Smoke monster) that humans are fundamentally good. When Alpert asks why he doesn't intervene, Jacob responds: "It is all meaningless, if I have to force them." Throughout the show, characters are faced with choices: whose group will they join, and whom can they trust? While the notion of fate vs. destiny rises especially in the quantum dynamics of season five, ultimately *Lost* argues that we are not pawns, but radically free creatures who make choices that matter. As

Desmond Hume explains to Charlie in the final bar scene: "There's always a choice." The cosmic variable is free will and decisive human action.

*Lost*'s moral imperative is that we need each other. Jack's original charge to the splintering group on the beach was, "If we can't live together, we're going to die alone!" Those who cut themselves off from community go mad: Rousseau, Claire, Jacob's mother, and Desmond in the hatch. Characters are not called to believe in a higher power but to believe in and love each other. Through their many misadventures, the survivors learn to trust each other even when such trust is unreasonable. The iconic exchange between two loners-turned-lovers, Sawyer and Juliet, captures this trust and interdependency well when Sawyer asks, "You got my back?" "Always" is her reply. Realizing this human interdependency is part of the awakening, as the ghost of Isabella explains to her beloved Ricardis: "Ya estamos juntos" (We are together). In the final moments of *Lost*, Jack's father explains to him why the core group of survivors is gathered together to cross over: "Nobody does it alone, Jack. You needed them and they needed you." Jack gets it, and he can let go. The awakened one closes his eyes and the historic series ends in a manner that would make T. S. Eliot smile: not with a bang, but a flutter of an eyelash.

JEANETTE REEDY SOLANO

# Dr. Phil

The reification of trauma as the be-all and end-all of American life has become a cornerstone of pop cultural philosophy. Celebrities now stand out when they *aren't* known for recovering from some kind of abuse; former child stars are imprisoned for being on a boat in France when they were supposed to be at rehab sessions in Santa Monica; action heroes are brought low when recordings of their violent and racist threats are exposed by their ex-girlfriends. Publicly airing one's dirty laundry is the new discreet. Oprah made it pay to talk about your pain in public; her acolyte Dr. Phil McGraw, born in 1950, made it seem like science. Both of them have surely helped masses of people to begin to think about life with new eyes, including the possibility of hope. At the same time, American talk shows that claim to be offering counseling services may be guilty of keeping people trapped in cycles of guilt at the poor behavior choices they've made—not least of which may be the decision to share intimate details of profound sorrow for an undisclosed honorarium and twenty minutes of fame on Dr. Phil's couch.

Phil McGraw grew up in Texas as the son of a psychologist. After his doctorate in clinical psychology from North Texas State, McGraw and his father joined Thelma Box's lucrative Pathways seminars. Success in self-help led to his first bestseller, *Life Strategies* (1999). McGraw also became a trial consultant, advising Oprah Winfrey on an upcoming Texas-based case. Her positive experience with him led to his regular appearances on her show as a relationship and life strategy expert. In 2002, Dr. Phil began hosting his own show (produced by Oprah's Harpo Productions), challenging guests to "Get Real." Long after abandoning his clinical license and practice, Dr. Phil became America's therapist-in-chief.

McGraw is the model of American perfectionist celebrity; the irony that good therapists will propose learning to manage imperfections as a path to healing seems lost in a show imbued with the hint of pastel-hued graphics, simplistic platitudes offered in place of thorough-going responses, and lie detectors exchanged for relationships built on trust. The repression of tragically broken emotions by the post-Second World War generation became the seed of the epidemic of family breakdown that first reared its head in the late 1970s. Dysfunctional families in the Boomer generation suffered from their fathers' emotional rigidity. Their elders' inability to talk about their feelings, keep a cap on explosive emotions, and manage the stresses of Reagan-era careerism gave birth to a swathe of people who needed more than their culture could offer. In the past, priests would have—theoretically at least—answered the need for rhetorical excursions into the deeper recesses of the psyche. Clergy had to give way to the cathode ray confessional, where things previously hidden were now used to garner TV ratings.

Now the public discussion of stories formerly kept under wraps has its benefits. But, we might also say, there's public discussion, and there's Public Discussion. Jerry Springer's spectacle contextualizes American life as the site of a constant battle between sisters competing for the same man; between lost daughters and estranged fathers; between people who already hate each other and want to show it in front of an audience. Dr. Phil is less sensational; representing himself as "a doctor" has seemingly led to some restraint on what actually gets discussed.

Dr. Phil's massive ratings signify our culture's gaping need for connection; but the genre of "therapy-tainment" risks enforcing unrealistic expectations about sexuality; money; possibility; and, most of all, status. The boundary between public and private worlds has collapsed. President Reagan personified a polygamous marriage between privatized capitalism, entertainment, and politics; the capitalization of human trauma is merely a logical extension of the 1980s. Putting life—warts and all—on stage may be an improvement on the time when sorrow was considered best buried behind suburban windows. But it's not the best we can hope for.

GARETH HIGGINS

# Pixar

Originally a division of Lucasfilm, Pixar established itself as a separate company in 1986 after its purchase by Steve Jobs, cofounder of Apple, for the paltry sum of five million dollars and the promise of additional future capital. In 2006 the Walt Disney Company purchased Pixar for $7.4 billion in stock, though Pixar remains headquartered in Emeryville in northern California.

Initially a computer hardware company, Pixar released the first entirely computer-generated feature film, *Toy Story*, in 1995. Director John Lasseter and the Pixar team demonstrated technical brilliance and artistic creativity. With an unprecedented string of commercial and critical successes, Pixar has extended its influence beyond films to merchandising via toys and other products based on its hit movies, particularly the *Cars* franchise (two movies from 2006 and 2011), which has generated an estimated six billion dollars in sales revenue, and the *Toy Story* franchise (three movies in 1995, 1999, and 2010), which has generated some nine billion. Pixar characters are also featured in Disney parks throughout the world and are icons in popular culture, as are some of their sayings (such as "To infinity and beyond!" uttered by the space toy Buzz Lightyear in the *Toy Story* films).

While none of Pixar's films are overtly religious in nature, several recurring themes resonate with traditional Christian morality. Some of these themes include hope, love, friendship, courage, and justice. Hope and love are two of the traditional theological virtues (the third is faith), while courage and justice are two of the cardinal virtues (the others are wisdom and temperance).

Andrew Stanton, director of the Pixar films *Finding Nemo* (2003) and *WALL-E* (2008), is a professed Christian and has stated that one theme in *Finding Nemo* is faith overcoming fear. Consequently, Marlin the clown fish learns that he cannot always protect his son, Nemo, from the challenges of the world, but can still do the best he can as a parent. *Up* (2009) admirably portrays the beauty of love and commitment in marriage, exemplified by Carl and Ellie, while also underscoring the hardships faced in life, including the death of a spouse and ensuing grief. Although *WALL-E* is essentially a love story, albeit between two robots, it also touches on serious questions regarding the philosophy of technology and human stewardship and responsibility in relation to natural resources.

Moreover, Pixar's characters are often transformed by realizing the value of relationships over material objects and self-centered or misdirected desires. In *Cars*, for instance, the main character Lightning McQueen is a prideful, self-centered race car who comes to value meaningful relationships over winning, acknowledging that a trophy is "just an empty cup." In *Up*, an elderly widower named Carl Fredricksen, who has enmeshed the memory of his wife with their home, later accepts that "it's just a house." In *The Incredibles* (2004), Mr. Incredible realizes that his family is his "greatest adventure," not his desire for the "glory days" as a superhero accustomed to working alone. The transformation of characters in Pixar films resonates with virtue ethics, where the emphasis is on building moral character.

Not afraid of grappling with serious themes, Pixar's films at times touch on topics that relate to religion and the meaning of life, including grief (*Up*), mortality (*Toy Story 3*), identity (*Toy Story, The Incredibles*), justice and oppression (*A Bug's Life,* 1998), fear and prejudice (*Monsters, Inc.,* 2001), and more. In addition, Pixar's creativity underscores the value of imagination and the human desire to create, which is, from the perspective of Christian theism, rooted in the belief that humans are made in God's image. Hence a rat named Remy, the hero of *Ratatouille* (2007), states "I know I'm supposed to hate humans, but there's something about them. They don't just survive, they discover, they create!"

Despite its influence on popular culture, Pixar is in some ways countercultural, offering positive, wholesome, traditional messages that emphasize hope while acknowledging the reality of difficulties in life. Foundationally, Pixar is at home when crafting meaningful, enjoyable stories, characters, and settings that tap into universal human concepts, fears, longings, and experiences. Philosophically and religiously speaking, these universal concepts most closely resonate with ethics, touching on vice, virtue, good, evil, human nature, and more.

ROBERT VELARDE

# *Project Runway*

"Auf Wiedersehen" had never sounded so bittersweet until it was accompanied by a double air kiss given to the losing designer by supermodel Heidi Klum on the biggest thing to hit fashion since Coco Chanel herself: *Project Runway*. Along with Klum, sidekick Tim Gunn provides the role of mentor to the designers complete with his own "make it work" catchphrase. Add the judges (designer Michael Kors and fashion editor Nina Garcia) and the stage is set for the fashion version of competitive elimination reality TV. Even though reality television had inundated popular culture by the time the show aired its first season in 2004, *Project Runway* produced record-breaking ratings on two networks, first on Bravo and six seasons later on Lifetime. It even won an Emmy in 2009 in the category of Picture Editing for Reality Programming.

Many credit *Project Runway*'s emphasis on the creative process as a large reason for the show's success. The challenges range in diversity, testing each designer's resourcefulness and imagination. Some of the more noteworthy challenges have been to create a look using unconventional materials, such as plants and flowers, food items, recycled materials, and even candy wrappers. Together with the time constraints and limited budgets, the ingenuity displayed on the runway is usually quite compelling. The documentary-style editing of the show allows the viewer to be invited into the creative process from several different perspectives, all within the sixty-minute air time of each episode. The allure of inspired design seems to draw in viewers, possibly because this opportunity for innovative thinking is something people yearn for but is often left unfulfilled in their own human experience. Perhaps people's attraction to the process of making something new is related to humanity's role as image-bearers for a divine Creator.

The idea of fashion and God intertwining might seem far-fetched. Yet for Christians and Jews, there is a clear precedent, as the first mention of clothing in the Bible takes place in the garden of Eden. Just after Adam and Eve took a bite of the fruit, their eyes were opened to their nakedness and "they sewed fig leaves together and made loincloths for themselves" (Gen. 3:7). After God finds them and describes the consequence for eating the fruit, he clothes them before sending them out of the garden in Genesis 3:21. The clothes, God's final provision for them before they leave, are of great significance, not only because of their protective function but because clothing is one of the most pervasive human symbols through which a person's position in society is signaled.

The practical needs of people to cover themselves eventually led to different trends in how communities dressed based on aesthetic interpretation of the materials and technologies available to them. The study of fashion from a historical perspective usually takes into consideration anthropological influences as well as its relationship with world history, tracing the roots of clothing styles by looking at geography, social setting, political situation, religious affiliation, technological development, and so on. What people wear on their bodies depends on many factors, including physical needs of the environment, availability of resources, associations within the community, and personal preference. Indeed fashion can tell more about a person's life than any other kind of material. Fashion has long been part of the human experience and bears great cultural significance, bringing together creativity, production, and aesthetics. *Project Runway* embodies this marriage by showcasing the creative process from a personal point of view, inviting the viewer to imagine, dream, and interact with the inspired outcome.

The creative process of the fashion, coupled with dexterity in the editing process is what truly makes *Project Runway* the hit reality show it has become. The composition of each show seamlessly combines the complexity of the design process, including limited resources and deadlines, with the emotional experience of each contestant and the intricate relationships among the contestants themselves. There is a tension between the designers competing against one another and the sincere relationships that are formed within the experience of the production. The designers are showcased as real and vulnerable, which leads the viewer into a deeper understanding of each person and his or her designs. There is a soulfulness to the show that does not exist in many other reality programs. Perhaps this authenticity is what truly draws viewers in and has encouraged the cult-like following of *Project Runway*.

MINDY COATES SMITH

## *South Park*

No animated television show dashed with more gusto through the door *The Simpsons* opened to religion than Comedy Central's long-running hit, *South Park*. With the help of a full-length movie in 1999 that grossed more than $52 million at the U.S. box office, *South Park* has firmly ensconced itself in American popular culture. Through the first decade of the twenty-first century, new episodes of *South Park* continued to draw nearly four million viewers per week, most of them teenage boys and young men. *South Park's* characters and creators landed on magazine covers and are the subject of hundreds of Internet Web sites. The show even won a coveted Peabody Award in 2006.

While it can be distasteful in the extreme, the show is especially popular with the 18-34 age demographic coveted by advertisers. The producers give fair, if absurd, warning: a disclaimer preceding each episode cautions that, due to offensive language and content, the show "should not be viewed by anyone." In 2005, the show extended its reach beyond cable, to syndication on broadcast stations, reaching an estimated 85 percent of the country, including forty-eight of the nation's top fifty markets. However, some of the episodes based on religion were considered so offensive to believers that they could not be edited for broadcast.

Pint-sized and potty-mouthed, the show's main characters are four fast-talking children in the third and fourth grade in a Rocky Mountain town of the show's title. Visually, Stan, Kyle, Eric, and Kenny are reminiscent of Charles Schulz's Peanuts gang, with round, oversized heads and short bodies. (In one of their Christmas specials *South Park* characters recite from the Gospel of Luke, just as Linus does in the Peanuts beloved annual holiday television special.) But, for the most part, the *South Park* quartet is nasty, naughty, and nihilistic. There is a creepy—if age appropriate—preoccupation with feces. And nothing is off limits for humor, from cancer to children with severe physical and mental disabilities.

For more than a decade, creators Trey Parker and Matt Stone simultaneously embraced and pummeled religion. Although not Mormon themselves, the pair grew up in Colorado with many Latter-day Saint friends, which has given them an understanding of and sympathy for that faith, to which they give theological parity with other world faiths (which account for the pair's long-running, Tony-award-winning Broadway musical *The Book of Mormon*). While still in college, the pair's first animated effort involved a short film in which Jesus used his halo to decapitate Frosty the Snowman, who was a serial killer. Over time, *South Park* became one of the most cosmological programs on the small screen, a show where scatology meets eschatology.

Religion appears in the series in many manifestations, some predictable and some unlikely. When characters are in desperate need, they cry out to God for help, or go to Jesus (a hapless, TV cable access show host) for advice—although not as frequently as they do to their school's cafeteria chef. When South Park residents—most of whom are Catholic—begin to spontaneously combust, one of their reactions is, "God must be angry with us." Infrequently, but occasionally, characters believe they have visions from God. Eric Cartman, the meanest of the crew and their foil, a misanthropic anti-Semite being raised by his sweet, promiscuous, single mother (in a home where crucifixes are prominently displayed), believes he has a revelation that God wants him to form a boy band and earn $10 million.

Woven through the narratives are fundamental questions about faith, often going deeper and far beyond *The Simpsons*. Like its Fox predecessor, *South Park* has dealt with the nature and purpose of God; the role of prayer; salvation; Hell; Jewish identity; cults; euthanasia; and the Christian missionary experience. But the Comedy Central show has also taken on religious broadcasting; Mormonism (an excellent episode that even LDS members circulate); Pentecostalism; the Roman Catholic Church's clergy sex-abuse scandal; anti-Semitism; spiritualism; and contemporary Christian music. *South Park* was one of the few shows to consider the controversy involving Danish cartoons of the Prophet Muhammad, although portions of the episode were censored by Comedy Central. Several episodes have eviscerated Scientology.

There is also syncretism: Moses, Muhammad, Krishna, Buddha, Lao Tzu, and Joseph Smith form, with Jesus, the Super Best Friends. They are equals and allies in combating evil. God their father, who says he is a Buddhist, appears as a cat with the head of a hippopotamus. "Every religion has their own version of God, and none of them makes sense," Stone explained in one DVD commentary. In a 1998 interview with the *Jewish Exponent* weekly newspaper, Stone, a self-described "agnostic Jew," offered a simple rationale for including so much theology in *South Park*: "Religion is funny."

MARK I. PINSKY

## *Survivor*

Few would have predicted such endurance for *Survivor*, which began as a summer replacement series on CBS in 2000. This groundbreaking reality show seemed destined for a meteoric rise and fall, yet it proved to be a survivor in its own right. In over twenty different seasons, it placed contestants into tribes on Samoan Islands and Nicaraguan beaches. The most divisive and popular contestants even came back for all-star editions.

What kept us tuning in? Probably not the weekly immunity challenges, which were little more than glorified obstacle courses. Although viewers enjoy the skimpy costumes and tanned bodies baking in the sun, we relish

the games contestants play with each other, forming alliances, plotting oust-
ers, hiding secrets. In the voyeuristic spirit of reality television, viewers are
invited into the huts.

Producer Mark Burnett led the reality TV revolution. He served in the
British army during the Falklands War, combat experience that may have
prepared him for navigating Hollywood. Burnett competed in a French
adventure race, Raid Gauloises, and turned the concept into his first television show, *Eco-Challenge*. He became the biggest brand name in reality TV
by following *Survivor* with *The Apprentice*, *The Restaurant*, *Shark Tank*, and
*The Voice*. Each program blurs the lines between sponsors and show. Burnett
reintroduced the oldest trick in the television business: getting companies to
pay for the programming by incorporating them into the storyline. With stunning vistas, *Survivor* became an alluring, season-long ad for the host island
or nation.

What makes it work so broadly? Survivor is first and foremost a game
that invites audience participation. In the Internet era, television has shifted
from a passive medium to an audience-driven activity. (It remains to be seen
whether religious institutions will follow suit!) The competition and voting
in reality TV prompts viewers to identify our favorites, to root for our champions. Over ten or twenty hours of television, we bond with the Survivors,
getting wrapped up in their personal, off-screen dramas as well. Romantic
subplots inevitably bubble up—as with contestants Rob Mariano and Amber
Brkich, who fell in love on *Survivor All-Stars*.

The show is predicated on inside knowledge. Audiences relish the chance
to listen to seemingly private conversations. We welcome the hushed con-
fessions, revealed to the camera but not to the other contestants. Indeed, we
know before they do who is next to be voted off the island. This format gives
us a taste of omniscience, the privilege of knowing more, seeing a slightly
bigger picture. *Survivor* also offers a taste of finitude. Contestants discover
what they are made of, finding their physical limits, but when they are voted
off the island, their torch is extinguished. It is a story of vigorous life and
sometimes cruel, unexpected "death."

*Survivor* could be seen as a Darwinian contest that promotes the survival
of the fittest. Contestants arrive as strangers but are soon grouped into teams,
identified as tribes. Each tribe faces tests that result in casting out the weak.
But the tests are mental as well as physical. The famously nude contestant
Richard Hatch became an unapologetic manipulator of people and things in
*Survivor*'s inaugural season. His lies were rewarded with a million dollar
prize. Yet Hatch ended up incarcerated for foolishly trying to hide his earnings from the IRS in real life.

*Survivor*'s winners have also included committed Christians, like season two's Tina Wesson and season four's Vecepia Towery. They brought prayer into the strategic mix. But don't the shifting allegiances and many layers of deceit inherent in the show contradict religious ethics? Should people of faith and conscience steer clear of *Survivor*? Contestant Joanna Ward from *Survivor: Amazon* couldn't separate her beliefs from the elements of the game. She wanted to keep the all-important immunity idol (a free pass to the next round) away from her tribe's camp. Perhaps she took the native/tribal roots of the show more seriously than the producers. She didn't want to encourage idol worship.

*Survivor* reminds us how often life resembles a game. From an early age, we enter into competitions and comparisons. The playground can be a cruel place where some are chosen and others wait in fear for their name to be called. As teams and tribes are formed, we are all given options in how to play the game. We may hope to be unguarded, but eventually we discover that not everyone is to be trusted. Wisdom arises from learning how to read a situation, understanding the players and the rules. Game shows like *Survivor* offer an opportunity to see all the ways people play each other—as fools, as tools, as means to an end. We hope others will treat us in a forthright manner, but we must learn to discern. Jesus instructed his disciples to be shrewd as snakes and innocent as doves. *Survivor* offers a safe place to put such principles into practice.

CRAIG DETWEILER

## Twilight and Stephenie Meyer

In 2003, an unknown writer named Stephenie Meyer had a dream in which a handsome vampire and an ordinary girl conversed in a meadow about how desperately he thirsted for her blood. Meyer turned this dream into the young adult novel *Twilight*, which she shopped to various agents and publishers before landing a lucrative deal with Little, Brown. *Twilight* became one of the best-selling books of the decade, spawning three sequels, a novella, and a series of blockbuster films.

It also engendered religious debate. While many on the religious right lauded the Twilight books for their emphasis on sexual abstinence (the brooding vampire in question, Edward Cullen, has singularly old-fashioned ideas about sex and marriage), many on the left criticized the books' 1950s gender roles and the all-consuming, unhealthy romance between Edward and his everygirl love interest, Bella Swan. Edward's moodiness, irritability, and desire to control Bella's movements aggravated many readers, as did her passive acquiescence and perpetual tendency to put her life at risk.

From a theological standpoint, *Twilight*—which opens with an epigraph from Genesis 3 and features a tantalizing depiction of a luscious red apple on its cover—wrestles with classic questions of good versus evil. Edward is supposed to be a monster, yet he continually strives to overcome his vampiric nature, joining with his adoptive family in a life of "vegetarianism," which in their case means refraining from human blood. Temptation is all around Edward, yet he strives to resist his urges—urges that become more insistent when Bella enters his life, since her blood "sings" for him. She is his soul mate, but he refuses to take her blood. It's only when Bella's own life is draining away in the fourth book, *Breaking Dawn*, that Edward consents to make her a superhuman vampire like himself.

Stephenie Meyer's Mormon beliefs are clearly discernible in the Twilight books (and not only in the conservative sexual ethic that has won the series praise from the right). Throughout, the emphasis is on what Mormons call agency, or human freedom. This is the ability to choose morality and resist evil, even at great personal cost. Edward, who is the primary moral agent in the series, exemplifies what the Book of Mormon calls overcoming "the natural man" by taming his innate impulses.

As well, the primary goal of the series is for a righteous family to live together eternally, a bond that actual Latter-day Saints make real through temple rituals "for time and all eternity." There are no formal rituals in Twilight, but the series promotes an ideal afterlife in which a husband and wife live together forever in perfected bodies following their mortal deaths. Edward and Bella strive for the same coupled eternal partnership enjoyed by other Cullens, including Edward's parents and his siblings with their mates. In the werewolf community that is home to Bella's Quileute friend Jacob Black, these eternal couplings also ring true. The male werewolves "imprint" once and for all time on a particular female, bestowing their affections in a monogamous and perpetual way.

It's also worth noting that both in Meyer's imaginings and in nineteenth-century LDS theology, Native Americans hold a special place as guardians of truth. They pass a specific kind of spiritual leadership from father to son, a guardianship that becomes activated in adolescence and stands between the Quileute people and their ruin. The affinity to the all-male Mormon priesthood, which begins at age twelve and is typically marked by fathers ordaining their own sons, is conspicuous.

Although books like *The Gospel according to Twilight* and *Touched by a Vampire* have rightly pointed to certain theological themes in the Twilight books, such as redemption, resurrection, and salvation, Susannah Clements has also argued that the novels instead stand in a line of cultural products that secularize the vampire. In Meyer's world, vampires are immune to crosses, stakes, and holy water; they can be destroyed only by dismemberment and complete immolation. This is in contrast to older cultural works such as *Dracula*, in which the vampire is depicted as a subhuman "other" who is morally repugnant and entirely subservient to the power of the Christian cross. In the Twilight series, the Cullen family displays a large cross in their chic American living room, a relic from the distant past of Carlisle, the family's benevolent patriarch. The message here seems to be that it is Carlisle's own good deeds that will save him (as, indeed, they have saved others) rather than any specific religious image or symbol.

JANA RIESS

# Rick Warren

No one changed the image and orientation of American evangelical Christianity in the early 2000s more than Rick Warren. The megachurch pastor is many things, but he is certainly no pretty boy. Unlike the nation's leading televangelists, he doesn't have perfectly coiffed hair, nor does he wear high-priced, well-tailored suits. He's a bit pudgy and, frankly, he's not always a terrific speaker. But what he does have is a message of humble, engaged Christianity that has struck a resonant chord, sweeping through the evangelical world—and well beyond.

In the grand tradition of megachurch pastors, Warren built his Saddleback Church from scratch, moving to a burgeoning area in southern Orange County, California, in 1979. Over time, he has expanded the congregation to more than 20,000 by sticking close to home—a 120-acre campus—and playing down his affiliation with the Southern Baptist Convention. Services feature upbeat, contemporary music, few crosses, and a low-key message. Warren says he teaches theology without using theological terms or telling people it is theology.

All this led, in 1995, to his first breakthrough book, *The Purpose-Driven Church: Growth without Compromising Your Message and Mission*, and a companion program of congregational development called "Forty Days of

Purpose." *The Purpose-Driven Church* was listed in "100 Christian Books That Changed the 20th Century," and *Forbes* magazine called it "the best book on entrepreneurship, management, and leadership in print."

In 2003, Warren became a media supernova with the publication of *The Purpose-Driven Life: What on Earth Am I Here For?* The book galvanized individuals and congregations, selling tens of millions of copies. "It's not about you," are the book's opening words. Warren listed five reasons why people are on this earth: 1) For God's pleasure; 2) For God's family; 3) To become like Christ; 4) To serve God; 5) For a mission. "It's when we realize these purposes for our existence that we'll start living."

Suddenly, Warren was the subject of numerous newspaper, magazine, and television profiles, becoming for a time something of a fixture on Larry King's CNN interview show. Yet, by deciding not to leverage this exposure into a regular, national broadcast audience, he escaped the increasingly problematic label of televangelist. *Time* magazine named Warren one of "15 World Leaders Who Mattered Most in 2004" and, in 2005, as one of the "100 Most Influential People in the World." Others began referring to him as "America's Pastor."

The *Purpose-Driven Life*'s royalties (and a cottage industry of multimedia spin-offs) enabled Warren to take several unprecedented steps. First, he gave back every penny he'd ever taken in salary from Saddleback. Then he announced that he would accept no speaking honoraria and began what he called "reverse tithing," giving away 90 percent of the millions of dollars he has earned from his best-selling books.

These moves, in turn, gave Warren the moral standing to criticize the huge salaries and lavish lifestyles of some preachers within the evangelical community. "The opulent lifestyles of televangelists make me sick," he said. Theologically, Warren has disparaged the "prosperity gospel," obliquely knocking Joel Osteen, another rising star in the evangelical firmament. "Success in any area often creates a spirit of entitlement—'I deserve this'—that is the exact opposite of servant leadership. It is evidence of insecurity and low self-esteem. Insecure people show off. Secure people serve." Toward that end, Warren has been at the forefront of utilizing new media to spread the gospel, making his sermons available for free on the Internet in order to assist pastors in small churches and in the third world.

As a secular media darling, Warren has placed himself at the head of a younger, emerging cohort of more moderate evangelical leaders. They are conservative but closer to the center than the far right. They appear less strident, pugnacious, and overtly judgmental than their predecessors. Warren and other leaders like him have moved to make evangelicals less a part of the Republican base. In 2008, he hosted a televised Civil Forum on the Presidency, inviting both Democrat Barack Obama and Republican John McCain. Warren also delivered the invocation at Obama's 2009 inauguration.

As part of what he hopes will be a modern Reformation, Warren has declared war on "the five global giants" of poverty, disease, spiritual emptiness, self-serving leadership, and illiteracy. He calls his solution the Peace Plan, a massive effort to mobilize Christians around the world to attack these giants by promoting reconciliation, equipping servant leaders, assisting the poor, caring for the sick, and educating the next generation.

MARK I. PINSKY

## *Wicked*

Apparently, it's good to be a little wicked.

In 2003, Broadway added another member to its billion-dollar club in the grand musical fantasy *Wicked.* Adapted (and significantly altered) from the novel by Gregory Maguire, *Wicked* cleverly reframes the story of *The Wizard of Oz* from the perspective of two friends, Galinda and Elphaba, who become the respective "good" and "wicked" witches of their land during social upheaval. The musical traces their paths toward goodness and wickedness—challenging our definitions of these terms—as they struggle to remain friends.

Like its fellow musical *Rent, Wicked* has brought an entirely new generation into the theater. At the heart of its fervent fan base—known for travelling thousands of miles to attend multiple performances—is the ten- to eighteen-year-old female crowd (and, presumably, their mothers). What beacon of hope does this musical present for this generation? It tunefully affirms in Elphaba that even the unlovable and ugly deserve love and redemption. And, countering our sex-worshiping, image-driven society, *Wicked* suggests that beauty isn't the chief good, but friendship, as it touts the unexpected respect and affection that Galinda and Elphaba develop for each other.

There's a broader message and appeal for this musical, too. Dr. Brian Howell points out in an article for The Center of Applied Christian Ethics that, culturally, we desire authenticity over absolutism. He says we can learn from *Wicked* that, "The greater sin is not in being declared wicked, but in accepting appearances of goodness." *Wicked* questions our definitions of loaded words like "good" and "wicked," asking us to consider who defined them and for what cause. Are they formed by truth or by power? While some have criticized a moral relativity in the musical, writer Mark Roberts says the show is calling us to deeper understanding and discernment.

One leader even recognized her own church's historical journey in Elphaba's quest. Reverend Lillian Daniel said, "We are a church that allows people to ask the hard questions. To challenge the status quo. Our church has not always been 'popular' and has been called 'wicked' when standing for the oppressed or for civil liberties for all."

But to reach a billion dollars in revenue, deeply personal connections and meanings must be suggested by a work. And *Wicked* has its share. Comic book writer Jim Krueger (*Earth X, Justice*) said he wept through the show, seeing Elphaba as a misunderstood Christ figure who works for all creation to be redeemed, only to be treated and killed as a criminal before coming back. Krueger celebrated the community of the disenfranchised being transfigured and even saw a little of our modern church in Galinda.

In the midst of all this redefining, reaffirming, and challenging, *Wicked* sounds an anthem of renewal in "Defying Gravity." Elphaba takes flight in this showstopping number, literally soaring high above the stage, and sings of defying limits, rejecting falseness, and trying to make a change. Though the music alone is enough to send one away triumphantly humming, the lyrics add personal reflection and social commitment.

Jesus spoke of authenticity, transformation, and renewal. He might have been talking to Galinda, or the modern church, when he scolded the Pharisees in Matthew 15 for honoring him with their lips but having hearts that were far away. He put the law's spirit above its letter—much to the Pharisees' consternation—and asked for their authentic hearts and souls, not just commands obeyed perfectly so that they might be called "good." In a parallel passage in Mark 7, he attempted to reverse how their tradition defined "clean" and "unclean" by telling them that food could not make a person unclean. Jesus said that true wickedness can come only from within, reaffirming that wickedness was not an outward description or label (as the citizens of Oz presumed in unjustly condemning Elphaba).

In gloriously staged grandeur, *Wicked* returns us to a fabled fantasy of our American youth in new and invigorating ways. In morally ambiguous times, it dares to challenge our definitions of goodness and wickedness and affirms the deep value of friendship. When many of us—not just ten- to eighteen-year-old girls—long for authenticity and renewal, *Wicked* echoes the call of

Jesus for authenticity and for a redefinition of some terms, even if it flies in the face of tradition or current powers. In light of this, doesn't it feel good to be a little wicked?

R. W. BONN

## Tiger Woods

Golfer Tiger Woods was seemingly destined for greatness. At the age of two, Woods was featured on *The Mike Douglas Show* putting against Bob Hope. By the age of eight, he not only broke 80 for the first time but also won the first of six Junior World Golf Championships. Driven in part by his infamously overbearing father, Woods became the youngest golfer to win the U.S. Amateur Championship and is the only repeat winner of the tournament. For golf's fan base, these early achievements simply prefigured the inevitable: Woods would surpass Jack Nicklaus's record of eighteen major championships.

Winning a golf tournament is no easy task. It is demonstrably more difficult to win a major championship, and that is to say nothing of winning eighteen. Most professional golfers would consider their career a success having won a single major. Yet, given his fans' desire to witness the remarkable, and coupled with Woods's preternatural talent and unquenchable ambition, the measuring stick for his career is qualitatively different than that of ordinary human beings. As Woods himself would attest, greatness was the only option. Anything less would be nothing more than an interesting failure.

Needless to say, the relationship between athletes and their fans is often tenuous, held together by little more than a combination of super-human athleticism and blind admiration. Woods, for example, is the world's wealthiest athlete, not simply because of the winnings he earned while racking up seventy-one PGA tour wins, but because of the record-setting endorsement deals he has signed. More than a golfer, Tiger Woods is an industry, and Americans buy what he is selling. In fact, as *Forbes* confirmed in 2009, Woods is such a successful spokesman that he is the first professional athlete to earn over one billion dollars.

Yet, Woods is not just an athlete; he is also a contemporary celebrity. And in the world of modern celebrity, immaculate personas are short-lived, for the public simply knows too much. Every misspoken word, every stolen glance, every illicit relationship is dissected, amplified, and broadcasted through every imaginable form of media. An individual's flaws thus fall under the scrutiny of an increasingly disparaging public whose passionate adoration of celebrity athletes is rivaled only by its collective contempt for their failings.

Woods's tragic flaw was his unchecked desire for beautiful young women. In spite of being the world's wealthiest athlete and bearing two children with his model-wife, Elin Nordegren, Woods's career and his life began unraveling in 2009 in the wake of his multiple extramarital affairs. Because of the extraordinary nature of his infidelities, not only did his wife leave him, but he also lost numerous endorsement deals and plummeted to the lowest world ranking of his professional golfing career. As stunning as Woods's life and career once was, his collapse was equally spectacular.

The public's conflicted relationship with Tiger Woods raises not simply cultural but innately theological questions. What can we forgive? Are there wrongs that cannot be made right, mistakes that preclude absolution? Moreover, as individuals and as an adoring public, how do we forgive? What does it do to us if we refuse? Like numerous other athletes whose sordid private lives have been publicly exposed, Tiger formally apologized and vowed to return to the religious roots that once grounded his life. Yet, despite these acts of contrition, Tiger Woods remains guilty in the eyes of an unforgiving society.

This refusal to offer Woods respite highlights the truly subversive nature of forgiveness. As Miroslav Volf reminds us, forgiveness always involves an act of remembrance, and to truly forgive, we must remember rightly. As is the case with athletes like Tiger, we often remember sadistically, guided by a vindictive desire to repay evil for evil. Ironically, in doing so, we actually fail to remember at all and thus commit a wrongdoing of our own making. If this is the case, might the ongoing criticism of Woods reflect not simply an inability to forgive but a deficient memory within the cultural imagination? To be sure, we hold on to the memory of wrongdoing for the right reasons—for the sake of the victims—because forgetting is tantamount to allowing perpetrators to commit their wrongs all over again. Nevertheless, forgiveness is about more than simple justice for the victim. It involves more than allowing perpetrators off the hook. It is about our health and vitality as a community of persons-in-relation. Thus, a step toward forgiving this billionaire athlete—however gratuitous that may seem—is in fact a step toward a reintegrated community, the restoration of our collective memory, and, indeed, our own redemption.

KUTTER CALLAWAY

## *World of Warcraft*

*World of Warcraft* (*WoW*) stands as the evolutionary heir to the mythical themes of Atari's *Adventure*, the immersive three-dimensionality of *Doom*, and the complex statistics and systems of *SimCity*—on steroids. In *WoW*, players choose to play fantasy roles drawn from imaginary races and classes such as Dwarven Rogues, Night Elf Priests, or Undead Warlocks. Banding together in raiding parties and guilds, players design collaborative strategies for dungeon delving, monster slaying, and guild dominance. As in the ancestral *Dungeons and Dragons,* players earn experience points for exploration, combat, and quests. Beyond the formal game, players also enjoy real-time social interaction through chatting and other forms of exchange.

By all estimates, the popular massively multiplayer online game (MMO for short) *World of Warcraft* enjoys a monthly subscriber base of nine to twelve million players. Each player invests an average of twenty hours per week in game play, paying a minimum of thirteen dollars a month for the privilege. Conservatively speaking, the annual economy of Azeroth—*WoW*'s fictional world—outranks at least twenty-five percent of global nations. The annual production of Azeroth generates more than eight billion hours of labor. *WoW* has also attracted celebrity players as diverse as William Shatner, Mr. T., Macaulay Culkin, and the creators of *South Park*. This phenomenon begs the question: what could motivate a video game player to spend this kind of time, energy, and money on a fictional life within a virtual world?

Blizzard Entertainment's *WoW* attracts players for a diverse range of complementary reasons. For example, Stanford researcher Nickolas Yee organizes the "motivations of play in online games" into three categories: achievement, social, and immersion. Following Yee's framework, some players enjoy *WoW* for its challenges of technical advancement and competition. Others enjoy *WoW* for the sake of socializing, relationship building, and teamwork. Still others seek out *WoW* in order to lose themselves in the play of exploration and identity. Some researchers argue that "synthetic worlds" like *WoW* are an extension of real life—not a replacement for it—while others perceive *WoW* as a "third place," not unlike a coffeehouse or church.

On the other hand, *WoW* suffers its share of critics. Advancement in the game demands "grinding"—a negative reference to mind-numbingly repetitive game play. The "daily grind" of *WoW* often consists of tedious tasks such as killing the same monsters over and over again, looting their corpses and selling their gear, and gathering and selling raw materials such as herbs and ore. Not surprisingly, the dullness of grinding has given birth to a real-life labor class of "gold farmers." Gold farmers do the grunt work within the game and then sell the digital spoils for real-world cash to other *WoW* players who are either too busy or too bored to do the work themselves. Rowenna Davis, a reporter for *The Guardian*, writes of lucrative businesses in China, "gold farms," that demand ten-hour shifts from their employees/players with only one free day a month. Thus, *WoW* offers the online community a witches' brew of community and capitalism. Myth and mundanity. Transcendence and tedium. Our nondigital lives also consist of a similar mixture—worship and work, belonging and boredom. It's no small wonder that in the leisurely spaces of our own making, we tend to replicate the possibilities and predicaments of contemporary society.

*WoW* is just one cultural canvas among many on which we paint our lives. Pick your favorite platform—baseball, scrapbooking, gardening, or multiplayer online role-playing games. Admittedly, many (if not most) of these platforms garner more respect than does *WoW*. Video games currently occupy the lowest rung of popular culture, but for how long? Consider television programs, Hollywood films, rock music, and comic books. All of these were once cultural ghettoes. Across time, however, imaginative persons began to see the aesthetic—and spiritual—potential of these new art forms. How long will it be until video games are similarly reimagined?

One day, the community of video game artists will have built their own best practices for spiritual game design. In all likelihood, their games will not be completely divorced from the mundane or the ordinary. However, they will have discovered how to design soul-nourishing stories, images, sounds, and procedures. There will be contemplation and discernment, mutuality, reconciliation, and creativity. Human potential can be developed, situated within a transcendent horizon of hope and longing. Many of these qualities have already been introduced in legendary designer Richard Garriott's *Ultima* series, particularly episodes IV, V, and VI, which are fondly remembered in the canon as *The Age of Enlightenment* series.

The tutorial for spiritual game design has already been played. Now, we wait for someone to take it to "the next level."

MARK HAYSE

# Zombies

The zombie is most commonly understood as a genre of literature, film, and games in which the dead come back to life as mindless ghouls to prey on living humans. The idea was primarily adopted from Haitian Vodoun (aka "voodoo") religion, in which a sorcerer raises the dead and controls the zombie, which has no will of its own. The modern zombie also has myriad literary influences, particularly vampires or humans brought back from the dead, such as in *Frankenstein* (1818). More recent influences include sci-fi works like the 1954 novel (and 2007 film) *I Am Legend*, as well as films from the 1930s to 1960s that feature the dead returning to life. Television viewers invited zombies into their homes on AMC's breakout series, *The Walking Dead*.

The zombie as most of us know it today has been quintessentially defined by American writer and director George A. Romero, whose 1968 film *Night of the Living Dead* instantiated nearly all the current conventions of the genre. In his book *Gospel of the Living Dead*, Kim Paffenroth outlines these features of Romero's zombies:

1. Zombies are autonomous, and not under someone else's control (a break from the Haitian origin).
2. Zombies reproduce by killing other living people, who then become zombies.
3. Zombies eat the living, but usually only partially, so that something remains to be zombified.
4. Zombies do not relent in their attack, but are easy to kill (by destroying the brain).
5. Because of the predictability of zombie behavior, the suspense in the genre comes mostly from human interaction.

While some of these conventions have been modified over the years, most critics agree that overall the zombie genre is more prone to social commentary than other horror subtypes. Zombies have been read as communist sympathizers, as slaves, as slave rebellion, as threatening bodies, as brain-dead followers of primal urges, as females, as antiproductive, and as cyborgs, to name a few. Where most contemporary zombie films tend to focus their critiques, though, are in the areas of racism (esp. *Night of the Living Dead*), classism (esp. *Land of the Dead*, 2005), consumerism (esp. *Dawn of the Dead*, 1978), scientific/government hubris (esp. *28 Days Later*, 2002), and individualism (all). Paffenroth even suggests that these indictments of Western, especially American, culture will forever keep the zombie film from being entirely mainstream.

Theologically speaking, such social criticism highlights human sin and brokenness. Most zombie films end up asserting that other living humans are a greater threat than the hordes of cannibalistic walking dead, not only in the metaphorical suggestions and parallels to real-life systemic injustices but also in the power struggles among the survivors. which often lead to them killing each other. In *Day of the Dead* (1985), *28 Days Later*, and *Planet Terror* (2007), military power especially is condemned, as soldiers vainly attempt to maintain the pre-zombie hierarchy of the government establishment.

More recently, however, there has been an optimistic turn in the genre by suggesting not only that humans cannot survive without cooperation but that true communion can be created even out of apocalyptic tragedy. The low-budget *Dance of the Dead* (2008) centers around a suburban high school prom night, which is interrupted by corpses who have been reanimated by waste from the local nuclear power plant (a throwback to Cold War-era anxieties). The attack forces kids from different high school cliques to work together in order to survive (the prom queen, the underachiever, the geek, the rebellious outcast, the cheerleader, etc.). In the process, many of the barriers engendered by mutual stereotypes come down and new relationships are born.

The highly successful picture *Zombieland* (2009) starts in a world already overrun by zombies. In such a context, the four human survivors, although at first antagonistic, must learn to trust each other. When they are given the chance to go their separate ways, they ultimately refuse. This communal commitment is exacerbated by the frequent voice-overs of the main protagonist Columbus (Jesse Eisenberg), who suggests that "we all are orphans in Zombieland." His comment and the plot of the film in general are clear metaphors for modern American life, which so often consists of boredom that is remedied through the accumulation of stuff, which often results in the loss of genuine human encounter. At the end of the film, Columbus has finally stumbled on to something else, however. His new friends, he tells us in voice-over, "were the closest to something I'd always wanted, but never really had—a family. . . . We had hope, we had each other, and without other people, well, you might as well be a zombie."

ANTHONY R. MILLS

# Conclusion:
# The Mystery Discerning Business

Thanks for going the distance with us. We hope you enjoyed reading the entries as much as we enjoyed writing them. Thumbing through our varied subjects, questions may have arisen. Is that really what that show was about? Would that author or filmmaker agree with our interpretation? How do we dialogue with popular culture from a theological perspective? Although two general approaches have often been taken, we wish to propose a third. As our dialogue partners, we will use Os Guinness, Bob Briner, N. T. Wright, Bill Romanowski, and Richard Mouw. Each has provided for the Christian community useful books on our engagement with culture as Christians.[1] They are important colleagues when it comes to theology and popular culture, even if we propose a more positive and sustained theological engagement than any of these might be comfortable with.

## A Traditional Approach

Many Christians have argued that when dialoguing with popular culture, we should start with our theology and use our faith to judge the meaning of all else. After all, Christian theology has the truth. We simply need to ask as theologians how any outside material—a cultural artifact, icon, or personage—matches up to the God we know, and to what he has revealed we should do. That is, we come to popular culture with our own presuppositions and we use what we already know to judge what we experience there. As these more conservative Christians interact with popular culture, they usually take one of three strategies, all of which effectively cut themselves off from the possibility of hearing God speak within culture, and from the possibility of experiencing any new truth, beauty, or goodness that God might be providing, not only through creation but through the creativity of those who bear God's image.

Toward this end, some simply try to boycott. Surely this is a valid last resort (e.g., with pornography), but it has often also been abused by the church. Book burning has never proven a very effective strategy. Moreover, in a media culture, boycott often creates publicity and helps gather a crowd, just the opposite result of what Christians intend by their actions. The boycotts of the movies *Dogma, The Passion of the Christ, Life Is Beautiful,* and *The Last Temptation of Christ* all proved counterproductive.

Many who take such a position see themselves as a remnant, a small group of Christian believers in a world that has become basically hostile to the gospel. Christians are therefore those who must separate themselves from the dominant patterns of our culture as we stand for the truth over against all that is false. Such Christians are also usually pessimistic in their assessment of culture's possibilities, believing that this world will not improve significantly until the *eschaton*. Here are many of our Christian brothers and sisters in the Pentecostal, holiness, pietistic, and Baptist traditions.

A second strategy used by some culturally conservative Christians has historic roots in the church going back to Origen and later to John Calvin. We are told that we can plunder the golden calves of our popular culture (Exod. 3:19–22; 12:33–36), extracting what we know to have value and rejecting the rest. Os Guinness writes, "By all means plunder freely of the treasures of modernity, but in God's name make sure that what comes out of the fire, which will test our life's endeavors, is gold fit for the temple of God and not a late-twentieth- [early-twenty-first-] century image of the golden calf." Guinness writes that we should "keep in mind Peter Berger's contemporary warning that they who sup with the devil of modernity had better have long spoons. By all means dine freely at the table of modernity," says Guinness, "but in God's name keep your spoons long."[2]

From our perspective, such a plundering mind-set has two problems, one theological and the other artistic. Theologically, God didn't keep his spoon long! The incarnation is the antithesis of Guinness's advice. Because of his close proximity with those of questionable morals and reputation, Jesus was mistaken for a wine bibber and glutton. He even found faith in a prostitute's chaste love; he did not keep her at arm's length. It is not long spoons that we need, but sensitivity to the voice of the Spirit of God, who is heard in and through his creation and creatures. All we need is eyes to see, ears to hear, and a heart to love.

Artistically, plundering also seems a deficient strategy in that it usually reduces the cultural expression to an illustration of a truth already known. It assumes that we as Christian critics have a superior position of judgment. In the process, it cuts off the chance for new insight, for a new glimpse of truth, beauty, or goodness. At best, plundering reduces some expressions of popular culture to a reinforcement of what the Christian already knows—like the line drawing illustrations in a children's book that reproduce but do not extend what is already written on the page in words. (One might helpfully contrast such reproductions with the pregnant drawings by Leonard Baskin that accompany *The Iliad* or *The Odyssey*. These drawings can stand alone in their power and meaning, even as they find further depth in their dialogue with the text.)

"Boycott" . . . "plunder" . . . "convert." Here is a third strategy that some culturally conservative Christians have adopted. Perhaps the most influential, recent example of this conversionist strategy has been Bob Briner's popular book *Roaring Lambs*. The book has been helpful in encouraging many Christians to take jobs in popular culture. Briner calls for individual Christians to enter culture as informed citizens and to articulately advocate for a Christian point of view. Christians are to be "salt," he says. "Being salt does not always mean we 'evangelize,' but by replacing evil with good, we enhance the climate for evangelism."[3]

Briner goes on to say that we must reclaim culture, not in a triumphalistic sense, but out of the strong Christian conviction that here is where Christians belong. He sees our churches as growing, our colleges bulging, our magazines and book companies thriving, and our media companies bringing teaching and music into homes. "In short, our subculture is healthy. *It* doesn't need more attention. It's the *world* that needs help."[4] Most readers realize that Briner was overly optimistic when he wrote this. The sad fact is that today the church needs help too. Many churches are dying on the vine. Many Christians sense the need for a fresh wind of the Spirit. Many say that they are more apt today to encounter God's Spirit in a movie than through a sermon. When was the last time a sermon made you cry (not because of its sentimentality, but because it ushered you into God's presence)? We would like to think that the answer is, "Recently," but we fear that for most it is not.

Whether boycott, plunder, or conversion, these conservative Christian strategies are usually (though not always) well-intentioned and can be useful in certain circumstances. But today these traditions that have sought to separate themselves from pop culture seem largely ineffective in their execution and intended result, even as those in the wider culture have judged such expressions of Christianity often to be manipulative and offensive. In the end, such approaches seem reductive, both of theology and of popular culture. Interestingly, such a critique is increasingly being recognized, even by fellow conservative Christians.

# A Reformed Corrective

Given such real limitations both missionally and formationally for those who would distance themselves from the creativity of those around them, others have tried instead to reverse the strategy. Recognizing that God's *common grace* is behind and in our culture, this second position has sought greater engagement with culture. It has helped the church relate to the wider culture, even if it has not fully escaped some inherent tentativeness. Bill Romanowski's widely read book, *Eyes Wide Open*, is a popular example of this position. Richard Mouw, in his insightful, book, *He Shines in All That's Fair*, asks: "Is there a non-saving grace at work in the broader reaches of human cultural interaction, a grace that expedites a desire on God's part to bestow certain blessings on all human beings, elect and non-elect alike—blessings that provide the basis for Christians to co-operate with, and learn from, non-Christians?"[5] Mouw thinks there is. But, true to his Reformed position, he also remains cautious. We must listen to the dissenters too, for we remain sinful people, and the contest between the church and the world still rages.

One can trace this theological position, as Mouw does, back to John Calvin himself. Calvin believed that God continues to work in and through the world for two primary reasons—to preserve the world by holding back sin (*Institutes*, II.3.3) and to promote civic righteousness, creating a basic sense of order and fairness through law (II.2.13). Such an understanding of common grace was rooted in Calvin's legal studies, going back to Roman jurisprudence, especially the writings of Seneca. Calvin wrote that there is "a universal apprehension of reason and understanding [that is] by nature implanted in men. . . . Because it is bestowed indiscriminately upon pious and impious, it is rightly counted among natural gifts" (II.2.14). This "peculiar grace of God" is found not only in Christian writers, but in "secular writers" as well. Thus Calvin can advise, "Let that admirable light of truth shining in them teach us that the mind of man (*sic*), though fallen and perverted from its wholeness, is nevertheless clothed and ornamented with God's excellent gifts" (II.2.15).

Calvin's understanding of human nature has done much to help the church engage honestly with the wider culture. Those adopting this second approach to theology and popular culture have been in the forefront of Christians who have sought to learn from the wider culture, even while seeking its renewal. Yet we have come to believe that even this second position is much too cautious and static, ultimately misunderstanding the present, dynamic role of the Holy Spirit in today's world. We say this for several reasons. First, Calvin's sources of common grace were largely ancient in origin; few were contemporary cultural leaders. Second, they also were mostly rational and not artistic in their focus. That is, Calvin limited his cultural engagement mainly to the ancient philosophers and rhetoricians. Though he spoke occasionally of artists, he did not reference them as he wrote. Lastly, Calvin's comments with regard to human cultural flourishing were always of a more general nature. There are no examples of his use of the secular culture of his day as a theological resource. It is simply the case that the cultural imagination of his day, not to mention human creativity more generally, play lightly within Calvin's theological formulations.

The implication of Calvin's cultural focus (historical in reference and largely rational in design) has had direct consequences on the continuing shape of cultural engagement by Protestants. In particular, there has been in our cultural interaction a propensity to favor the social sciences and philosophy over the arts. This has led us too often to shy away from primary, first-order aesthetic encounters as a source of cultural knowledge, instead rooting our cultural judgments more often in analytical, in second-order critical reflection. Writing, for example, in the nineteenth century, Danish theologian Søren Kierkegaard is particularly biting in his critique at this point, lampooning those who enter a foyer with two doors and choosing not the door marked "heaven," but the door marked "lecture about heaven." Buffered from direct engagement with God within and through our larger culture, we have thus tended to see the world primarily as being in opposition to God, even if there remain the occasional glimpses of divine grace. (And there is wisdom here: the world is greatly flawed.) But those who begin by focusing on humankind as artist and creator, thus rooting themselves in present transcendent experiences in and through contemporary culture, tend to hear in humankind's creational endeavors "rumors of angels," to use Peter Berger's phrase.[6] Rather than judging creation's cup as "half-empty" and in need of correction (which it is), they instead recognize it to be "half-full" with divine mystery and light (which it also is).

There is an additional factor at work here as well. Do Christians understand the Spirit as having, in the past, gifted the world at creation? If so, common grace is the residue, the remainder after the fall, through which God chooses to maintain civic order and world preservation. This is N. T. Wright's argument in *Simply Christian*. Justice, spirituality, community, and beauty produce longings, but not much content. Residual in creation's order, and perceived through the creature's fallen rationality (and imagination), these echoes of grace are signposts, murmurings. But they are largely without content. They lead one toward the center of the maze but leave us tantalizingly short.

Given humankind's sin and brokenness, Wright is surely right to be suspicious of any creation-generated source of knowledge today. But what if

God's continuing grace is understood as the ongoing dynamic gift of the Spirit working afresh and anew today, in and through creation? Is the truth, beauty, and goodness evident in culture today dependent solely on a past gifting of the Spirit that was then built into the creational fabric? Or do these virtues depend for their continuing vitality and transformative power on the ongoing present work of the Spirit? To use biblical language, when the Psalmist says that the heavens declare the glory of God, is this to mean that the heavens reveal God's past footprint if we would but have eyes to see; or does this mean that the Spirit of God continues to speak, to reveal God's presence, through creation and creature?

The difference is of crucial importance. Are we speaking of creation's divine residue, or is it divine providence, or even general revelation, that is still at work today? The ancient Egyptians believed that the world operated according to an overarching *ma'at*—a static world-order that even the gods were beholden to. Egyptian wisdom was thus an attempt to help humans line up with this past, created order. But when Israel borrowed from Egypt's wisdom, it was not to affirm an overarching order built into the fabric of the universe. Rather, it was to try to reflect the desires of the divine "Orderer"— the Spirit of God who has continued after the fall to work in the world and whose creativity continues to be revealed.

By tending to emphasize grace as already residing in creation and therefore natural to humankind in all times and places, this second theological tradition has consistently underemphasized human creativity because of the belief that sin compromises our natural endowment. This meant that for Calvin, for example, the human mind was judged to be "limping and staggering" (II.2.13); it was "choked with dense ignorance" (II.2.12). Although such theology seeks to hold on to the root Christian antithesis as being between sin and grace, by having common grace as natural to humankind through a past creation and saving grace as the unique, present possession of the church/ the elect, a robust understanding of the work of God in the world today has been lost. The core antithesis has been shifted to that between those in the church and those outside it. And in such a scenario, the church trumps all else. General revelation finds itself largely washed out, and an emphasis on the creative Spirit of God speaking through human creativity is found to be lacking, or at least seriously weakened.

## A Biblical Alternative

In a 2002 chapel address at Fuller Theological Seminary, where he is president, Richard Mouw put the contrasting choices with regard to theology and popular culture into colorful language. He identified two questions that you can ask about the activity of those outside the church. You can ask, "What in hell are you doing?" Or you can ask, "What in heaven's name are you doing?" Both conservative and Reformed Christians have usually limited their focus to the former. By focusing on human folly, believing that popular expressions of truth, beauty, and goodness are permanently corrupted, such Christians effectively eliminate the possibility that the Holy Spirit might still be offering new insight through conscience, creation, and creativity— through what theologians label "general revelation." To fail to ask, "What in heaven's name might be happening today outside the church and without direct reference to Jesus?" is to muffle the Spirit, hobbling both our spiritual growth as Christians and our missional outreach to those outside the church.

Throughout the Bible, there are repeated examples of the Spirit of God at work outside the believing community. Unfortunately, most of these texts have been ignored or "interpreted away" by the church. One of the most interesting of these is found in Proverbs 30 and 31, where we have written in our inspired Scripture, "The words of Agur son of Jakeh" (30:1) and "The words of King Lemuel. An oracle that his mother taught him" (31:1). The proverbs that follow in both of these mini-collections were recognized by God's people as inspired words from God, on par with those inspired utterances from Moses, David, and Isaiah. And yet Lemuel is not one of Judah or Israel's kings and Agur is not a Hebrew name. Their proverbs were part of the popular culture of the day, cultural expressions that had their origin outside of Israel. Yet they were recognized also to be God's Word. These portions of Scripture evince that the Spirit of God was at work outside the believing community, inspiring writers sensitive to God's Spirit to write what Jews and Christians have recognized for millennia to be God's inspired Word to us.

There are other examples as well. King Abimelech of Gerar heard the Spirit of God in a dream and, as a result, did not take advantage of Abraham's wife Sarah, even though Abraham had lied to him about who Sarah was (Genesis 20). The text makes it clear that it was someone outside the people of God—Abimelech—who spoke for God to Abraham, the father of God's people. Similarly, the biblical text makes clear that it is Melchizedek, king and priest of Salem, who is God's spokesperson to Abraham, for he prepares a special meal for Abraham and blesses him. Then Abraham recognizes that Melchizedek is indeed God's representative by giving him a tithe.

Later, in 2 Chronicles 35:20ff. we have recorded King Josiah's encounter with Pharaoh Neco of Egypt. The text makes it clear that Josiah was a man of God who had walked in God's ways for a lifetime. He had reinstituted the regular reading of the Torah, sought the prophetess Huldah's advice, celebrated the Passover once again, and restored the Temple. But despite Josiah's mature faith, it is the Pharaoh who the text says was sensitive to the voice of God at a critical juncture, not King Josiah—"He did not listen to the words of Neco from the mouth of God" (35:22). As a result, King Josiah lost his life. Or again, one chapter later, 2 Chronicles ends not with an account of a faithful Israelite, but with King Cyrus of Persia saying that "The LORD, the God of heaven, has given me all the kingdoms of the earth" (36:23).

One could also reflect on Isaiah's recognition that God was speaking to his people through the Assyrians (Isaiah 10), God's dialogue with Habakkuk about the Chaldeans (Habakkuk 1–3), the goodness of the sailors in Jonah's boat (they act more like believers than Jonah), Paul's discovery of divine truth in two Greek poems about Zeus (Acts 17:28), and so on. Behind all such biblical accounts is the recognition that the Holy Spirit is providentially and presently at work also in the hearts of unbelievers. We have observed that some Christians have called such activity an "echo" of God's revelation, a "kind of grace" (see N. T. Wright). But surely it is more than this. Such narratives are examples not of a reverberation of God's past action but of God's continuing, present revelation to humankind. To be sure, such revelation is not described as salvific. Rather such accounts should be labeled "general revelation"—but revelation it is, nonetheless.

What Christians of every denomination and tribe should gladly testify to is the continuing work of God in the world through the Holy Spirit, including through popular culture. Often, Christians have deduced their doctrine of general revelation through a process of elimination. It has been an intellectual experience, not a heartfelt one. Christians have not allowed themselves to believe that they can experience God's presence at the movies, or listening to a symphony, or building a house for the homeless, for God is wrongly thought to be apart from that. Some have thought that such notions might somehow detract from the importance of hearing the full revelation of God in Christ. But is this true?

Though well-intentioned, the result of such mistaken caution has been damaging on two fronts. First, there has developed missionally a growing disconnect between those in the church and those in the wider culture as spirituality has become more widely recognized and embraced, particularly within the arts. Christians have too often been perceived as dismissive of the spiritual sensitivity of those around us and have lost an opportunity for sharing about how knowing Jesus might add to and deepen their spiritual insight (see Acts 17). Second, there has often been within the Christian community a stunting of spiritual growth because of our reticence to expand our theological sources to include wherever it is found the Spirit's ongoing gifting (see Psalm 19).

In his book, *He Shines in All That's Fair*, Mouw concludes his reflections by quoting Thomas Weinandy concerning the nature of theology. Theology, Weinandy writes, is best understood as "a mystery discerning enterprise," not "a problem solving" one.[7] Weinandy's insight came as he reflected on the nature of divine suffering. But his insight is just as relevant when considering how we might find God in pop culture. Too often we have approached the topics of how non-Christians contribute to our culture's expressions of truth, beauty, and goodness, as well as how we might hear God speak through such avenues, by treating the discussion as problems to be solved. Instead, we might recognize that our experience of the Spirit, our experiential pneumatology, might need to go beyond our problem-solving ability, instead inviting the discernment of mystery.

The Christian's mystery-discerning business is rooted in the Spirit, who like the wind blows where it will. This mystery goes far beyond how to include a Plato and a Seneca, or even an Einstein and a Marilyn Monroe in our theology of culture. If God spoke in biblical times through the Assyrians and Chaldeans, even in their godlessness and immorality, then the mystery-discerning business is bigger and broader than any Pentecostal or Presbyterian might imagine. If this is God's world—if God has the whole world in his hands—and if the Spirit of God is active in the world today, outside the church and without direct reference to Christ (as surely the Spirit is), then we must not make limiting claims about how God might or might not choose to reveal himself to us.

God's revelation in and through creation, conscience, and culture is not a mere echo, a residue left over after the fall so that humankind might not go to hell in a handbasket. Rather it is an expression of the Spirit of God's continuing revelatory presence among us. One important arena of that divine activity is the creative endeavors of humankind. Popular culture might well become, in God's mysterious plan, the vehicle by which God speaks to those both within and outside the church. This would seem, in fact, to be the witness of increasing numbers of people as we move ever more strongly into what some call postmodernity. Surely it is the witness of biblical account after biblical account. For those who have eyes to see and ears to hear, God's Spirit is indeed present. It is a mystery not to be ignored.

ROBERT K. JOHNSTON

# Notes

1. Os Guinness, *Dining with the Devil: The Megachurch Movement Flirts with Modernity* (Grand Rapids: Baker Books, 1993); Bob Briner, *Roaring Lambs: A Gentle Plan to Radically Change Your World* (Grand Rapids: Zondervan, 2000); N.T. Wright, *Simply Christian: Why Christianity Makes Sense* (San Francisco: HarperSanFrancisco, 2006); William D. Romanowski, *Eyes Wide Open: Looking for God in Popular Culture* (Grand Rapids: Brazos Press, 2007); Richard Mouw, *He Shines in All That's Fair: Culture and Common Grace* (Grand Rapids: Eerdmans, 2001).

2. Guinness, *Dining with the Devil*, 90.

3. Briner, *Roaring Lambs*, 43.

4. Ibid., 32.

5. Mouw, *He Shines in All That's Fair*, 14.

6. Peter Berger, *A Rumor of Angels: Modern Society and the Rediscovery of the Supernatural* (Garden City, NY: Doubleday, 1969).

7. Thomas Weinandy, *Does God Suffer?* (South Bend, IN: University of Notre Dame Press, 2000), 32–34, quoted in Mouw, *He Shines in All That's Fair*, 89.

CPSIA information can be obtained at www.ICGtesting.com
Printed in the USA
BVOW020837101012

302598BV00002B/2/P